Histories

Studies in Critical Social Sciences Book Series

Haymarket Books is proud to be working with Brill Academic Publishers (www.brill.nl) to republish the *Studies in Critical Social Sciences* book series in paperback editions. This peer-reviewed book series offers insights into our current reality by exploring the content and consequences of power relationships under capitalism, and by considering the spaces of opposition and resistance to these changes that have been defining our new age. Our full catalog of *SCSS* volumes can be viewed at https://www.haymarketbooks.org/series_collections/4-studies-in-critical-social-sciences.

Histories

Ancient, Modern, Personal and Political

Tom Brass

Haymarket Books
Chicago, IL

First published in 2025 by Brill Academic Publishers, The Netherlands

Published in paperback in 2026 by
Haymarket Books
P.O. Box 180165
Chicago, IL 60618
773-583-7884
www.haymarketbooks.org

ISBN: 979-8-88890-905-8

Distributed to the trade in the US through Consortium Book Sales and Distribution (www.cbsd.com) and internationally through Ingram Publisher Services International (www.ingramcontent.com).

This book was published with the generous support of Lannan Foundation, Wallace Action Fund, and the Marguerite Casey Foundation.

Cover design by Jamie Kerry and Ragina Johnson.

Printed in the United States.

Library of Congress Cataloging-in-Publication data is available.

For Amanda,
Anna, Ned, and Miles;
and in memory of my parents

Contents

Acknowledgements

Histories examined here extend from the ancient to the modern, encompassing also the political and the personal. The reason for examining recent trends in the historiography of the Roman empire is because it is there, at the starting point of the historical trajectory on which the whole of Marxist theory is based, that attempts are being made to undermine its foundations. This is where an attack on Marxism currently takes place, in the form of a twofold attempt to redefine ancient Rome as in some sense modern. On the one hand, by non-Marxist historiography that invokes modern social science concepts in order to construct a tension-free image of Roman society, while on the other by a self-proclaimed Marxist approach which similarly recasts ancient Rome as a flourishing capitalist economy.

Against this revisionism the efficacy of Marxist theory about class and much else besides is reasserted via an examination of how and why discourse about work, gender, and property relations features at the rural grassroots, together with a critical analysis of how and why discarding Marxism has contributed to the current empowerment of populism. In keeping with this, the 'new' populist postmodernism questioned anthropological practice so as to replace the voice of the ethnographer with what is claimed inaccurately to be an unmediated – and thus authentic – voice-from-below. Whether studied or not, however, lives deemed ordinary fuse the personal with the political.

Additionally, these histories entail addressing the way in which the nature, origins and future of capitalism are explored, not only because in these different accounts lie clues as to its transcendence (or not), but also positioning the self within the narrative. This is the reason why the authorial subject features, less so in the early chapters but more prominently in the later ones. It is an approach based on a dialectic between self and context, enabling the construction of two interrelated narratives: about the self (and other) in the case of anthropological fieldwork, and about the other (and self) in the form of life fragments.

Special thanks are due to the following people. To Professor David Fasenfest, the Series Editor, for encouragement; to Judy Pereira of Brill Publishers, who guided the book through production; and to my daughter Anna Luisa Brass, who provided the drawings for the front cover and those within the book. A number of chapters reproduce materials which have appeared previously in different journals. Others have not been published before, and appear here in print for the first time. Like all my previous monographs, this one is dedicated to two sets of kin. To my family: Amanda, and Anna, Ned and Miles. Also, to the memory of my parents: my father, Denis Brass (1913–2006), and my mother, Gloria Brass (1916–2012).

Richmond-upon-Thames
May, 2025

Figures and Tables

Figures

Tables

Introduction: Histories Revisited

> It is a long-term struggle we are part of. It is a further stage of the same conflict which erupted into the Spanish Civil War.
>
> AUGUSTO PINOCHET responding to Henry Kissinger about the reason for the overthrow in Chile during 1973 of the democratically-elected Popular Unity government of Salvador Allende, underlining the extent to which it is not just the left which sees history in terms of class struggle.[1]

Covered in this volume is a wide range of historical debates, extending from ancient Rome to modern society, attempting to make sense of what connects them and why. Along the way it considers – inevitably – the reasons for the continuing rise and rise of populism, and why the left (with few exceptions) was both taken by surprise at its rapidity and as a result has thus far not formulated a politically adequate response to this process. Included are considerations of methodological issues linked to fieldwork, and what these have to say about studying populism and – more broadly – historiographic analysis.[2] The personal aspect referred to covers two things: fieldwork, in particular how the focus of the anthropologist shifts from an observer to a participant; and livelihood trajectories that are described as ordinary.

Not the least important aspect of history is that, in examining the present through the prism of the past, it provides lessons as to what from the latter conjunctures to avoid politically. One question arising from this concerns the reason why those who analyse the development of modern capitalism should think it useful to go back and study ancient Roman history; is there any point in Marxists examining the present through the lens of the past? If one cannot explain what sort of economic system it was, and why, it is impossible to talk about its connections to the present – its similarities to and dissimilarities

1 See Document 14, Secret Memorandum of a conversation between Pinochet and Kissinger regarding US–Chilean relations, 8th June, 1976, cited in Kornbluh (2003).

2 Among the issues considered is whether it is any longer possible for anthropologists to study inhabitants whose identity they do not share, now seen as an illicit form of 'orientalist gaze' (Said, 2002: 296–97).

from the latter – and thus also how systems change and what drives this.[3] In a word, the study of ancient history is too important to be left to classicists.

A perennial methodological difficulty, therefore, concerns the manner in which the voice-from-below is accessed: that is to say, whose voice are we hearing when confronted with an account containing this sort of evidence.[4] It is noticeable that nowadays academics who construct what they claim are 'new' models about political consciousness at the rural grassroots in Asia and Latin America, why it exists, how it emerged, and to what effect, do so without any fieldwork experience in such areas. This problem has not escaped the notice of others, particularly those who have indeed gone to the field, conducted this kind of research, and based their paradigms on what they found there.[5] Clearly, this is different from the sort of methodological difficulties facing historians of ancient society: whereas modern practitioners of social history construct models about the nature of rural grassroots existence in places where they could have – but have not – done research, this option is not and never was open to historians of ancient society. It can be argued that among the social sciences, only anthropology has a practice capable of a sustained access to the voice-from-below.

As an academic discipline, social anthropology has a history of championing the cause of those it studies, to the extent of supporting grassroots resistance to any planned development projects by the state. Informed by the well-meaning but misleading idea that such contexts have remained the same over eons, opposition to change tends to overlook two things: that social contexts apparently static historically are rarely so, and that small-scale agrarian units defended against the outside as seemingly corresponding to egalitarian

---

3 Much the same point about the usefulness of social anthropology is made by Evans-Pritchard (1951: 122ff.).

4 Hints about just such a methodological issue are encountered in Goad (1998: 101), who writes: 'The working class doesn't write a lot of history books. The working class doesn't produce many movies or radio shows. The working class doesn't tend to hire media consultants or theatrical agents. The working class has played an itty-bitty role in fashioning its popular image. That's because the working class was too busy working. The working class has plenty of reasons to be angry. Unfortunately, only the working class realizes it.'

5 Interviewed in 1987, Kapuściński (2007: 235ff.) made precisely this point, observing: 'Twenty years ago, I was in Africa, and this is what I saw – I went from revolution to coup d'état, from one war to another – I witnessed, in effect, history in the making, real history, contemporary history, our history. But I was also surprised. I never saw a writer. I never met a poet or a philosopher – even a sociologist. Where were they? Such important events and not a single writer anywhere? Then I would return to Europe and I would find them. They would be at home, writing their little domestic stories ... None of these books had anything to do with our world, our reality – nothing.'.

rural structures invariably hide internal oppressions and exploitative relations. From this approach, moreover, it is but a short epistemological and political step to privileging 'otherness' *per se*, on the same relativistic cultural grounds as does the 'new' populist postmodernism.[6]

Ever since the social anthropological practice of participant/observation fieldwork was indicted by the 'new' populist postmodernism as an inappropriate form of orientalizing gaze, anything written by British social anthropology about the 'other' it studies is tainted. Notwithstanding its extension to cover peasant communities, therefore, by the 1980s fieldwork was declared by the 'new' populist postmodernism as illicit, declaring that even to gaze – let alone to interpret what is seen – was no longer acceptable as a form of research, on the grounds that as no objectivity is possible, such a practice can only be subjective. Because of this, argued postmodernists, those entitled to gaze and interpret what they see can only be from the same society, nationality, or ethnicity.

Among the historical lessons that ought to be learned by the rise and consolidation of the 'new' populist postmodernism is how easily it is possible to abandon radical politics by intellectuals who quickly turn away from an erstwhile challenge to capitalism *as a system*, and replace this with bits-and-pieces tinkering round the edges of what exists, inferring or arguing that nothing much can be done (and so one shouldn't waste time trying) to replace accumulation as an economic process.[7] A more charitable description of this sort of response is that it corresponds to nothing more than a form of 'internal exile' or 'inner immigration', whereby survival requires that political focus shift either onto an oppositional discourse that is not as challenging, or else

6 An instance of privileging national 'otherness' in a way that casts doubt on the idea of social science as a discipline seeking common answers to universal questions is the assertion by Pocock (1971: xi, original emphasis) that 'Indian anthropology must be truly Indian in the first place and not, necessarily, ask the questions which foreign anthropologists have asked, according to *their* intellectual needs, of Indian society'.

7 At the outset of the cultural turn, this tectonic shift in the role of intellectuals was spotted by Narr (1980: 63) who, observing that 'no social scientist today would have the ability, courage, or self-confidence to offer the public an authoritative assessment of the present state and future direction of our society', then writes: 'The abdication of philosophers and social scientists leaves a vacuum which is readily filled by superficial formulae which define and condone the uses of unrestricted power. Intellectuals in shying away from their foremost duty – to make complexity comprehensible, to clarify choice, to explain the structure and symbols of reality – may unwittingly sanction the ideologies of the "terribles simplificateurs" which function as powerful tools of domination. The gap left today by the failure ... of critical thinkers has been abundantly filled by vulgar books which pander to the public simplistic concepts of the "post-industrial", "post-modern" or "technotronic" society.'

a withdrawal from politics altogether.[8] A less charitable one is that a revolutionary challenge to capitalism – such as that from Marxism – is abandoned when it becomes an obstacle to entry into academic employment or promotion within the university hierarchy.

Against the usual complaint, still heard frequently nowadays in academic circles despite evidence to the contrary, that Marxism and Marxists have always ignored or downplayed the element of gender when analysing grass-roots movements, Trotsky long ago recognized the important role of women in opposing and mobilizing to counter the entrenched forces of reaction.[9] He would not have been surprised by the heroic action of women in Iran protesting about the attempts by clerics to impose on them what is advocated by backwards-looking religious ordinances. Equally relevant currently is his critique of those such as agrarian populists, who insist on the feasibility of a pro-peasant stratagem recuperating pre- or non-capitalist institutions and cultural traditions within an actually-existing capitalist economic system: that is, change at the micro-level only, leaving the macro-level more-or-less intact.[10] In a similar vein, his critique of the tendency to romanticize peasant society anticipated the idealised view rural life presently held by 'new' populist post-modern exponents of identity politics.[11] This negative appraisal still applies

8 This response can be explained as follows: 'inner emigration has re-emerged in Russia today as an antidote to renewed authoritarianism. And in many other countries, too, people appear to be losing interest in the news, retreating from public life and prioritising their inner world ... This desire to switch off is understandable ... people [in a US opinion poll] felt the need to limit their consumption of political news [because it] can lead to feelings of "hopelessness", "helplessness" and "existential anxiety"'. See '"Inner immigration" is no escape from today's reality', *The Financial Times* (London), 7th March 2025.

9 'When I read about the success of one of your female fellow students in Kazan among the illiterate Tartar women,' noted Trotsky (1969a: 10) in a speech at the Communist University of the Toilers of the East in 1924, 'I was reminded of my recent short visit to Baku where I heard for the first time a Turkoman Communist woman, and had an opportunity to observe in the hall the enthusiasm of such women, who having heard our message of liberation, had awakened to a new life. I realized then for the first time that women will play a more important role in the liberation of the East ...[t]his will be the case for the simple reason that Eastern women are even more oppressed and entangled in age-long prejudices than men.'

10 'To rationalize life, i.e. to transform it according to the dictates of reason, is not possible without the rationalization of production, for the roots of the conditions of life lie in economics', argued Trotsky (1924: 31, 32), adding: 'This is a fact which marks our successes in the domain of custom and habit dependent on our successes in the domain of economics.'

11 'There is a simple rudeness of peasant origin, which is unattractive, certainly, but not degrading. It becomes unbearable and objectively reactionary only when our young novelists boast of it as of some extremely "artistic" acquisition', writes Trotsky (1924: 72), who

to agrarian populists like James Scott, who celebrate existing forms of traditional culture, insisting these should not just be retained but strengthened and protected, a position that is the opposite of Marxism, which seeks to transcend the existing since it is 'a mark of the old slavery'.

The conditions giving rise to populism tend to focus on the personal, the individual and his agency (charisma, demagoguery), rather than the processes which confer acceptability on what the individual-who-speaks-to-and-for-us says. Considered less often, therefore, is the prefiguring role of intellectuals generally, and academics in particular, in creating a theoretical space for this sort of political discourse. Writing a century ago, Trotsky presciently warned against resurgence of nationalism, aided and abetted by those he called 'bourgeois exploiters of Marxism', pointing out that 'Marxism, of course, is not an academic science, but a lever of revolutionary action'.[12] The task, as he saw it, was not just to expose the ideological, political, and economic contradictions inherent in the capitalist system but also then to point out how their resolution necessitates a transition to socialism.[13]

Faithful to Here?

Currently, what passes for Marxism is indeed curious, including as it does the bizarre claim that capitalism is an ever-present system which has existed in all contexts at every historical epoch.[14] As odd is the claim to be a Marxist and Leninist while simultaneously discarding concepts like the industrial reserve and peasant differentiation. Another variant of this kind of self-deception is that, *mirabile dictu*, some on the left are still promoting the desirability not of socialism but rather more capitalism, on the spurious grounds that the latter has not yet run its course, and should be supported in doing so. Shifting the

---

then points out that '[t]he foremost elements of workers regard such false simplicity with instinctive hostility, for they justly see in the coarseness of speech and conduct a mark of the old slavery.'

12 On this see Trotsky (1969a: 8, 9) who elaborates: 'Russia was backward, not only economically, but also politically. Marxism preached the inevitability of capitalism, and those bourgeois-progressive elements which wanted capitalism for its own sake and not for the sake of socialism, accepted Marxism, having previously deprived it of its revolutionary sting.'

13 The nature of this political task is explained by Trotsky (1924: 96): 'The first step towards a new order of things must be ... the showing-up of the contradiction between the new requirements of life and the old habits – a contradiction which becomes more and more unbearable. This is what the revolutionary party has to do.'

14 For this and the following contradiction, see Chapters 1 and 2, this volume.

political focus in this manner, from advocating socialism and opposing capitalism to what amounts to its converse, resisting if not opposing socialism whilst favouring more accumulation, is perhaps the most egregious kind of view advanced in the name of Marxism.

Although such 'Marxists' present their arguments, more often than not to interviewers, as though these have remained consistent over time, the exact opposite is the case. Moreover, as these approaches have in effect discarded everything and anything to do with Marxism, why then do they continue to present these views as Marxist? And perhaps more importantly, why do others believe this to be the case? Such instances illustrate yet again the veracity of a particular shortcoming in academia: the tendency to address a case made by an author without challenging, contextualizing, or even perhaps having read what the latter has published. Revealed on these occasions is the gap between what is claimed to be the case and what really is the case.

Equally strange is the claim by Francis Fukuyama that the approach informing his end-of-history thesis is analytically no different from that of a Marxist project, just with a different outcome, that 'liberal democracy and free markets constitute the best regime'.[15] He still seems incapable of making a theoretical and historical connection between on the one hand liberalism, democracy, and the accumulation process, and on the other identity politics, populism and nationalism. This is because he fails to understand the nature of the trajectory followed by capitalism, and how once they escape the bounds of the nation and becomes global in scope, the free movement of labour and capital – promoted by the kind of *laissez-faire* economic policy of which he approves – triggers the very populist response he fears.[16]

An unmistakeable characteristic of the recent past, therefore, is the proliferation of attempts in the social sciences to promote or set up a variety of non-Marxist Marxisms, even on occasion anti-Marxist Marxisms. Symptomatic of this kind of approach is a proposal that Marxism ought no longer to be seen as the 'other' of populism, in effect melding ontologically and politically with the latter. In the name of these kinds of 'Marxism' one is offered an epistemology devoid of historical specificity, whereby capitalism is now considered to be a system found everywhere at all times, unconnected moreover to anything resembling a socialist transition. The absence of the latter, central to Marxist teleology, is evident from a comparison of the extent to which the prospects for a future socialism have diminished in leftist narratives. On the one hand, therefore, an early 1990s discussion saw this political transformation as both

---

15 Fukuyama in discussion with Fasting (2021: 71, 73).

16 This misrecognition by Fukuyama is explored in detail elsewhere (Brass, 2024a: Chapter 6).

desirable and achievable internationally, and thus as an outcome that was still possible, albeit in terms that were guardedly optimistic.[17] Some three decades on, however, even this earlier tone – conditional, but positive – has changed, noticeably so: the situation now faced by the left is one in which 'rather than *transforming* their states, these social democratic parties were *transformed* by capitalism'.[18]

In terms of non-Marxist alternatives to populism, at the serious end of the spectrum are found theorists like Paul Klugmann, Robert Reich, and Joseph Stiglitz, all of whom oppose Trump on the grounds that capitalism as a system requires saving from his kind of policies which – if they persist – in the end will undermine if not destroy the global economy. At the non-serious end of the spectrum, however, the poverty of current opposition to Trump and his bevy of techbro oligarchs is hard to miss. Thus, for example, Naomi Klein and Astra Taylor frame their antagonism without mentioning the role of capitalism, and the very idea of Marxism and socialism as alternatives are for them quite simply beyond the pale.[19] What we have instead is advocacy of touchy-feely togetherness, along the lines of we-should-all-be-nice-to-each-other, which fails to consider either the causes of or the economic reasons for populism and

17 This sanguine prognosis is evident in the following statement (Qadir and Gills, 1992: 11): 'Socialism is by no means dead, but must now be reformulated, and this reformulation must first and foremost address the problem of development in the global economy as a whole'.

18 See Albo and Maher (2025: x–xi, original emphasis), who consider the prognosis for current socialism, asking: 'What political forms were called for ... How could they play a role in regrouping fragmented and diminished social movements, and bring them together to form a broader socialist politics? What would a socialist transition ultimately entail?', all questions that are answered by them in an unmistakeably pessimistic manner: 'And then, just as quickly, these hopes were dashed. The opening, it seemed, was illusory.'

19 See Naomi Klein and Astra Taylor, 'The rise of end times fascism', *The Guardian* (London), 13th April 2025. Arguing that 'The governing ideology of the far right has become a monstrous, supremacist survivalism. Our task is to build a movement strong enough to stop them', Klein and Taylor then maintain that: 'Perhaps what is needed is a modern-day universalization of that concept: a commitment to the right to the "hereness" of this particular ailing planet, to these frail bodies, to the right to live in dignity wherever on the planet we are, even when the inevitable shocks forces us to move. "Hereness" can be portable, free of nationalism, rooted in solidarity, respectful of indigenous rights and unbounded by borders ... To have a hope of combating the end times fascists, with their ever-constricting and asphyxiating concentric circles of "ordered love", we will need to build an unruly open-hearted movement of the Earth-loving faithful: faithful to this planet, its people, its creatures and to the possibility of a liveable future for us all. Faithful to here.'

Trump's rise to power, or the complicity of those who, like Klein and Taylor, themselves hold populist views drawn from the cultural turn.[20]

Oft-heard from baffled liberals is the complaint that many trust, subscribe to, and consequently support what populists like Trump and Musk are doing, evidence about its being based on misinformation notwithstanding. The questions then asked by the former are: how can this possibly happen, and why do people believe such untruths? Marxists answer the same questions differently, pointing to prefiguring links in a chain of causation. Long before the 2025 election, therefore, oligarchs and other wealthy elements began to purchase media platforms (newspapers, television stations, etc.), thereby laying the ground for a process of ideological formation: generating, disseminating, and reproducing false consciousness among the masses.[21] Having done that, it is now rather late in the day to begin asking – as do liberals and other progressives – how on earth was it possible to arrive at this (for them) inexplicable situation.

Those taken by surprise at Trump policies in 2025 seem not to be aware of the extent to which these are guided by the populist playbook, not least the element of nationalism.[22] Hence the imposition of tariffs on China is justified

20 Hence the view of Klein and Taylor that 'we counter their apocalyptic narratives with a far better story about how to survive the hard times ahead without leaving anyone behind. A story capable of draining end times fascism of its gothic power and galvanizing a movement ready to put it all on the line for our collective survival. A story not of end times, but of better times; not of separation and supremacy, but of interdependence and belonging; not of escaping, but staying put and staying faithful to the troubled earthly reality in which we are enmeshed and bound. This basic sentiment, of course, is not new. It is central to Indigenous cosmologies, and it lies at the heart of animism ...'

21 The irony of this outcome is unmissable: I recall when not so long ago the sociological orthodoxy was that rich people acquired newspapers and television stations not in order to produce and control opinion, but rather only for their own personal prestige, as a way of displaying their wealth. The inference then was that press and media ownership was somehow unconnected with a desire to shape or sway politics, a sociological interpretation that has not wholly vanished even now.

22 The imposition – or threat thereof – by Trump of tariffs on market rivals in order to protect American jobs mimics both the approach and objective followed by the Pan-German League over the late nineteenth and early twentieth century. Supportive of German colonialism and opposed to internationalism of whatever kind (financial capital, proletarian), the organization advocated unity between German workers and German capitalists, fostering a sense of national identity (*Nationalstaat*) that extended beyond the borders of Germany, on the grounds that it would form an exclusive market for German commerce, thereby protecting the employment prospects of German workers. The fear (Wertheimer, 1924: 100) was that 'our people (*Volkstum*)' would not – unless united – be able to 'present as solid a front as possible' so as to 'oppose the united commercial power of our enemies': unless this was done, 'the world will be closed to us commercially'. This combination – nation = capital + labour – is not only central to the populist playbook

by the constant refrain that such an economic policy is undertaken by him to protect the livelihood of the American worker. In short, to prevent the latter from further exposure to labour market competition from abroad, in the form of labour costs which undercut those of American labour, and drive restructuring based on outsourcing and the consequent loss of local jobs. Similarly, the widespread axing by Musk of state agencies and employees is consistent with a long history of populist discourse expressing opposition to the state as the embodiment of bureaucratic 'interference'.

In part, 'new' populist postmodern theorists failed to recognize the extent to which their own views – about the innateness and politically non-transcendent nature of traditional non-class identities – prefigured these same policies, which took comfort from positions they themselves had advocated earlier. This returns one to the issue of just how Marxist have Marxists been, and if not, what has been the wider impact, especially outside academia. Downplaying, postponing, or rejecting not just socialism but also the means of its realization – revolutionary agency – is itself an effect of misunderstanding what was going on, as a result not asking the right questions, and consequently supporting as progressive the wrong political objectives. All these difficulties inform what is otherwise a laudable attempt by Ash Sarkar to examine recent British politics using a Marxist approach.[23]

Ignoring History

Part of a broader case made over some decades by me, about labour regime change, has concerned the main reason why capitalism survives: the post-war expansion of the industrial reserve, itself an effect of two developments. First, the Green Revolution in Third World countries, which drove peasants off the land, making their labour-power available to capital either in their own nations or as migrants in metropolitan capitalist ones. And second, the rise internationally of the *laissez-faire* economy from the 1980s onwards, deregulating markets and facilitating the global movement of labour and capital. This combination led in turn to a populist backlash in many of these contexts, where increased labour market competition empowered producers but

across different periods and contexts, but also had as its political legacy the rise of the far right in Germany and Italy during the 1930s and 1940s. Then, as now, it underlines how the historical role of populism is to see off or pre-empt a from-below challenge to capital, thus ensuring its continued reproduction.

23 Sarkar (2025).

disempowered workers, who turned increasingly to conservative or far-right parties undertaking to control borders and migration. Capitalists, however, exercised pressure on governments to retain access to the industrial reserve, an objective abetted by academic exponents of postmodern theory, whose championing of identity politics helped shift the debate about labour markets from protecting the existing workforce against further competition to one about culture and human rights of the migrant 'other', an argument supportive of open-door policy.

Ostensibly, the case made by Sarkar appears to be going down the same path, arguing that its intention is to show how the embrace by the left of identity politics undermined working class solidarity and organization, but in the end this supposition about what she intends to say proves to be illusory. Writing from a Marxist viewpoint, her object is to show not only how what she terms minority rule 'directs working-class anger away from wealth and political inequalities, and towards identity minorities who've been made into scapegoats', but also how 'the left embraced an individualistic and competitive model of victimhood'.[24] This, she maintains, was because 'the left *unwittingly* forged the political weapons being used against it by our political opponents.'[25] Against this interpretation, my view is the exact opposite: adopting the weapons of those opposed to the left was not done 'unwittingly' in the sense of an accidental occurrence, but in some instances the result of abandoning Marxism in order to progress in academia and then endorsing postmodernism as an alternative radical theory.

Announcing from the outset that she is going to investigate and indict the left for its complicity with identity politics, Sarkar observes that 'it's time to be brutally honest about something that's been happening on the left: we have absorbed the tenets of liberal identity politics'.[26] Opinions expressed about the latter, among them that 'subjective judgements ... are given sacred status', and that 'we have opened the door to victimhood being appropriated by the right', are indeed accurate, but not actually new.[27] They overlook the fact that some on the left have been saying just these kinds of things for quite a while

24 'I became a Marxist', Sarkar (2025: 6, 260) informs us, concluding: 'Here's why I'm not a liberal, or a social democrat. I believe that the politics we've got are a balance of class forces in society'.

25 On these points, see Sarkar (2025: 9, 21, emphasis added).

26 Sarkar (2025: 20). This is a claim repeated at the end of her analysis (Sarkar, 2025: 248): 'Throughout this book, I've been showing you the various methods through which working-class power has been inhibited, splintered and weakened. It's down to how the left has internalised an individualistic and competitive model of victimhood ...'

27 Sarkar (2025: 27–28).

now – in my case for at least three decades – so this call to arms, although welcome, is somewhat tardy. It overlooks the existence of a prefiguring trajectory composed of the few leftists who saw this coming and called out the 'new' populist postmodernism, warning about what the political consequences were likely to be. Some acknowledgement of these academic precursors would have been comradely, not least because those holding views critical of identity politics have frequently experienced hostility on account of this, much like Sarkar herself.[28]

Because these earlier debates are not referenced, Sarkar unknowingly does two things. She not only reproduces much of the previous case made against identity politics, but also mistakenly regards as political friends those who are really foes. Thus, for example, the views of Stuart Hall and Michel Foucault are cited by her endorsingly, despite the fact that their privileging of 'otherness' helped pave the way for the cultural turn.[29] What is termed by her 'the liberal turn in identity politics' is characterized by three 'preoccupations'.[30] These consist of irreducible differences between identity groups, each of which have competing interests that are legitimized by 'lived experience'. Significantly, all these are the characteristics of postmodern theory, which privileges as innate not only identity difference and its accompanying competing interests but also subjectivity based on 'lived experience'. Epistemologically, a solipsistic theoretical framework which proclaims 'reality is whatever I say it is', the inference being that no interpretation beyond the self counts; in short, there is no objective material reality 'out there' against which subjective perceptions can be measured.

Oxford Debating Nerds

Curiously for a self-professed Marxist, but perhaps because of her background in journalism, the approach of Sarkar is dismissive of anything to do with academia, to the extent of at times corresponding almost to a form of anti-intellectualism. Decrying media employment bias towards those with a public school Oxbridge educational background, therefore, Sarkar looks at the issue of identity politics through a very narrow lens, confining her analysis

28 See, for example, Brass (2025a: 399, n. 14).

29 Sarkar (2025: 18–19). On the complicity of Hall and Foucault with 'otherness' and the cultural turn, see Brass (2017: 162–65; and 2021: 58–59).

30 For this and what follows, see Sarkar (2025: 32).

largely to what happens in television and print journalism.[31] The latter focus is embodied in statements like '[t]he media's distorted portrayal of social justice causes, with its emphasis on hysteria, absurdity and antagonism, is a core component of the Minority Rule moral panic.'[32] As a result, she underestimates the role of academia in framing and then consolidating an alternative narrative to Marxism, and how it was the intellectual and institutional locus where the shift in hegemonic discourse first took place, influencing what was then said in the media.[33]

From the start, therefore, she adopts a defensive attitude towards deliberations occurring in higher education, a stance informing comments such as '[t]his book isn't an academic examination of the forces that shape our society', and '[s]orry to the Oxford debating nerds out there, but it's not a battle of bon mots in the marketplace of ideas'.[34] In keeping with this, a subsequent attempt to get to grips with defining class is referred to by her as an endeavour that 'might not be the product of in-depth peer-reviewed research.'[35] Not undertaking 'an academic examination', however, is an insufficient reason for not investigating the pre-figuring debate that has taken place in universities about issues that are central to the case she wishes to make. Such animus is not merely debilitating, both in a political and an intellectual sense, but her resolutely journalistic approach is as a result confined to – and hampered by – the kind of sources relied upon: those cited are limited mostly to press and internet accounts.

A result of not addressing relevant discussion circulating in academia, and seemingly being unaware of what has been said there previously, both for and

---

31 Sarkar (2025: 76).

32 Sarkar (2025: 99), who makes no reference to earlier critiques of media bias, such as the empirically detailed and pathbreaking analyses produced by the Glasgow University Media Unit (Philo *et al.*, 1976; 1980; 1982). Without knowing what has been said there, it is easy to imagine that an issue being addressed is entirely new, not having been discussed before.

33 About the early debates regarding the cultural turn and subsequent influence these exerted beyond academia, a historian comments: 'Postmodern debates over the futility of searching for "facts" were largely internal to the humanities and social sciences in the 1980s and 1990s, and were not something that a broader audience of people reading or listening to popular history were especially concerned with. Whereas now controversy is politicised in a way that does spill over. Although history has always been a contested practice and discipline, it has acquired heightened charge in the context of certain types of public debates.' See 'A history of History', *CAM: Cambridge Alumni Magazine*, Issue 104, Lent term 2025, p. 29.

34 Sarkar (2025: 6, 18).

35 Sarkar (2025: 138).

against identity politics, is that Sarkar tends to perceive as new the longstanding positions and arguments prefigured in these earlier debates.[36] Hence the tendency to present an argument as though it was being made for the first time, along the lines of 'I'm going to show you how ... I'm going to explain how our perception of reality is manipulated ... I'm going to examine how ... I'll break down how class and race have been ... What this chapter is going to show you ...' and 'What I'm going to show you over the course of this chapter ...'.[37] This is a pity, because the issues she addresses are important, and had they been contextualized adequately in terms of background disputes, together with their causes and political effects, the case Sarkar makes – and rightly seeks to bring to the attention of a wider public – would have been that much stronger.

Frightened Conformity

As it is, references by Sarkar to complicity with identity politics are mainly about the political right, not the left. Contrary to the claim to have indicated how it was the left that was complicit with identity politics, therefore, her focus is principally on discourse emanating from the political right.[38] By far the most numerous and strongest criticisms she makes, therefore, are aimed at institutions or individuals on the right of the political spectrum: state agencies (the CIA), corporations (Coca-Cola, Lockheed Martin), media platforms (Fox News), commentators (Melanie Phillips, Piers Morgan, Matthew Goodwin, Lionel Shriver, Douglas Murray), and politicians (Enoch Powell, Ronald Reagan, Marine Le Pen, Nigel Farage).[39] All to the good, certainly, but the right is nowadays something of a target rich environment where political criticism is

36 Books about identity politics she does cite tend to have been published around the 2020s, conveying the misleading impression that questions about this issue surfaced only recently. Among the ones referenced (Sarkar, 2025: 31–32, 37, 45, 271 n. 6, 273 n. 30) are Brown (2021) and Dabiri (2021).

37 Sarkar (2025: 20–21, 28, 68).

38 'Far from rejecting identity politics', notes Sarkar (2025: 60), 'the modern political right understands the power of weaponised grievance and becoming the victim.'

39 See, for example, her criticisms of right-wing commentators (Sarkar, 2025: 11, 16, 53–54, 69–74, 79, 87, 91–93, 97, 99, 102, 187, 241–42, 193–94, 199) and right-wing politicians (Sarkar, 2025: 14, 110–112, 133, 135, 147, 151, 162, 164, 174, 177, 226, 235–37, 264). She points out that 'a world in which the CIA ... can celebrate "intersectionality" is no more absurd than one in which Coca-Cola and Lockheed Martin attempt to brand themselves as allies in the fight against injustice'.

concerned, and the case against it is long-standing and well-known. Less familiar, but as important, is one confronting what currently passes for leftism.

That identity politics and Marxism diverged is attributed by her both to 'public shaming [which] has cultivated an atmosphere of frightened conformity', and to the former being 'a largely middle class preoccupation, due to its spread in elite universities'.[40] Because of this, '[t]he left has a persistent habit of immobilizing itself over matters of identity'.[41] All these processes – conformity, middle class preoccupation, spread in universities, no less than demobilisation – are the *effects*, not a cause, of the political shift away from Marxism and towards a dominant focus on non-class identity. The unasked questions, therefore, are: what led to this change in the political approach of leftists, and why was it located in academia?

Unlike that of Sarkar, my argument has been that the cause is to be found in three interrelated processes occurring in academia: first, the post-1960s entry of leftists into university jobs, as Marxism vanished from the streets and into academia, where it changed into a subject for study rather than for action; second, the transition in the nature of the oppositional narrative, from class to non-class identity, as advocacy of Marxist theory became an institutional obstacle to employment or promotion within the university system; and third, how Marxism was then replaced by a less threatening form of 'radicalism', consisting of paradigms influenced by a postmodern framework, embodied in conceptual approaches like subaltern studies, multitudes, empire, and global labour history. This in turn was leapt on by capitalism, which used identity politics as a way of legitimizing its continued access to the industrial reserve.

Ominous Trends

Stemming from the same cause – not addressing prefiguring debates about identity politics – is the disappointment experienced by Sarkar in 2019 at the defeat of Jeremy Corbin and the electoral success of Boris Johnson.[42] Missed

40 Sarkar (2025: 44, 45, 46), who observes: 'As identity politics became untethered from Marxist thinking ... it became less concerned with transforming society, and more focused on being represented in it'.

41 Sarkar (2025: 20).

42 'I was ... certain that the left was on the brink of making history', confesses Sarkar (2025: 134–35) about the initial 2017 gains made by Corbin, but adds: 'In hindsight, I was self-deluding and hubristic. I got swept up in the fantasy of what a socialist government could be like ... But what I should have been paying attention to was what it would take to win the next election, rather than what Labour would do if they won.'

by her 'were ominous trends' signalling the loss by Labour of northern seats in the 'Red Wall' – 'traditional Labour heartlands' – and their move to support Conservatives, 'sign of things to come'.[43] Clearly, she was taken by surprise at this seemingly inexplicable electoral shift, Conservatives winning erstwhile safe Labour seats.[44]

Misrecognized, however, was the fundamental reason for – and the logic driving – this change in voting patterns, a shortcoming that can be traced to a lack of acquaintance with debate about the 'new' populist postmodernism, and how it reinforced capitalist ideology. Hence the problem in her case was not – as she thinks – that her views then were not shared by the majority of the population, but much rather that she had quite simply misjudged the politics of the situation.[45] The fault was that a consequence of being unaware of what Marx and Marxism had said about the industrial reserve, and its deleterious impact on workers, 'young, left-wing graduates' like her endorsed what amounted to the continuation of open-door policies, and were then taken aback when these were rejected by the working class. The reason for this is not difficult to discern.

Following the economic deregulation pursued by European governments, workers found themselves in a labour market where it was increasingly necessary to compete for jobs with those coming from outside the nation. For their part, capitalists similarly faced with having to compete in global markets were quick to take advantage of cheap migrant labour in order to cut costs and remain profitable or even viable. In the UK, conservative policy to 'take back control' of borders attracted the electoral support from working class inhabitants of 'Red Wall' seats who felt their present or future employment and livelihood prospects jeopardized by this enhanced labour market competition. The process to which they were opposed, therefore, was a burgeoning industrial reserve army of labour, the intensification of competition for jobs, and the

---

43 The initial success of Corbin in 2017 notwithstanding, '[c]oncealed by the headline figures ... were ominous trends ... the six [seats] which went the other way [from Labour to Tory] were all located geographically in the Midlands and the North of England – traditional Labour heartlands. This was a sign of things to come.'

44 'Just two years later, in the 2019 election', she concedes (Sarkar, 2025: 135), 'I learned my lesson the hard way, much the same way falling flat on your face teaches you something valuable about looking where you're going.'

45 'I wrote articles arguing that Labour should take more of a pro-EU stance than a pro-Brexit one', reports Sarkar (2025: 135), who maintains that 'I forgot the number one rule in politics [that] there were more people in the country who weren't like me than those who were ... metropolitan elites like me had lost the working class ... It was the fault of us young, left-wing graduates that the country had taken such a sharp lurch to the right'.

forcing down wages and conditions, a response that Marx and early Marxists would have understood.[46]

Accordingly, a precursor of this electoral switch was the earlier abandonment by many leftists not only of what Marxism teaches, but also of one of its main theoretical concepts, together with the political consequences of this desertion: the industrial reserve, its populist backlash, and the political empowerment of conservatives and the far right. Historically and currently, where different ethnicities/nationalities compete for the same jobs, antagonism generated by such economic rivalry tends to be expressed in terms of non-economic identities, a process that marginalizes (or eliminates) class unity and thus benefits employers. To prevent migration contributing to English labour market competition, undercutting wages and stifling working class solidarity and organization, Marx himself gave serious consideration to severing the link with Ireland.[47]

Equally clear, therefore, is that even in 2019 Sarkar perceived neither identity politics nor migration (= industrial reserve) as a problem, and that recognition of it as such dates after – and perhaps even as a result of – that election.[48] Until then, it seems, she continued to endorse the very same concepts of 'otherness' as the one structuring identity politics.[49] Further evidence supporting this contention is the throw-away remark made in the course of a 2016 video, when in reference to statistics demonstrating a shrinking white but rising non-white population, Sarkar declared 'Yes lads, we're winning'.[50] Dismissing the subsequent criticism that the remark was divisive, she commented it was

46 Part of the difficulty is that Sarkar (2025: 152) regards accepting immigration as evidence for true working-class consciousness, which the history of Marxism shows is not the case.

47 Pointing out that working class emancipation in England depended on capitalist development in Ireland, Marx (Marx and Engels, 1934: 289–90) argued that international solidarity entailed support by English workers for Irish equivalents in their struggle for economic and political independence, as distinct from migrating to where this had already occurred.

48 Although noting that worker and migrant are played off against one, to the disadvantage of both, a process encouraged by an employer-friendly media, Sarkar (2025: 138) nevertheless omits to connect this either with increased labour market competition linked to the industrial reserve, or with the rise of the 'new' populist postmodernism, and the espousal of the latter by leftists discarding Marxism.

49 See, for example, the acceptance by her (Sarkar, 2025: 151) of '[t]he simple fact ... that I'm comfortable with immigration because the humanity of ethnic minorities is not alien to me', which explains why she has so much difficulty trying to account for the emergence of identity politics in terms of causation.

50 On this episode see Sarkar (2025: 221ff.), who expresses contrition for her comment. Nevertheless, as the title of her video suggests – 'Against Integration' – she was defending 'otherness', in effect privileging the discourse of identity politics.

merely a joke, and that the antipathy encountered gave her an insight into the demographic panic of Great Replacement discourse.

Not the least problematic outcome of this uncertainty on her part about identity politics are the contradictions that it generates. Having expressed opposition to integration, and indicating that it is a view she continues to support ('I basically still back the premise'), at other points in the same book Sarkar is critical of using 'race as an identity'.[51] As inconsistent is the divergence between two equally contradictory statements made by her. On the one hand, therefore, the view that racism is inherent in the UK population, a perception embodied in the belief that Enoch Powell's 'Rivers of Blood' speech generated 'images have been embedded in the national unconscious ever since'.[52] On the other, however, the opinion of Great Replacement discourse held by Sarkar is that 'I don't think this is representative of how most people think about their fellow citizens'.[53] In keeping with this aporia is her supportive view of Jonathan Portes, who advocates open-door policy on the grounds that migrants are good for economic growth – that is, for the continuance of the accumulation process.[54]

Themes

Of the sort of histories that feature in this volume, the first part (Chapters 1–4) addresses not only that of ancient Rome, and the questions arising from this, but also how this compares with – or departs from – that of the present. The issue of systemic decline ('doomology') is examined further in relation to other aspects of the Roman empire. One of these concerns the way film images portray this process in popular culture, equating social decay with a decadence that is offset by the rise of Christianity. Another involves a comparative analysis of the dynamics constraining or driving forward the development path followed by the Roman Empire and the modern West, which argues that common to both conjunctures and contexts is the rise of the periphery and its historical displacement in each instance of core economies on the wane.

51 On these contradictory positions, see Sarkar (2025: 222, 237), who observes, rightly, that 'It's a mistake to cling to the idea of race as an identity ... But if we try to see race as a mirror to ourselves, treating its distinctions as though they really reflect who we and others are ... we will have renewed racism's diabolical grip on our lives and politics.'

52 Sarkar (2025: 236).

53 Sarkar (2025: 242).

54 Sarkar (2025: 201).

The second part (Chapters 5–8), which looks at the link between the political and the personal, examines the reason why populism has emerged and established itself historically, its rejection of class analysis and current advocacy of identity politics, together with the implications of these developments for Marxism. That class and the struggles arising from this are still crucial is demonstrated in the cases of Peru and India, specifically with regard to an ethnographic understanding of the dynamics at work in rural society in such contexts. It also features in the more mundane world of the ordinary life, as foregrounded in the politics of the personal.

Examined in Chapter 1 is an example illustrating a recent tendency in the social sciences to autobiography, consisting of personal accounts positioning the self in a political discourse, academic debates, or simply culture. Purportedly from a leftist viewpoint, the issues covered by the case in question range from reinterpretations of the historiography of ancient Rome to film genres. Not considered by its presenter is the way these two subjects combine, and consequently how each is shown through a revisionist lens. Hence modernist images in historiographic accounts which portray Late Antiquity as an early and benign form of capitalism are matched by film depictions of ancient Rome as the locus where agency is the equivalent of the modern superhero epic. The latter transformation can be linked in turn to the way plot, narrative, and script are increasingly displaced by a CGI driven focus on the spectacle.

Many of the same aspects resurface in Chapter 2, but now covering a wider historical canvas. Changes of mind notwithstanding, the case examined – said to be a Marxist one – claims that at all periods and contexts (among them the Roman Mediterranean, the Islamic world, China) production relations are 'disguised wage labour', and thus evidence for the presence there and then of capitalism. Problems with such an interpretation extend from downgrading class and class struggle, via misunderstanding the definition of free and unfree labour-power, comparing some agrarian systems with other equivalents in unfamiliar settings, to endorsing non- and even anti-Marxist historiography.

Considered in Chapter 3 is the present-day relevance of Marxist theory to the study of ancient society, why this is still important theoretically and politically, and what – if anything – remains of a Marxist approach to explanations of how, why – and, indeed, if – the Roman empire declined. This involves a critical examination of the kinds of concepts, sources, methods, and claims made by recent interpretations of Roman society. Unlike earlier historiography, including that of Marxism, which portrayed ancient Rome in negative terms (decentralisation, ruralisation, overtaxation, poverty and crisis), current approaches depict it much rather in positive hues (slavery benign, freedom and capitalism widespread). If true, the latter possess implications for the whole of

Marxist theory based on systemic transition and the historical specificity of capitalism. The current state of classics and ancient history, much influenced by anti-Marxist postmodernism. suggests that old theoretical and political battles fought by Marxism, and long thought settled epistemologically, will have to be fought anew.

Following up on aspects discussed hitherto, Chapter 4 examines a recent and interesting contribution to the decline thesis, based on a comparative study of the Roman Empire and the modern West. Its argument is that in each instance the periphery has come to dominate the core, the former supplanting the latter economically. In a conceptual framework shared with 1960s development theory, migration is regarded as negative in the case of ancient Rome but making a positive contribution to economic growth in the modern West. Downplayed, however, is the role of labour market competition and populism in the unfolding crisis of present-day capitalism.

Chapter 5 considers how opposition to the second Trump presidency is hampered by its deployment of the same kind of populist approach as his, regarding the innateness and non-transcendent nature of traditional culture, national or ethnic identity. A conservative discourse intended to counter from-below revolutionary agency, populism has been a from-above attempt historically to mobilize plebeian support on the basis of shared non-class identities. In the absence of leftist opposition to an expanding industrial reserve, workers have supported populists electorally, thereby empowering the political right. Advocating mobilization on the basis of identity politics, the 'new' populist postmodernism has been complicit with this process. Divided between anti- and pro-'otherness' in general, and open-door migration in particular, popular culture now declares either that opposition to capitalism is no longer possible, or that it entails opting out, reverting to a 'barbarian' past. That the populism underwriting the latter approach continues to be regarded as progressive is a view which continues to circulate in the social sciences, its exclusionary and anti-modern politics notwithstanding.

Outlined in Chapter 6 is that, contrary to the populist claim that Marxist theory about class no longer explains development, research conducted in rural Peru much rather validates its grassroots presence. Hence the structure and ideology of drinking groups operating in an agrarian cooperative demonstrate the historical importance of these sites as places in which the meaning of work, gender, and property relations were formulated and reproduced. Among the issues decided in such contexts was the dissolution of cooperative member status and the privatisation of its land. Drinking group participation was also a method whereby poor peasants not only gained access to decision-making about crucial economic resources, but also expressed their different class identity from rich and middle peasants on the one hand, and landless agricultural workers on the other.

Chapter 7 addresses the historical changes in social anthropological practice, and how its difficulties emerge in fieldwork diaries. In the period following the 1939–45 war, and especially the 1960s development decade, the focus social anthropology was no longer solely on autochthonous tribal populations but extended to include peasant societies. The latter – like the ethnographer him/herself – had histories, which now became part of the narrative. Unlike the monograph, the fieldwork diary records details of anthropological practice itself, and the separation between these two sorts of account diminished, as the ethnographer moved to the centre of the narrative. Attention paid to the self conducting research was influenced by postmodernism, which challenged the very notion of fieldwork, arguing that instead of the ethnographer, fieldwork should be the unmediated expression of an authentic voice-from-below. Excerpts from my Peruvian and Indian fieldwork diaries record issues that became important (peasant differentiation, bonded labour, outmigration), and also difficulties (problems with health, academia, research assistants, bureaucracy).

Finally, and on a more personal note, Chapter 8 presents episodes from three ordinary lives: mine, and those of my parents. These were shaped politically by externalities: the Spanish Civil war, the 1939–45 conflict, and the student movement of the late 1960s. At the time John Cairncross spied for the Soviet Union, correspondence reveals that his girlfriend was my mother; for his part, whilst in Germany my father witnessed the rise there of fascism. Episodes affecting me include political difficulties arising both from cartoons I drew and critiques I wrote in defence of Marxism.

PART 1

Histories: Ancient, Modern

CHAPTER 1

Recovering the Subject(s)? Self and Others on Parade

> [A]nd just as the thought of a single writer is born of the collaboration of earlier with contemporary history, so that same thought, when (as we inaccurately say) it issues from him and communicates itself to others, passes through an historical development that is no longer his, but that of all who welcome it and improve upon it, or even reject it and misunderstand it and controvert it and ignore it: in a word, think for themselves.
>
> An observation by BENEDETTO CROCE, reminding writers that, despite what they themselves may think, the ideas they have are neither their own, nor invariably correct, or indeed new.[1]

Introduction: Why Write?

Surreptitiously, a discernible pattern is unfolding in the sphere of academic publishing. Approaching one's eighth decade, and consequently faced with intimations of mortality, a number of those in the social sciences are appending biographical details, or indeed mini-biographies, to what they write. The object is, transparently in most cases, a settling of accounts with regard to what has – or less frequently has not – been said, undertaken, or achieved throughout life, in an attempt possibly to construct what it is hoped will serve as an enduring narrative about the self.[2] Not the least important aspect of such an endeavour is to paint an image of the self-as-cultured, an identity extending

1 Croce (1927: 112).

2 Recent examples include Breman (2023: 1–28) and Joyce (2024). Much rarer is the successful kind of self-critical and informative narrative found in the straightforwardly autobiographical account by Hart (2022). As the archaeology of the self presented in Chapter 8 of this volume shows, it is possible to anchor a personal history in the wider context, emphasizing the agency not of the self but of those around one.

beyond the record of what the individual concerned has actually published by delving into other intellectual areas and subjects, all of which are referenced with an air of authority.

Considered here is one such instance: the provision by Jairus Banaji of 111 vignettes covering a variety of different subjects from what is said to be a leftist political viewpoint.[3] Although these purport to address a wide variety of cultural issues, he tends to focus on what might be termed high culture, and for the most part eschews cinematic depictions by popular culture. Given his focus (here and elsewhere) on questions of Roman historiography, this failure to consider how and why ancient Rome is depicted in popular culture in the manner it has been – and in particular on film – is a curious omission, and an opportunity missed in a publication such as this.

This chapter consists of two sections, the first of which delineates his choice of vignettes, and questions the way in which some of these are interpreted by him. The second examines what might be regarded as a story not told, or a series of vignettes addressing how and why ancient Rome is portrayed on film – that most influential form of popular culture.

I

Many of the vignettes consist simply of long quotes from one or two sources, interspersed with brief comments by Banaji himself. All too often, therefore, what is a complex issue is reduced to a précis, giving rise to frequent observations of the following kind: 'so here's a quick summary of what is said there', 'what follows is a rehash of these sources', 'This entry is too long already so there's no room to say anything about how …', 'Here is a highly condensed summary of it', 'more on that elsewhere', 'Here is a short summary of …', and 'Here's a rapid summary of the plot'.[4] Difficulties arising from such brevity are themselves compounded by the element of repetition, whereby the same information reappears across different vignettes: for example, on Sartre and Pasolini. Among the questions that the entries themselves invite are why them but not others, and just how politically leftist is the approach.[5]

3 See Banaji (2023).

4 For these observations, see Banaji (2023: 73, 84, 89, 94, 95, 98, 122).

5 Inescapably, and perhaps even unfortunately, the title can be interpreted as an oblique reference to the 1971 film *And Now For Something Completely Different*, directed by Ian MacNaughton, which featured humorous routines by Monty Python's Flying Circus. If so, the danger is that the reader may think the vignettes as being less serious politically than would otherwise be the case.

Politics?

An answer, in part, requires situating them with respect to arguments found in all that Banaji has published hitherto. The vignettes read like nothing so much as the kind of entries found on Wikipedia, lacking complexity, depth, and thus also a critical approach to the issue covered. At best, they can be regarded simply as enthusiasms (along the lines, uncomplicatedly, of 'I like what *x* or *y* says …'), at worst as attempts to justify arguments or positions advanced hitherto by Banaji himself ('*x* or *y* upholds or agrees with what I've said all along …').[6] Of the latter tendency there is much evidence, which keeps on surfacing throughout, not least in the way issues to do with both domestic labour and the Nairn-Anderson theses are presented.

Banaji endorses social reproduction theory, which argues for the production by unwaged and gender-specific domestic labour of value, contributing thereby to capital accumulation, from which process – it is claimed – it is in effect inseparable.[7] Consequently, housewives are described by feminist theory as 'indirectly waged', and for this reason valorise capital, no less than does a male worker employed directly in the labour process. On this reckoning, the owner of a construction company or a corner shop can be deemed to be part of the same category, since by providing food/shelter for male workers they too contribute 'indirectly' to the reproduction of the commodity labour-power, and thus also to the valorisation of capital.

That Banaji supports this interpretation is unsurprising, since it is no different from his own argument that each and every relational variant throughout history is nothing other than a form of 'disguised wage labour', the view on which rests in turn his claim that capitalism has been present everywhere and at all times. These kinds of view dissolve not just the distinction between productive and unproductive labour, central to Marxist theory, but also between classes, together with their form of consciousness and struggle. This is because such interpretations, widely encountered in non- and anti-Marxist social sciences analyses, rope into the same category as the proletariat those elements Marxism is adamant are external – if not antagonistic – to it, like individual peasant proprietors, small traders, and the lumpenproletariat.

---

6 The approach is similar to another form of enthusiasm: the schoolboy collector who compiles an album composed of cards featuring sportsmen or film stars.

7 Banaji (2023: 90–92).

Capitalism?

Two of the longer vignettes address the Nairn-Anderson theses, concerning the role of gentrified bourgeois culture in the economic retardation of British society.[8] Against the view of Christopher Hill, who maintained that a bourgeois revolution was incomplete, Nairn argued that it has taken place, only under the aegis of a capitalist alliance with the existing landlord class. Unlike other places in continental Europe, therefore, no struggle between industrial bourgeoisie and rural aristocracy took place or, indeed, was necessary. Replaying the trope attributing the historical decline of English manufacturing to cultural attitudes, Banaji maintains that what is needed is a 'rationalisation of the superstructures', since the crisis is one of hegemony, or 'the particular forms that bourgeois power has always assumed in England.' On account of this, 'England remained refractory to Marxism. The whole of this ideology (mystified deference-based notions of class, traditionalism, empiricism and provincialism) are [*sic*] easily discernible in England today.'

Objecting to the Nairn-Anderson theses, however, Banaji privileges a contentious interpretation of his own: namely, that it was English commercial and not industrial capital which survived and prospered, a view which fits in both with his analogous objection to the systemic decline of the Roman Empire in Late Antiquity, dismissed by him as 'catastrophism', and with his insistence on the historical ubiquity of capitalism.[9] Significantly, perhaps, no mention is made by him of other causes of economic decline: external ones such as increasing competition for market share from other capitalist nations; or internal ones, like class struggle waged 'from below', offset by the deleterious role of media power in shaping and consolidating the ideology of conservatism.

All relational forms are reduced by him to what is termed 'disguised wage labour', an interpretation that in turn underpins his claim about the historical ubiquity of capitalism across time and space. Consequently negative arguments about the decline of the Roman Empire, advanced by Marxists among others, are dismissed as 'catastrophist', and replaced with a sweetness-and-light

8 Banaji (2023: 94–95, 100–102).

9 Marx, of course, was resolutely opposed to the view that the economy of ancient Rome was capitalist. Those who question the labelling of the economy in the Roman empire as capitalist range from Giardina (2007: 23), who is critical of a 'lapse into the … excess of postulating the existence of an "ancient capitalism"', to Roscams (2008), who is similarly critical of historiography that 'gets perilously close to another favourite technique of bourgeois scholarship when discussing past empires – finding capitalist enterprise in pre-capitalist societies.' For more on this issue, and why it has implications for Marxist theory more generally, see Chapter 3 in this volume.

version of the Principate as a flourishing economy, a positive view Banaji shares with Fergus Millar.[10] Because the Greek East became Roman, asserts Banaji, 'the empire achieved a sort of functional and ideological integration that the British were never able to establish in any of their imperial domains, least of all in India'.[11] Not only does this replicate the problematic claim advanced by Mary Beard about Late Antiquity as an exemplar of multi-culturalism, in the modern/positive sense of a tension-free society, but it also overlooks the negative effects of labour market competition, then as now, as true of ancient Rome as of colonial/independent India and present-day UK.

Marxism?

In keeping with this approach, Banaji questions the Marxist view that 'capitalism is invariably seen [by Marxism] as essentially European in its origin and development', promoting instead the idea of 'an earlier capitalism in the Muslim world'.[12] Indeed, the anti-Marxism informing some of the vignettes – anyway surprising to encounter in a self-declared leftist text – is difficult to avoid. This is evident from the very start, when Banaji writes that the main purpose of his approach is 'a need to break the mould of stereotypical and impoverished versions of the left's imagination and of the memory of the left' by recovering what in his view is 'a modern left [devoid of] the sclerotic traditions bound up with the parties (and smaller groups aspiring to be parties)', described by him as 'stranded objects' that were 'simply doctrinaire and sect-like'.[13] He accepts, however, that many of those recovered in this fashion were not actually 'on the left', but 'whose work mounted a powerful challenge to prevailing state doctrines'. The trouble with the latter is that it opens the door to populism, the conservative underpinning of which Marxism has always opposed.

Anti-Marxist observations surface regularly throughout the text. The work of Arghiri Emmanuel is commended because it dismissed Lenin's theory about imperialism; support for the latter 'hallowed text' by 'left-wing orthodoxies' is

10 Acknowledging that it was Peter Brown, like Fergus Millar one of the revisionist historians of ancient Rome, who conceptualised the term Late Antiquity, Banaji (2023: 79–80) nevertheless omits to mention not just its influence on his own approach but also its theoretical and methodological affinity with postmodernism (on which see Brass, 2021: Chapters 5 and 6).

11 Banaji (2023: 36).

12 Banaji (2023: 67–69).

13 Banaji (2023: 1).

similarly disparaged by Banaji as 'this kind of intellectually lazy reverence'.[14] Analogous references of a belittling sort include the following: 'crude base/superstructure models which were being rehashed at the time Tawney wrote [*Religion and the Rise of Capitalism*]'; Marxism in his opinion 'has to be understood in a diffuse cultural sense', in a way that 'no rigid party line or narrow doctrinalism would have sanctioned'; and, finally, 'Did Visconti make "Marxist" films?… Simply asking [this question] shows how nonsensical the issue becomes if framed in this way'.[15] However, no explanation is provided by him as to why this question is nonsensical.

That the propensity of Banaji constantly to change his mind about questions of theory, and in effect reinvent himself, continues undiminished as before, is also in evidence. The vignette about the views of Henryk Grossman considers two antithetical processes: on the one hand the link between capitalist crises, the fall in the profit rate, and systemic breakdown; on the other the presence of counteracting influences ('modifying countertendencies') off-setting just such a movement towards crisis.[16] Among the latter is an expanding industrial reserve army taking the form of immigration, a process identified as restructuring, arguments endorsed by Banaji himself. The irony is unmissable, since earlier he questioned the conceptual efficacy both of the industrial reserve ('a race to the bottom') and of restructuring, seen by him now as central to the accumulation process.[17]

Unknown Unknowns?

Scattered throughout the text are self-aggrandizing asides, irksome and unwarranted inferences as to the lack of knowledge on the part of the reader. Hence the reference to *Critique of Dialectical Reason* as 'Sartre's most difficult work', one with, according to Banaji, he himself has had a 'lifelong fascination', but is nevertheless a text the 'sheer inaccessibility' of which in his view means it is a closed book to everyone else ('least read text of contemporary social theory').[18] In keeping with this kind of approach is the unintentionally patronising comment that 'Marker's *La Jetée* has attracted tons of analysis, some of it fairly

---

14 See Banaji (2023: 30–32).
15 For these views, see Banaji (2023: 67–69, 80).
16 Banaji (2023: 96–97).
17 On this earlier view, see Brass (2012: 715 note 15).
18 Banaji (2023: 1).

subtle'.[19] It is also the case that the slavery/capitalism link is well-known, and not as obscure or unresearched as Banaji appears to think.[20] Likewise, the case of David Abraham, a young historian denied academic employment on account of his Marxist politics, is not as isolated an example as Banaji imagines.[21]

Despite commencing in the by now familiar self-referential manner – noting that the *Alexandria Quartet* was 'one of the earliest pieces of literature I read as a boy' – the vignette dealing with Lawrence Durrell on Alexandria is in a political sense more problematic.[22] Banaji cites with approval the view that Durrell was a racist writer 'who did not know Alexandria', since he 'always had this "strange" aspect in his portrayal of [Alexandrians], with an eye to satisfying the desires of Western readers, who have a certain fascination with the sensational strangeness or exoticism of the East'. The difficulty with this is hard to avoid. Objecting to how 'the West' categorizes 'the East' does not prevent him from categorizing 'the West' – 'the desires of Western readers' – in a similar manner.

The tone of other asides convey – again, no doubt unintentionally – an egocentric air that on occasion involves name-dropping. Thus the vignette about Fergus Millar, Camden Professor of Ancient History at Oxford, is accompanied by a remark that its subject 'would go out of his way to be welcoming to new graduates in the Classics Faculty, as I know from my vivid memory of a reception (in Michaelmas 1987) where Fergus appeared affably out of nowhere ...'.[23] Being able to engage with what Perry Anderson writes about British history and Wittgenstein is made possible because, we are informed, Banaji himself 'did philosophy at Oxford in the late sixties'.[24] Similar in tone are observations that: 'I got to know K. Damodaran ... who had been so important in the (undivided) Communist Party of India'; 'who knows if Pasolini walked past my building [in Bombay]'; that 'the film critic Bruno Fischli (with whom I showed this and other films about German fascism to student audiences in India in the

19 Banaji (2023: 116).
20 Banaji (2023: 83–84).
21 See Banaji (2023: 84–85). Much the same has happened to others who – against the grain – remained Marxists (among them Isaac Deutscher, Trevor Aston, George Rudé, E.H. Carr, and Jack Stauder), a fate that contrasts with those who abandoned Marxism so as to enter, remain in, or rise up the hierarchy that is academia. Banaji, of course, is not among the latter category.
22 Banaji (2023: 76–78).
23 Banaji (2023: 35).
24 Banaji (2023: 79).

early 1980s) wrote …'; and that 'I've met someone who knew Hedayat back in the late forties.'[25]

While it is certainly difficult to avoid regarding what is said by Banaji as a form of display, along the lines of 'eminent personages I have known', this approach is undermined by the triteness of some entries and/or references, either presenting information about their subject that in many instances is common knowledge, or alternatively declaring a familiarity for which no evidence is presented.[26] For no discernible reason, therefore, Banaji cites the Portuguese writer Miguel Torga, an early champion of whose work was my father, who first translated his poetry and short stories into English.[27] One is left wondering what, if anything, of Torga's work Banaji has actually read.

The emphasis informing the section on Marxist themes in film is also odd, consisting for the most part of vignettes on European directors, among them Eisenstein, Tarkovsky, Ivens, Godard, Visconti, Pontecorvo, Marker, and Fassbinder. Although a film by Tarkovsky is commended as the epitome of anti-war cinema, this label applies more accurately to films like *Neighbours* (1952), directed by Norman McLaren, and *Night and Fog* (1956), directed by Resnais.[28] Despite being told by Banaji that the films of Orson Welles 'are allegories of fascism', no mention is made of what is his most successful cinematic depiction of the subject, *The Stranger* (1946), about how the Nazi responsible for planning the holocaust, now living under a false identity in small-town America is tracked down by a war crimes investigator.[29] Also missing is the film *Chimes at Midnight* (1965), a nostalgic celebration by Welles of Falstaffian feudalism informed by the agrarian myth.[30] In short, politically it is not what might be termed a Marxist film: great Shakespeare, but poor Marx.

---

25 For these observations see Banaji (2023: 59, 74–75, 120, 133).

26 That to dictators and tyrants 'appearances matter infinitely more than truth' is hardly news, as Banaji (2023: 87–89) seems to think it is. As difficult to avoid is error: for example, The Red Army Fraction, a revolutionary leftist guerrilla organization active in West Germany during the 1970s is wrongly termed by Banaji (2023: 127) 'The Red Army Faction'.

27 See Banaji (2023: 119). On the work of and by this Portuguese writer, see Torga (1950). In a 1987 special issue of *Adam: International Review* (Nos. 481–486), devoted to the writings of this author, the editor Miron Grindea (p. 4) noted of Torga: 'His oeuvre is still to be discovered in this country. What little of his work has so far been published in English is due to Denis Brass, one of the best interpreters of both his poetry and prose.'

28 On the anti-war film of Tarkovsky, see Banaji (2023: 114–15). The film by Resnais is referenced by Banaji (2023: 126) only elsewhere, and in passing.

29 Banaji (2023: 24–25).

30 As a film based on Shakespeare it stands alongside Kurosawa's *Throne of Blood* (1957), Kozintzev's *Hamlet* (1964), and Olivier's *Henry the Fifth* (1944) and *Richard III* (1955).

II

Among the vignettes, Banaji might have devoted one to addressing how ancient Rome is depicted in popular culture (especially film and television), the reason for this, and what impact it has, but he omits to do so. That the portrayal of ancient Rome on film now matches the way its form of society is interpreted by revisionist historiography may be illustrated primarily with reference to *Gladiator II* (2024), directed by Ridley Scott, also responsible for the prefiguring epic, *Gladiator* (2000). Just as the latter picture ancient Roman society in terms of a modern form (CGI), so Banaji reinterprets its content in the name of a modern epistemology. Each departs from what are presented as now transcended previous approaches: on the one hand earlier films (or television serials) either based on or following closely historical and/or literary sources which inform the script and narrative, while on the other the prior 'catastrophist' views opposed by Banaji (and postmodernism).

Privileging the Image

Both *Gladiator* and *Gladiator II* are a testament to the primacy of the image, and how display as a means of communication with the cinema audience in effect displaces speech.[31] Language takes on a different form, as it is technology which defines authenticity, by increasingly enabling its physical construction. Thus, the focus on CGI seemingly obviates the need any longer to have a coherent narrative, and the script becomes virtually insignificant. In a sense, therefore, the film replicates the function of the gladiatorial games themselves, privileging spectacle over any other aspect of the issue in question, more or less decoupling the latter from its history. In much the same way, capitalism as a system can be projected backwards historically, enabling revisionist interpretations of ancient Roman society to extend the epistemological boundaries of what such a context is said to have been, seeming thereby to licence claims that it was merely another example of what is understood to be the capitalist system.

31 As in the case of *Gladiator* itself, *Gladiator II* subscribes to agrarian myth discourse (on which see Brass, 2001: 24; and Brass, 2010a: 107, n.5). Not only is the 'hand over wheat' image from the former also repeated in the latter film, but the beginning scene of *Gladiator II* locates its main protagonist at home in a rural setting, feeding chickens on his smallholding.

Gladiator and *Gladiator II* correspond to CGI-driven tales, more akin to film epics that combined ancient history with fantasy and science fiction, to the extent that one would not have been surprised to see a helicopter emerge from the clouds and land in the Colosseum. Notwithstanding claims that, with the exception of its two main protagonists – Lucius and Acacius – *Gladiator II* is based on history, its overly reliance on CGI puts it in the same company as overtly fictional cinematic epics, ranging from the last two *Indiana Jones* movies, via the *Lord of the Rings* trilogy (2001–2003), directed by Peter Jackson, and the *Harry Potter* series (2001–2011), directed by Chris Columbus and others, to *The Great Wall* (2016), directed by Zhang Yimu.[32] As the directors themselves remind us, where the epic is concerned in the last analysis it is economics which determines the way films are made.[33] Hence the following observation by one of them: 'Nobody can afford to buy three or four thousand extras. It's not economically feasible anymore because you have to costume them, you have to transport them, you have to feed them, and you move very slowly when you are trying to direct a large group of people live. Doing that today [the 1990s] is next to impossible.' He continues: 'But doing it digitally, you get a small group of people, say one hundred people, and you replicate them and move them around, and you can have exactly the same effect for one-tenth of the cost.'

It is necessary to underline that criticism of the filmic dominance now exercised by special effects, as exemplified by *Gladiator II*, does not constitute technophobia.[34] Very clearly, a story and its narrative can be enhanced by CGI: the latter, however, should not displace – either in part or wholly – the former, as it seems to do currently. The poor quality of the dialogue in *Gladiator II* is hard to miss, consisting of trite utterances such as 'I don't fight for power. I fight to free Rome from men like them'; 'The people have not seen hope in a long time'; and 'I always get what I want'. When combined with the lack of character

32 Hence the fusion of ancient history with science fiction both in the film *Indiana Jones and the Kingdom of the Crystal Skull* (2008), directed by Steven Spielberg, where the narrative ends with a flying saucer emerging from an ancient city in the Peruvian jungle, and also in *Indiana Jones and the Dial of Destiny* (2023), directed by James Mangold, which features time travel to Sicily in 212 BC, and the siege of Syracuse. For their part, *Lord of the Rings*, *Harry Potter*, and *The Great Wall* are all instances of the fantasy genre.

33 'Today [1990s], a film like The Fall of the Roman Empire has the poignant beauty of a lost art', notes Scorsese (Scorsese and Wilson, 1997: 90), adding: 'For this was the autumn of the great American epics. They simply became too expensive to make.'

34 Clearly aware of the problems that a dominant CGI poses for film, some directors deny that the prognosis is negative. Hence the view of Francis Coppola (Scorsese and Wilson, 1997: 94): 'There is a misconception that we are surrendering something of art to a technology that will do it for us ... The technology is always an element of creativity, but is never the source of creativity and so my attitude is to embrace technology as it comes'.

development, the impact of this double absence is deleterious, to the extent that the characterization in *Gladiator II* even compares unfavourably with the way individuals representing ancient Roman archetypes – slave, senator, soothsayer – appear in television comedy series (Marcus, Grumio, and Stylax from *Plebs*, or Lurcio from *Up Pompeii*).[35]

An Element of Creativity?

This is not to say that pre-CGI film portrayals of ancient Rome were all marked by appropriate characterization, dialogue, scripts, narrative, and history.[36] Central to many of the early depictions on film of narratives taken from Roman history was the coming of Christianity, a theme which privileged a discourse about religious ideology and conservative politics.[37] Thus, for example, *Quo Vadis* (1951), directed by Mervyn LeRoy, counterposes the good of characters that are Christian (Lygia, the heroine, Aulus Plautius, a retired Roman general, the apostles Peter and Paul) to the evil of their oppressors and persecutors (the Emperor Nero, his wife Poppea, the Praetorian Guard).[38] Between these binaries, and occupying a liminal position, is the victorious Roman commander Marcus Vinicius, whose transition from hostility to acceptance of Christianity forms one of the main dynamics of the story. The same is true of *Ben Hur* (1959), directed by William Wyler, in which religion fuses with nationalism, pitting Jew against Roman.[39]

---

35 Macrinus, who in *Gladiator II* is depicted simply as a lanista who trains gladiators for the arena, and is eventually killed by the main protagonist Lucius, historically not only was himself emperor in the period 217–18, but also 'gained a reputation as a jurist [and] served as ... financial administrator of [the emperor] Severus' private estates' (Grant, 1997: 123). This sort of backstory is not merely unmentioned, but as portrayed on screen by Denzil Washington seems to be little more than an astute denizen, more at home in present-day New York city.

36 For useful analyses of the way film deals with ancient Roman themes, see Elley (1984) and Wyke (1997).

37 'These religious films', observes Wyke (1997: 63), were 'steeped in the rhetoric of the Cold War [whereby the] widescreen gaze of God is constructed in alignment with contemporary American political interests and in opposition to the perceived godlessness of the Antichrist, Communism.'

38 Although, as Elley (1984: 115) notes, '[t]he Rome vs Christianity formula is the most commonly accepted form, in the general filmgoers' eyes, of the historical epic,' current privileging of CGI has shifted this discourse, keeping the focus on the arena but discarding or downplaying its religious connection.

39 Reading *Ben Hur* from a religious standpoint, Cawkwell (2004: 141–42) regards the film simply as an illustration of a spiritual journey undertaken by its subject.

A similar kind of clash between indigenous religion and imperial power informs a subplot in the film *The Fall of the Roman Empire* (1964), directed by Anthony Mann.[40] The Senate is persuaded by the philosopher Timonides to allow a captured tribal chieftain, Ballomar, and his German followers, to be settled on land in Italy and become farmers. However, together with Timonides himself, most are killed on the orders of the emperor Commodus, and those that survive – including Ballomar – are condemned to die in the Roman forum, where they revert once more to their original tribal beliefs, calling on their own gods for salvation and revenge. Like *Gladiator* and *Gladiator II*, moreover, *The Fall of the Roman Empire* also subscribes to agrarian myth discourse: whereas that of both the latter is the plebeian variant, *Gladiator* corresponds to the aristocratic variant.

On the northern border of the Roman empire, the emperor Marcus Aurelius addresses the gathering of leaders from every corner of its domain, telling them that – regardless of location, ethnicity and religious belief – they constitute 'a family of equal nations' and as such demonstrate 'the unity that is Rome'. Appearing in the middle of the development decade, *The Fall of the Roman Empire* displays or gives voice to many of its concerns and views. Anti-war views expressed both by Marcus Aurelius and by Timonides are in keeping with those advanced during the 1960s by opponents of the Vietnam war.[41] Similarly, peasant economy is highlighted and privileged, while slavery is declared to be unprofitable.[42] The religious beliefs (= pagan) of the 'other' are

40 A 'novelization' linked to the film was written by Whittington (1964), while the screenplay itself is available in a variety of formats on the internet.

41 Hence the tenor of a speech by Timonides: 'Fellow Romans. I am a teacher, and as a teacher I know that when I have tried to teach the same lesson for a hundred times and still the pupil does not understand, then I am forced to the conclusion that perhaps there's something wrong, either with the lesson or with the teacher. A hundred times we have taught those we have called barbarians what it means to make war with Rome. We've burned their villages, we've crucified their leaders. we've enslaved their young. Fires go out, the dead are buried, the slaves die, slowly. But their hatred that we leave behind us never dies! Hatred means wars. Wars mean tribute torn from our provinces, taxes, hunger, disease. How costly that is! How wasteful! And yet the answer is simple. We must have no war.'

42 In a key scene, Timonides addresses the Senate, arguing for settling captives as smallholders with citizenship rights: 'Let us transform my friends from men of war to men of peace. Let us put them on our abandoned farmland. Not only will they produce food for themselves, but this I pledge you. One day they will send food to Rome'. To this a senator replies: 'Yes, I agree. Put them on those lands. Let them produce for us but as slaves. That is the way it has always been.' Timonides then points out that 'it is no longer profitable to keep slaves. Slaves do not produce as much as free men. Let us do what is profitable, and right. Let us share the greatest gift of all. Let us give these men the right of Roman

given parity of esteem with those of the dominant power (emperor worship).[43] As regards culture and national identity, the German captives are assured – again by Timonides, the 'voice of sanity' – that there is 'no reason to change your ways', while Marcus Aurelius himself refuses to label them 'barbarians'. For its part, the coming of Christianity theme goes unmentioned.[44]

Pax Romana?

Occupying a liminal space, *The Fall of the Roman Empire* looks back to epics like *Quo Vadis*, *Ben Hur*, and *Spartacus*, but also forward to *Gladiator* and *Gladiator II*. Unlike the latter, its characterization, narrative, script, and dialogue are passable, but like *Gladiator* and *Gladiator II* it is not devoid of spectacle.[45] *The Fall of the Roman Empire* – like *Gladiator* and *Gladiator II* – depicts all the images associated with film epics: not only legions mobilizing on the norther frontier and fighting battles there, but also the funeral of Marcus Aurelius and individuals fighting in the arena.[46] As in *Ben Hur*, also depicted are triumphal processions and a chariot race. However, there is a noticeable contrast in the way fights are portrayed: whereas in *Spartacus* and *The Fall of the Roman Empire* the bouts are choreographed, following the

---

freedom. And they will spread the word that Rome has accepted them as equals, then we will have our human frontiers. The Roman peace that Marcus Aurelius promised.'

43 These views are expressed by Marcus Aurelius thus: 'We've had to fight long wars. Your burdens have been great. But we come now to the end of the road. Here, within our reach, golden centuries of peace. A true Pax Romana. Wherever you live, whatever the colour of your skin, when peace is achieved, it will bring to all, *all*, the supreme right of Roman citizenship.'

44 The sole reference is when the dead Timonides is revealed to be wearing a crucifix.

45 *The Fall of the Roman Empire* and *Gladiator* feature the imperial transition from Marcus Aurelius to Commodus, and the main protagonist in each film is a Roman general: Livius in *The Fall of the Roman Empire*, and Maximus in *Gladiator*. As in the case of Livius, Maximus too falls foul of Commodus. Unlike the former, however, Maximus becomes a professional gladiator, eventually performing in the Colosseum where – again like Livius – he fights and kills Commodus. Symptomatically, therefore, the trajectory followed by Maximus in *Gladiator* takes him to the arena: Livius survives combat with Commodus, but Maximus dies. Whereas *The Fall of the Roman Empire* contains a pessimistic conclusion, the inference being that nothing much in Rome is going to change, *Gladiator* (and *Gladiator II*) projects an unrealistically optimistic ending.

46 The pre-CGI Roman Forum constructed for the film was one of the largest sets ever made. Situated in the mountain range to the north of Madrid, descending to the Spanish capital in 1968 it could still be seen from the train in the distance, quite alone, consisting of scenery without anything behind it, much like the towns that appear in Hollywood westerns.

individual combatants around the arena, in *Gladiator* and especially *Gladiator II* the equivalent clashes are of short duration, consisting for the most part of visceral decapitations, underlining the displacement effect of CGI.

Like *Quo Vadis*, but unlike *Gladiator II*, *The Fall of the Roman Empire* traces in depth and over time how friendship between Livius, a successful general, and Commodus, the son and heir of Marcus Aurelius, turns to enmity. This particular characterization, explored at length, is central to the narrative. On becoming emperor, Commodus rejects the policy of equality among the nations followed by Marcus Aurelius, telling the senate to 'forget the weakness of my father', and announces both that he intends to change Rome, focussing on games and gladiatorial contests, and that he will double the amount of taxation appropriated from the colonies, famine there notwithstanding.[47] Together with Livius, Lucilla, and Timonides, Marcus Aurelius symbolizes the benign aspect of ancient Rome, in contrast to Commodus, who represents decadence, oppression, exploitation, the abuse of imperial power, and ultimately the process of decline.[48] Hence the final voice-over, accompanying the credits, proclaims: 'A great civilization is not conquered from without until it has destroyed itself from within'.

By contrast, *Spartacus* (1960), directed by Stanley Kubrick, makes no explicit reference either to religion, nationality, or the agrarian myth, its focus being on the opposed class position of the protagonists: on the one hand Crassus, representing the wealth, power, and oppressive might of Rome and its state; on the other, Spartacus and the slaves, who although possessing a variety of national/regional origins, are united in terms of a desire to be free, to return to their homelands, and to engage in any struggle and hardship necessary in

47 Such differences are highlighted in an exchange between Lucilla, who observes 'Rome has changed. It's now crawling with gladiators', and her brother Commodus, who retorts 'Sister, I thought you'd retired as a Vestal virgin', to which she replies 'and abandon Rome to you?', which he in turn dismisses as nothing more than the idea of a 'female philosopher'.

48 This contrast is set out below:

Marcus Aurelius **Livius** **Lucilla** **Timonides**	**Commodus**
'Good'	'Bad'
Thought	Action
Persuasion	Force
Co-existence	Domination
Equality	Hierarchy
Respect 'otherness'	Reject 'otherness'

order to achieve these ends. Even here it can be argued that a nationalist/religious theme is present as a subtext – and thus not wholly absent – since 'the *Spartacus* associated in particular with its executive producer and star Kirk Douglas constructs a more discrete historical parable in which a Moses-like hero courageously attempts to lead his surrogate Israelites to the Promised Land.'[49]

The crucial role played by narrative, and script, for the depiction of ancient Rome can be demonstrated with reference to the BBC television series *I, Claudius* (1976).[50] Lacking the features informing film representations of Roman epics, it nevertheless convinces because of a coherent plot and characterization.[51] As such *I, Claudius* is the antithesis of portrayals such as *Gladiator* and *Gladiator II*, underlining thereby the negative effect of privileging image and spectacle over literary sources. Although the impact on a cinema audience of recreating on screen the Colosseum or battles fought on land and at sea is akin to the sublime, the dramatic impact of the latter soon pales when accompanied only by mediocre characterization, plot, and script. Hence the contrast between the dramatic tension that *I, Claudius* managed to sustain and reproduce over its thirteen episodes and the rapidly dwindling interest in what happens to any of the protagonists during *Gladiator II*.

Conclusion

The dismissal by Banaji of examining film through a Marxist lens notwithstanding, it is possible to apply such an approach to two of the themes covered by the vignettes: ancient Rome, together with the way its history is depicted

49 See Wyke (1997: 68–69, 70), who notes that Spartacus 'appears on screen as a leader of a mass migration ... rather than as a revolutionary aiming to overthrow the oppressive Roman state, and his revolt appears driven more by religious piety than by class struggle'.

50 It helps, of course, to have script based on accounts written by Suetonius and Robert Graves. An earlier but uncompleted version based on these sources is the subject of a 1965 television documentary, *The Epic That Never Was*, which recounts how in 1937 Joseph von Sternberg started directing a film of *I, Claudius*, starring Charles Laughton, abandoned when the female lead playing Messalina was involved in a car accident. What remains of that film – scenes in which Livia tells Caligula that Claudius is 'the last decent man left alive in Rome' and Claudius threatens to replace senators with 'men who love Rome better than their purses' – suggests Laughton was every bit as good in the part of Claudius as was Derek Jacobi in the same role four decades later.

51 A mean-spirited trope is that the television series of *I, Claudius* was notable mainly for its wobbly scenery, which misses the point entirely. Although restricted for the most part to interior sets, the quality of the narrative, acting, characterization, and plot more than made up for the purported lack of production values.

on film. Like the gladiatorial games themselves, cinematic representations of imperial Rome allocate primacy to the spectacle, whereby image displaces speech, and with it, narrative. In the domain of popular culture, therefore, the focus of the Roman film epic has shifted, becoming increasingly CGI-driven, a change accounted for by economics: labour has become more expensive to hire, so crowd scenes are constituted digitally instead. Much like the reinterpretation of the Roman economy itself as a form of capitalism, therefore, film depictions of ancient Rome increasingly mimic those of the superhero epic located in a technologically advanced future.

In film, images of ancient Rome merge with those of superhero epics, focusing as they do on the empowered and empowering individual. Just as mythology requires a hero, an individual whose agency drives the narrative, so history requires the crowd, the mass action of which is designed to further progress. Subsumed in the larger collectivity, the individual and his/her interests are realized within this wider unit, as part of a movement, in contrast to situations where the latter is depicted merely as the product of an 'extraordinary' individual, as in the case of the hero or superhero. Central to film culture, therefore, the hero/superhero operates as the individual beyond and outside the crowd, which is portrayed as debauched, fickle, easily swayed, and politically untrustworthy. Hence in film the crowd as such remains, but as the locus of the ordinary, and consequently the antithesis of the superhero and the desirable.

In the end a compilation such as the one considered in this chapter boils down to a familiar combination: people I like, those I know, and/or individuals who think like me. An inevitable effect of the latter is the way the epistemology and politics are themselves positioned in the narrative. Given the general tendency on the part of Banaji to frequent changes of mind, constructing a persona both for himself and for those depicted through the medium of these vignettes is fraught with difficulty. Memorialising becomes a form of situating oneself on uncertain ground: a past that is itself constantly shifting in terms of interpretation, and consequently a process difficult to separate from myth-making. A crucial factor contributing to this problem is the contradiction between what are the two main aspects of his approach: on the one hand privileging his own interpretation of what Marxism really is, a theme that informs many of the vignettes; and on the other, then attaching the term leftism to the way the issues are presented, and the subject(s) recovered. The outcome is a Marxism that many Marxists – including this reviewer – would find unrecognizable as actually being Marxism.

CHAPTER 2

Marxist Mosaic or Non-Marxist Kaleidoscope?

> But though I've voted for six different parties in my life – and some independent candidates in local elections – I don't regard myself as ever having changed my mind.
>
> A lack of self-awareness on the part of the novelist JULIAN BARNES.[1]

Introduction: Repositioning the Subject

Dante expressed his disapproval of certain occupations and individuals by placing them in the deepest circle of Hell, where some were to be found with their heads buried in the ground. Where then in a hierarchy of the delusional, at the bottom end of which one finds politicians, estate agents, and snake-oil salesman, should the academic be located? By now well-known and much written about, is the notorious case of how Isaiah Berlin not only blocked Isaac Deutscher, a revolutionary socialist, from a university post simply on political grounds, but also continued to present himself thereafter – and wrongly – as 'a man of the left'.[2] Even in the present, this capacity for delusion on the part of academics should not be underestimated. A case in point is that of Henry Bernstein, who claims to be a not just a Marxist but also an upholder of Leninist theory, despite simultaneously dismissing the work by Marx on the industrial reserve and by Lenin on peasant differentiation.[3] Such claims

1 Barnes (2025: 26).

2 On this academic episode, see Ignatieff (1998: 234–35), Hitchens (2000: 141), and Caute (2013). 'Isaiah muddied the waters considerably by claiming he remained a man of the left', remarks Ignatieff (1998: 235), adding: 'In reality, as the Deutscher affair shows, he was not of that political family at all.'

3 The claims by Bernstein (2024) to follow the case made by Lenin in *The Development of Capitalism in Russia*, and its model of class differentiation, are quite simply wrong, as is all too clear from what he has argued elsewhere (on which see Brass, 2021: Chapter 4). In another article (Bernstein, 2018), therefore, he dismisses not only the possibility of capitalist accumulation in the countryside but also the presence of kulaks as unimportant. In keeping with this, Bernstein questions the central point made by Lenin, that peasants are differentiated

notwithstanding, the evidence confirms that Bernstein is neither a Marxist nor a Leninist but much rather an agrarian populist.

It is also possible to regard the author of the book analysed here, Jairus Banaji, as delusional in the same sense as Berlin and Bernstein: believing himself, and believed by others, to be a Marxist while at the same time rejecting virtually every component and concept that is central to such an approach.[4] Although, as will be seen, subject to changes of mind on a continuous basis, the arguments made by Banaji are deployed in support of the following claims: since every known production relation is, in essence, a form of 'disguised wage labour', which because it is paid is categorized (initially, at least) as free; this in turn leads inexorably to his conclusion that capitalism itself must be an ubiquitous systemic form; consequently, it is located by him in every context and epoch throughout history. Accordingly, a critical analysis of the views presented in what is a very large tome will focus on aspects of these arguments which are problematic, so much so that they bring into question his claim to be a Marxist.

This chapter consists of two sections, the first of which examines the many changes of mind informing the views held by Banaji, while the second considers how this in turn is linked to misunderstanding the conceptual apparatus of Marxism.

I

Onwards and Upwards?

Right from the start, the (surely misleading) impression conveyed is that the world is beating a path to his doorway. Hence the tenor of the following observations: Sebastian Budgen is thanked 'for suggesting the idea of this book, *indeed insisting on it*', while 'David Yaffe wrote to me saying …' and 'Nigel Harris

along class lines, and then rejects Marxist critiques of populism as unwarranted, arguing instead that populist ideas must now be accepted by Marxist theory. Within the same 2024 interview, moreover, contradictions abound. Bernstein endorses Marx's view about surplus population, yet further on what is termed inaccurately 'functionalist readings of Marx's concept of the reserve army of labour' are dismissed by him as a 'problematic assumption'. Bernstein depicts the issue as if he himself is part of the political solution, whereas from a Marxist perspective he is much rather part of the problem.

4 The book in question is Banaji (2024). Those who might regard the application to Banaji of the term 'delusional' as unwarranted should be aware that the same term is frequently applied by Banaji himself to those with whom he disagrees (Banaji, 2024: 439ff., 575, 589, 699).

stayed in touch with me till at least 1978'.[5] As the chapter proceeds, and seemingly unaware of the humour involved, Banaji goes into full Pooterish mode: his own political centrality to events is underlined, extending from minor ('a Third Worldist student society that ... I had started') to maximalist form ('I moved to Bombay [and] formed the Revolutionary Bolshevik Circle ... the purpose [of which] was to establish a better Trotskyist group than anything that existed then in India [and later] called ourselves the Platform Tendency [which] were years of high theory and a movement away from "Leninism"').[6] A case perhaps of move over Vladimir Illich and Lev Davidovich, here comes Jairus.

In a tone which is far from modest, Banaji informs us of a progress that is nothing if not triumphant: that 'the college had given me his [Rostovtzeff's] two massive volumes on the [Roman] empire as a prize'; that a 'letter from Robin Blackburn ... says "we were heartened to receive the two chapters from your book ..."'; that the JNU staff, including Romila Thapar, 'showed an obvious sympathy for what was a clear attempt [by Banaji and others] to create an alternative Left that was better read'; and that he was engaged both in 'building a modernist vision of ... late antiquity that turned its conventional image upside down', and likewise a 'paper on Sasanian aristocracy ... researched and written to refute the widespread scepticism that existed among scholars ...'[7] Fittingly, this exultant litany is rounded off in an unsurprising manner: 'In the years that followed [2001], *Agrarian Change* [*in Late Antiquity*] began to have some impact on scholarship in the field and it was gratifying to see one historian describe it recently as "the most important book on the Roman economy in the last generation"'.[8]

---

5 See Banaji (2024: x, 5, emphasis added).

6 Banaji (2024: 5, 9). The same political theme resurfaces later in the book (Banaji, 2024: 83ff.), all of a part with the kinds of things found in a recent volume (Banaji, 2023), as is outlined elsewhere (Brass, 2024d). It contrasts with the self-critical and self-deprecatory autobiographical narrative written by Hart (2022).

7 See Banaji (2024: 4, 6, 7–8, 14, 15–16). The approach of early Marxists was somewhat different: emphasizing not individual achievement but rather the emergence of political ideas or intellectual progress from the wider social milieu of which they were a part. 'I do not like any form of self-advertisement', wrote Paul Mattick (Roth, 2015: 305–306) in the late 1960s, 'I do not like to draw attention to myself. Besides my ideas and attitudes are not personal qualities but the result of circumstances shared with many people.'

8 Banaji (2024: 16). Unsurprisingly, perhaps, no reference is made to the negative assessments of that book (Banaji, 2001), not just by me (Brass, 2005) – about which he complained in the 2012 Radical Notes discussion (see below) – but also by Grantham (2004), an economist who states that '[t]he logic of this argument is very obscure' because Banaji's 'monetary analysis is hopelessly contaminated by the attempt to explain the variations in the relative value of copper, silver and gold coinage ...[t]he monetary history of the later Roman empire deserves better'.

Hard to avoid is the resulting divergence, between on the one hand the confident assertions of the kind found above, as outlined in Chapter 1 of his book, and on the other the problematic arguments encountered in the Chapters that follow, which cast doubt on claims to have upended, overturned or refuted existing models. Attempts to present them differently notwithstanding, personal achievements as depicted by the journeyman academic are in most instances mundane, invariably ordinary. As significant as what is said, therefore, is what is not said. Contrary to the impression of an epistemologically unbroken progression, one corresponding to an intellectually pristine trajectory, Banaji's ideas have been marked by constant revision, so much so that it is not possible to be sure what he claims is the case today will be what he thinks it is tomorrow.

Consistency?

Inferences as to uninterrupted theoretical consistency notwithstanding, in a footnote is found a passing reference to the mode of production debate in India during the 1970s, without mentioning either his own contribution to the deliberations or to the fact that in the course of that discussion he found it necessary to change his mind not once but twice.[9] Thus the retraction by him of criticism aimed at Paresh Chattopadhyay 'as badly misdirected'.[10] Having been an enthusiastic supporter of Utsa Patnaik (then as now an exponent of the semi-feudal thesis), Banaji changed his mind and became an opponent of her views. The same is true of his initial endorsement of the 'colonial' mode of production, which he also jettisoned subsequently, a *volte face* again mentioned only in passing, but not explained thereafter.[11]

Nevertheless, the term itself pops up again in the book, where the 'colonial' mode is in an unspecific way coupled with the semi-feudal thesis.[12] These kinds of about face were prompted by criticism from others, who pointed out the flaws in the argument he made or the position he held. Modes endorsed, then discarded included not just semi-feudalism, the 'colonial' mode, and the peasant mode, but also the tributary mode.[13] In a similar vein

9 Banaji (2024: 10, note 22).

10 For this retraction, see Banaji (1978: 419).

11 Banaji (2024: 6–7).

12 Banaji (2024: 66).

13 Details concerning this uptake/discard pattern informing modes of production, together with the awkward theoretical and political issues generated as a result, are outlined elsewhere (Brass, 2011: Chapter 4; Brass, 2021: Chapters 5 and 6; and Brass, 2022a: Chapter 3).

the late antique economy has been labelled variously 'proto-industrialisation', 'proto-modernity', 'quasi-capitalism', and capitalist. Initially Banaji poured scorn on historians who maintained that capitalism existed in ancient Rome. Terms such as 'bourgeoisie' and 'entrepreneurs' applied to 'groups of capitalists' who were engaged in economic activity such as investing in land and labour were dismissed by him originally as unjustifiable 'clichés in Roman historiography'.[14]

Currently, however, these very same 'clichés in Roman historiography' are ones to which Banaji himself subscribes: his view now is that capitalists were ever-present throughout ancient Rome, the economy of which was 'organized on capitalist lines'.[15] It is a claim, moreover, that he applies to all the subsequent modes. That it is the receipt by labour of a wage is considered evidence for the presence of capitalism not just in ancient society but in every other epoch and context is underlined by Banaji in the clearest possible manner: 'Does an economy contain elements of capitalism? Signs that we are certainly dealing with an economy that contains "elements of capitalism" would be: the widespread use of paid labour (which was certainly true of the Roman Mediterranean, but also of the Islamic world and China)'.[16]

Marxism, Methodology?

In the name of Marxism, therefore, Banaji promotes not just bourgeois contract theory, but also the un-Marxist (not to say anti-Marxist) idea that a

On why the tributary mode appealed as a concept, Banaji (2024: 433, original emphasis) observes that 'there was sufficient historical connectivity between the different forms and exemplars of the tributary mode for us to call "Asiatic production" an *epoch* ... while they lasted the "Asiatic" or tributary regimes had considerably more vitality than Marx ever attributed to the Asiatic mode.'

14 The mid-1970s dismissal of ancient Rome as capitalist is reproduced in the book (Banaji, 2024: 291): 'For a long time the history of classical antiquity worked with a similar illusion: what impressed the historians of the Roman world was the formal existence of capital, the fact that groups of capitalists were well-attested for the late Republic and early Empire, that they "invested" heavily in various speculative forms of activity, from the supply of slave-labour to the buying and selling of land or the "farming" of provinces. "Bourgeoisie", "entrepreneurs", "slave-holding capitalism" became clichés in Roman historiography.'

15 See Banaji (2024: 397ff.). Whereas earlier he appeared to endorse the view about the systemic decline of the Roman empire (Banaji, 2024: 21ff.), now that same interpretation is dismissed by him as 'catastrophism', a result perhaps of his having found there instead a flourishing capitalism.

16 Banaji (2024: 404).

benign capitalism has existed everywhere from the beginning of time. It is an approach where there is little or no room for crisis and decline of the Roman empire, for feudalism, for transition between different modes of production, and certainly for socialism at the end of it all. Instead, we have, amongst other things, a sweetness-and-light version of ancient history, under the rubric of late antiquity. As Peter Brown, the most important exponent of this historiographic approach makes clear, essentially the term 'late antiquity' covers non-economic developments in the Roman empire, whereas those like Banaji extend the concept to the economy itself. Just as Brown sees a flourishing of religion and culture as positive aspects of the period in question, so Banaji replaces systemic 'catastrophism' with a benign and eternal form of capitalism.[17] The accompanying epistemological difficulties are hard to disguise.

Acknowledging the influence of social anthropology and sociology on his own research, 'to whom I had owed so much in recent years', Brown conveys the impression that the study of ancient society can, much like modern social science, uncover what its people thought and why.[18] Hence the presence at ceremonial by the masses is taken by him as evidence for 'their assent to power', and thus also for the fact that they were 'not cowed'.[19] The difficulty with this is that it attributes motive to inhabitants of the Roman empire whose

17 In the words of Brown (2023: 369), 'The term "late antiquity" had originated among art historians [and] was best applied to the social and cultural developments ... of Greco-Roman civilization ... it was a challenge to the view that the last centuries of the Roman Empire could be seen only as a period of decline and fall – as Edward Gibbon and many others had seen them. In fact, the ancient world continued for many centuries; and these centuries were marked by unexpected creativity in religion, art, and literature.' For more on this issue, see Chapter 3, this volume.

18 On this see Brown (2023: 465–66, 467), who then adds: 'The efforts of the world history group influenced my own work deeply at the time. So far, my readings in anthropology and the comparative history of traditional societies ... had a bookish quality'. This overlooks just how problematic have been social anthropological claims about the nature, structure and dynamics of 'traditional societies'. The idealisation that stems from this inter-disciplinary transfer is clear. 'Appealing to the studies of modern anthropologists working in the villages of Egypt and the Middle East,' observes Brown (2023: 478), 'I argued that the ascetic movement did not arise from the misery of the peasantry. Far from it: the ascetic movement emerged, on the village level, from [the] new prosperity and by new possibilities for social mobility.'

19 As Brown (2023: 472) notes, 'a heartening recent development in late Roman and Byzantine studies that stressed the role ceremonial, drama, and movement in the life of the cities. The work of recent scholars had reversed many earlier negative judgments on the later empire. They showed that the ceremonies of the imperial court were not mounted only as overbearing shows of power, as Gibbon and many others had thought. They also had a popular element. Those who engaged in them were held to have given their assent to power ... They were not cowed spectators ... but an urban populace seeped

views cannot be accessed methodologically. In short, unlike contemporary social anthropological practice based on participant/observation at the rural grassroots, which to some degree elicits what the latter think and why they act, historiography of ancient Rome is for obvious reasons unable to do the same. This methodological distinction, together with its implications for the research into the reception by inhabitants of long-gone societies who left no record as to how they themselves perceived ceremonial and what it meant for them, is crucial.

Production Relations?

Yet another change of mind concerns the nature of production relations, a fundamental prop of his entire approach.[20] The centrality of this aspect is evident from the claim by Banaji that, because the production relation found throughout Late Antiquity was hired labour, consequently the mode of production in existence then was capitalist. Symptomatically, here he accepts that late Roman estates were based on labour tenancy, a view which he appeared to question earlier. Labour tenancy is labelled by him 'as a type of free worker', attempting thereby to retain his original definition, but claiming this is an 'inherently ambiguous position', which backtracks somewhat on his initial categorization of such production relations as 'disguised wage labour' that was free.[21]

Contrary to what Banaji states, however, the free/unfree dichotomy is central to how Marx and other Marxists have interpreted the logic driving accumulation, not least in determining the balance of forces in the class struggle. As will be seen below, where Roman estates are concerned his mistake is to have followed the neoclassical economic definition based simply on entry into a production relation, not the Marxist version of entry into + exit from. Again, as will be seen below, although the concept 'labour' covers free workers and

in centuries of festival. It was not the emperors who made the ceremonies. It was the ceremonies that made the emperors.'

20 Further aspects of this problem, together with their implications for his argument regarding production relations and capitalism, are considered below.

21 His interpretation of the estate workforce as composed not of tenants but of hired labour that was free has been questioned by others. On the basis of the same Egyptian papyrological sources as Banaji used, therefore, Freu (2013) has established that hired labour was not as common as thought, and was anyway confined to specific agricultural tasks (herding cattle, viticulture, irrigation). Her evidence does not support his contention that estate tenants were simply wage labourers.

slaves alike, differentiated in terms of production relations means that unfree labour cannot be seen as being part of a proletariat as a class in the sense understood by Marxism, any more than can peasants generally, CEOs hired by corporations, or lumpenproletarians.

Moreover, Banaji shifts the definition of tenancy from the economic to the ideological, arguing that such elements 'had the attributes (if not the consciousness) of a small peasant', but who were nevertheless 'dominated' by landlords who imposed on them 'slave-like conditions'.[22] What he is describing is in fact an unfree production relation, his earlier insistence that tenants are 'free' notwithstanding. Banaji then states that it is this 'ambiguity' which accounts for the 'confused picture of such workers' held by 'modern scholarship'; a breathtaking claim to make, as if he himself was in no way responsible for this self-same confusion. Part of the difficulty, unmentioned by him, is that Banaji fails to differentiate tenants in terms of class: that is, between rich peasants who borrow for productive purposes, and poor ones who borrow for subsistence.[23]

Where capitalist restructuring is concerned, Banaji adopts contradictory positions. On the one hand, therefore, he has in the past questioned the conceptual efficacy both of the industrial reserve ('a race to the bottom') and of restructuring, observing that '[t]he biggest myth of globalization is to believe that a race to the bottom is somehow inherent in the logic of capital'.[24] On the other, however, not only does the same concept pop up throughout the book, but it is used by Banaji to explain how Henryk Grossman accounted for the manner in which counteracting influences ('modifying countertendencies') enabled capitalism to prevent systemic crisis.[25] Among the latter is an expanding industrial reserve army taking the form of immigration, a process identified as restructuring, arguments endorsed by Banaji himself.

---

22 See Banaji (2024: 363), who comments: 'All this suggests that late Roman estates made regular use of labour tenancy in one form or another, and that the inherently ambiguous position of the labour tenant as a type of free worker who had the attributes (if not the consciousness) of a small peasant, but whose terms of employment allowed owners a wide margin of flexibility, including the power to dominate them and enforce slave-like conditions, accounts for the confused picture of such workers that we find both in the legal sources and in modern scholarship.'

23 Why this difference is crucial is set out elsewhere (Brass, 1999).

24 Banaji (2000: 9).

25 See Banaji (2024: 61–62, 65ff., 68, 74, 183, 359, 508, 559, 657) and Banaji (2023: 96–97).

Sedulously Aloof?

Mildly intriguing, certainly for this reviewer, is the content of Chapter 32 in the book, about Indian Maoism, and the way it too differs from the case made by Banaji in the course of an earlier interview.[26] Since both date to 2010, their textual interconnectedness is in all other respects much the same. In the interview, Banaji compared the Naxalite movement in India to that of Sendero in Peru, arguing that each subscribed to the same mobilizing discourse. The latter was the semi-feudal thesis: the similarity between Sendero and the CPI/ML stemmed from a common Maoist belief in the existence of a pristine peasantry, and the parallel between the nationalism of Maoism and the reassertion of indigenous tribal/peasant 'otherness'. Unmentioned, however, was that all these arguments, together with the same ethnographic source and the case about the Sendero/Naxalite resemblance, had been made elsewhere two decades earlier.[27] That initial comparison by Banaji, along with the critique based on it, no longer features in the analysis of Indian Maoism presented in this book, and seems to be yet another instance of a change of mind on his part.

Equally problematic is the inference that he 'published almost nothing in the [nineteen] eighties', because he was too busy with other things either to engage with or to be affected by postmodern theory ('[t]hroughout these years I remained sedulously aloof from Subaltern Studies and postcolonial theory ... and was blissfully unaware of the intellectual fashions sweeping through academia on the other side of the Atlantic').[28] Apart from an unfortunate *de haut*

---

26 Leonard and Singh (2010).

27 The article making the earlier case is Brass (1991), based on ethnographic data contained in Duyker (1987). The latter is also cited subsequently by Banaji in Leonard and Singh (2010). Attention was drawn to this similarity (Brass, 2012: 709, 713 n6), and although the text by Duyker appears in this book (Banaji, 2024: 691–94, 700), the Sendero/Naxalite comparison does not.

28 For this claim see Banaji (2024: 14), who appears to have forgotten his participation in an *ad hominem* discussion about me posted on the Radical Notes website on 7 September 2012, in the course of which I was accused by one contributor of 'a serious mental illness' and by another of 'delusional rantings' on account of my blaming 'everything on post-modernism and chayanovian populism always and everywhere', an approach one contributor recalled also informed 'a similar article [by me] about subaltern studies'. This view went unchallenged by Banaji, who in a somewhat desperate attempt to invalidate a critique (Brass, 2005) complained that I had 'reviewed [his book] *Agrarian Change in Late Antiquity*, undeterred by the fact that [I] had little knowledge of the field.' Of the many ironies stemming from this spurious argument are two in particular. First, what 'qualifications' did Marx, Engels, Lenin, Trotsky and Luxemburg have – or, indeed, need – for writing about the things that they did? And second, Banaji intervenes in the discussion of topics – such as the rural historiography of Latin America – where he

en bas tone, this is debateable for a number of reasons, not least the overlap between 'new' populist postmodern epistemology and his own revisionist view about late antiquity. Acknowledging that 'postcolonials were cursing the Enlightenment', and further that postcolonial theory was 'absurd', Banaji accepts that, after all, he did engage 'with that great upheaval', but only to the extent of questioning the decline thesis as this was applied previously to ancient Rome, in his view an Enlightenment legacy of Gibbon.[29] Moreover, his claim to having had nothing to do with subaltern as a concept notwithstanding, Banaji still deploys the term in the book without explaining what it signifies.[30] What these contradictory positions suggest is that, in retrospect, he wants to be seen as on the side of the angels – those who recognized the shortcomings of postmodern theory – despite remaining 'sedulously aloof' from and unaware of the 'cultural turn'.[31]

Having rejected the notion of labour being unfree, describing such production relations as 'so-called', Banaji seems of late to have rowed back on this, to the extent that he now accepts that labour – not just that of chattel slaves – can indeed be unfree. Accordingly, dismissed out of hand by Banaji in 2003 as 'so-called', unfree labour reappears in analyses published during 2007/2008, now no longer 'so-called' but an epistemologically standard form of production relation.[32] Conversely, the category of free labour is belatedly recognized as being less straightforward than previously thought, as suggested by the ensuing terms applied to it ('the indeterminacy of free labour', its 'incoherence').[33] So central is the issue of free/unfree labour, both to his view about capitalism and to his approach more generally, that it requires unpacking further.

II

Misunderstandings by Banaji about systemic modes, production relations, labour regimes, and much else besides, together with changes of mind necessitated as a result, have their roots in his contribution to the mode of production

himself 'has little knowledge of the field', a lack and its consequences that are considered below.

29 Banaji (2024: 15).

30 For these references to the subaltern, see Banaji (2024: 382, 744).

31 Noticeable is the number of those who now declare that they have always been aware of the conservative or reactionary political antecedents of postmodern theory, thereby claiming – wrongly – to have played a crucial role in its unmasking. This is a theme analysed critically by me elsewhere (Brass, 2000a).

32 Compare Banaji (2003) with Banaji (2010: Chapter 7).

33 Banaji (2024: 433–34).

debate, where he concluded that '[t]he capital/wage labour relationship was thus widespread throughout the Deccan'.[34] Nineteenth century peasant smallholders working on their own land, selling not labour-power itself but rather the product of labour, are deemed by him to be in receipt of 'a concealed wage'; accordingly, these subjects are conceptualised as 'disguised wage labour', and thus described – wrongly – as a 'proletariat' composed of workers that are free. Undifferentiated internally, the rural household is perceived as a unitary form, composed of family members all of whom received 'a hidden wage' for growing crops on their own land. This, argues Banaji, enabled capital to integrate peasant economy into commodity production by a process of 'forced commercialisation' which did not entail dispossession of the direct producer.

What Marxism Is or Isn't

A major difficulty stems from how Banaji defines free and unfree labour, and the difference between them. Characterizing unfree labour as a proletariat overlooks the fact that for Marxism workers belonging to this category must be doubly free: separated not just from their means of labour but also from control exercised by an employer.[35] Banaji seems not to recognize this, since he makes the common error of arguing that Marx restricted the free aspect only to separation from means of production (land).[36] The only labour-power regarded by Banaji as unfree is chattel slavery, a view that similarly ignores the element of unfreedom present in other non-slave work arrangements, such as indenture, bonded labour, sharecropping, and tenancy. Contrary to the assertion that 'the distinction between free and unfree labour collapses in a grey area which is much better sorted out in terms of a notion of *how wage-labour markets are structured and how they work*, especially in agriculture', it is precisely in relation to markets 'and how they work' that the free/unfree dichotomy operates.[37]

Overlooked, therefore, is that Marxism situates this dichotomy within class struggle, a process whereby labour that is free can become unfree, and *vice versa*. In short, Banaji misrecognizes the dynamic at work, one to which he himself purportedly attaches significance when – as below – he speaks of 'organization

34 See Banaji (1978: 407). The prefiguring role of this view is clear from what is said by him in the book (2024: 13): 'I had a sense that the work I had done on the Deccan peasantry and the ideas gained from that about how peasant households fare under imperial systems would exert a strong influence on my reading of Late Roman sources.'

35 See Marx (1976: 271–72).

36 Banaji (2024: 434).

37 Banaji (2024: 436, original emphasis).

and control of the labour process in concrete settings'. Where competition is acute, not just between capital and labour but also between enterprises, producers replace free workers with unfree equivalents, or convert the former into the latter, a transformation that corresponds to deproletarianisation.[38] The reverse dynamic, also the outcome of struggle, consists of the emancipation of unfree labour, and its conversion into free counterparts. Thus, the free/unfree dichotomy does not, as Banaji insists it does, 'collapse'.

Another significant break with Marxist theory concerns the way production relations are defined as unfree. For Banaji, the element of unfreedom is characterized solely by the involuntary entry into a work arrangement (= entry into), an interpretation shared by neoclassical economists. The latter, like Banaji, restrict the unfree element simply to the inception of an employment contract: that is, to the involuntary manner in which a labourer enters a work arrangement. That a worker is then unable to withdraw from this work arrangement without the consent of the employer does not influence its conceptualisation as unfree. By contrast, in Marxist theory the definition of a production relation as unfree stems from the condition governing the reproduction of the *whole* relation: entry into + exit from. Not considered by Banaji, therefore, is that the presence of a debt relationship between employer and worker compels the latter to borrow in order to survive, thereby extending the duration both of the debt and – consequently – of employment. In such circumstances, unfreedom based on coercion operates not just at the beginning of the production relation but also its end.

Debt, Coercion as Free Wage-Labour?

Not the least of the many ironies with such claims are two in particular. First is the emphasis placed by Banaji on payment received by labour as evidence of its free character, and thus also its categorization as a 'proletariat' signalling in turn the presence of capitalism, when in fact it was precisely through this method – 'payment' (= debt) – that workers were bonded, and rendered thereby unfree. And second, the acceptance that '[t]he labour relationships of the Byzantine large estates reflected the subjection of free labour in forms that gave large landowners well-nigh absolute power over their employees', which underlines the confusion informing the way he deals with issues to do with the labour regime, and how to characterize production relations.[39] What

38 On deproletarianisation see Brass (1999, 2011).
39 Banaji (2024: 358).

is classified as 'free' labour-power is, he agrees, a work arrangement in which landowners exercised 'well-nigh absolute power over their employees', which suggests that the workers in question were much rather unfree.

For this reason, the theoretical problem with the concept 'disguised' wage labour, deployed by Banaji in debates about the mode of production and late antiquity, is clear. Because it reifies the wage, this term confuses the fact of payment made to a worker (= wage labour) with labour-power that is free. The two aspects are, of course, distinct: one has to do with the kind of production relation linking a worker to his/her employer, while the other concerns the form taken by the remuneration for labour expended. Ignoring this conflation, Banaji privileges-by-essentializing payment, insisting '[t]hat the deployment of these forms of hired labour was characterized by considerable *coercion*, including debt bondage ... is incidental to the essential nature of the relationship as a domination of *wage*-labour.'[40]

Epistemologically, the problem generated by conflating payment of a wage with labour-power that is free is obvious. Throughout history, many different kinds of workers who were relationally unfree nevertheless received payment whilst in the employ of another. That they were paid did not of itself signal the presence of labour-power that was free, as many examples of payments made to workers who were also chattel slaves, indentured labourers, debt peons and attached or bonded, all attest. Hence the problematic nature of his accusation that Marxists 'have paid so little attention to ... the deployment of labour [viz.] the actual organization and control of labour processes'.[41] This is an astonishing claim to make, not least because the focus of virtually every article published in *The Journal of Peasant Studies* – to which Banaji himself contributed – over the period 1973–2008 was precisely on the organization and control of the labour process.

New Ways of Thinking?

There are other reasons for questioning what Banaji understands by Marxism. Noting that '[t]he last few years have seen some remarkable contributions to agrarian history', he merely asserts the validity of his opposition to the characterisation of labour-power as unfree, based as it is not on an examination of the arguments concerning such production relations, but only on citing the

40 Banaji (2024: 663–64, original emphasis).
41 See Banaji (2024: 436–38).

work of revisionist historians.[42] This contention is illustrated with reference by him to the analysis by Charles Gibson of rural Mexico from the sixteenth to the nineteenth century, an exemplar of the revisionist view that debt peonage was benign, not to say empowering for its subject.[43] Despite insisting that Mexican peonage was non-coercive, however, Gibson himself admits not only that unmet debts were passed from father to son but also that workers were prevented from leaving the hacienda without at first clearing such debts, a position hardly consistent with the idea – misleadingly endorsed by Banaji – of 'liberal peonage' based on the exercise of 'autonomy' and 'significant bargaining power'.[44]

Once again he appears to qualify this view somewhat later in the book, when observing that '[m]ost *peones* who worked on Mexican estates in the seventeenth and eighteenth centuries were not serfs but wage-labourers bound by debt [who] worked full time for the estates'.[45] Hence the concession that those described hitherto as 'free' because they received a wage are actually bonded labour. As is the case throughout Latin America where the hacienda system prevailed – unfree workers tasked with carrying out labour-service were meeting the rent owed by a tenant to the landlord.[46] Much the same argument is made by Banaji with regard the *inquilino* system of labour tenancy found on

42 Banaji (2024: 349ff.). 'Some of this work, notably recent Latin American history,' he declares, 'especially Charles Gibson's seminal rewriting of the history of debt peonage to allow for a greater sense of autonomy and resistance in the *gañanes* relations with their Spanish employers [supported] the idea that rural workers who had always been conceived simply as bonded labourers or slaves could actually exert significant bargaining power made it possible for other historians to insist on the distinction between more or less "liberal" forms of peonage ... and to open a space for new ways of thinking about "traditional" institutions.'

43 Gibson (1964).

44 See Gibson (1964: 537, 538, notes 186 and 193). Ironically, Banaji appears to row back from revisionist claims when observing subsequently (2024: 363, n81) that: 'The capacity of the landlords to enforce their will on their tenants depended largely on their capacity to limit the latter's mobility ... tenants' bargaining power was proportionate to their ability to move off the farm and seek better terms elsewhere'.

45 Banaji (2024: 436).

46 Writing in 1929, Tannenbaum (1968: 404) comments: 'The revolution has freed approximately one-half of the rural population from serfdom ... about 6,000,000 people were in 1910 located upon haciendas and ranchos ... the greater portion of these occupied a position of indentured servitude or peonage. This peonage took the form of restraint on account of debt'. Earlier the same source (Tannenbaum, 1968: 109) points out: 'As far as possible the hacienda maintained a permanent labour force ...[t]he serfdom that existed in Mexico for some four hundred years must be looked upon as in part an attempt to overcome a labour shortage. The reduction of lands of the villages has been an attempt not merely to get the lands of the villages but also to get permanent labour. It is generally

Chilean rural estates, where the landlord project was based on 'an expandable supply of labour (the labour of *families*)'.[47] Again, the precise manner in which this arrangement operated remains unmentioned: how did the household head – the tenant – ensure that kinsfolk (and also fictive kinsfolk) met his labour-rent obligations? Despite being labelled as 'free labour', evidence confirms that the Chilean *inquilinaje* was an unfree production relation: like the *gañan* in Mexico, it was a form of tenancy structured by debt (often at the estate store) which, as long as it remained outstanding prevented its subject from selling his/her own labour-power on a seasonal or casual basis for higher wages elsewhere.[48]

Straying into what for him is unknown territory – rural Latin America – prefigures the resemblance Banaji claims to exist between the hacienda system and Byzantine estates. No mention is made of the 'qualifications' necessary for this kind of comparative analysis: much rather the opposite, in that an unwillingness to undertake such comparison is now regarded as causing 'a conceptual atrophy', and 'is the biggest limitation on any progress' in the historiography of ancient society, which is very different from the view he expressed about not being 'qualified' to tackle such an approach.[49] In support of his claim that capitalism existed in ancient society he maintains both that landlords were interested in the economic operations on their estates, and that the workforce was paid.[50] While the first part of this claim is uncontentious – has anyone ever doubted that landlords were interested in the returns from their rural properties? – no reference is made to what sort of production relations structure the work arrangements these sources describe simply as 'paid labour'. All kinds of unfree labour-power received payment, and that workers referred to merely as 'paid labour' were bonded by debt (either to the landowner, a labour contractor, or petty trader) means that they were not free, and thus did not constitute a proletariat, as argued by Banaji.

agreed that the system ... was most fully developed in those sections of Mexico where labour was scarcest.'

47 Banaji (2024: 360, original emphasis).

48 On the unfreedom of the Chilean *inquilino*, see McBride (1936: 148–9, 150).

49 Lamenting the lack of comparative analysis carried out by historians of the ancient world, Banaji (2024: 350) notes that: 'The lack of interest in other periods of history spawns a progressive conceptual atrophy, and it is this drying up of our sources of conceptual understanding which is the biggest limitation on any progress in ancient economic history.'

50 The sources, argues Banaji (2024: 350–51, 352), 'tell us repeatedly that paid labour was used regularly and on a large scale, that the use of labour reflected rational considerations ... all signs of a precocious modernism ... the issue is not whether estates retained permanent workers but whether such workers, who normally received rations from the estate, were really wage labourers of some kind.'

Who Is the Enemy?

Rather than engaging critically with non- or anti-Marxist positions and theory, these days many self-proclaimed Marxists spend their time instead attacking Marxism itself. An additional reason for questioning the Marxist credentials of Banaji, therefore, is the extent of his condemnation aimed at leftist politics and parties.[51] Censure includes not just Communist groups and Stalinism, but also – and more especially – followers of Trotsky. All are blamed for shutting down theory, since 'most claims to orthodoxy were simply spurious'.[52] He continues in much the same vein, labelling as untenable '[t]he idea that Bolshevism offered a model for how a revolutionary movement is built'; in contrast to those connected with his sort of 'study circles', leftists of every kind are castigated by Banaji as 'doctrinal', to the degree that in his opinion it is not possible 'to imagine a renovation of the Left emerging out of the legacies of theoretical stagnation … that Stalinism bequeathed even to its most resolute opponents.'[53]

Yet another factor leading to this kind of doubt is the wide range of non- and anti-Marxist sources cited with approval by Banaji. In this category are found not just agrarian populists such as Bernstein, who like Banaji himself rejects many crucial aspects of Marxist theory, but also vehemently anti-Marxist historians such as Richard Pipes, together with neoclassical economists strongly opposed to Marxism, such as Robert Steinfeld, Robert Fogel and Stanley Engerman.[54] Much the same applies in the case of the espousal by Banaji of the tributary mode, a concept little different from the oriental despotism model formulated by the Cold war warrior Karl Wittfogel. Equally problematic is the endorsement by Banaji of the way unfree labour is interpreted by Jan Breman who, again like Banaji himself, has not only changed his mind about this production relation – a *volte face* that goes unmentioned in the book – but

---

51 The full extent of Banaji's animus towards leftism *tout court* can be gauged from the following blanket condemnation (Banaji, 2024: 29): 'For just as the intellectual terrorism of the modern Marxist corresponds closely to the mental habits of the Stalinist bureaucracy, there is a certain intimate relation between the ultramaterialist view of man common to the uncritical vulgar Marxists and naïve realists and the oppressive, static structures of the Stalinist hierarchy.'

52 Banaji (2024: 8).

53 Banaji (2024: 17).

54 Hence the positive references to Bernstein (see especially Banaji, 2024: 498ff.), to Pipes (Banaji, 2024: 430–31), to Steinfeld (Banaji, 2024: 435–36, 532), and to Fogel and Engerman (Banaji, 2024: 282, 428).

also wrongly perceives his own approach to agrarian issues as being influenced by Marxism.[55]

Conclusion

Unlike a kaleidoscope, in which the image is ever-changing, a mosaic is composed of small, coloured glass pieces forming a pattern that is fixed in place: the consistency of the latter is in marked contrast to the inconsistency of the former. Rather than a Marxist mosaic, therefore, the arguments and case made by Banaji over the years, and collected in this volume, can be said more accurately to be a non-Marxist kaleidoscope. As such it raises once again the contentious – but currently very relevant – political question of how much of the conceptual apparatus of Marxism is it possible to abandon, and yet still be considered (by self and others) to be a Marxist. There are those with whom one disagrees, but whose Marxist credentials are recognized; then there are those with whom one disagrees, and whose claim to uphold Marxist theory is disputed. It is to the latter category that, for this reviewer, Banaji belongs.

Evidence from the many essays in his book point to the extent of a dissonance between a prefiguring affirmation of consistency and a subsequent approach characterized by continuous backtracking, including about what Marxism is thought to be, what modes of production are, and what Roman history is. Over a whole range of issues, therefore, Banaji either rejects – or, indeed, opposes – what Marxism not only teaches but also ontologically requires: concepts that are central to this epistemology the meaning of which he changes or discards take in definitions of free and unfree production relations, the proletariat, and capitalism itself (its space and time). In many instances, rather than Marxist interpretations, endorsed instead are those advanced by anti-Marxist historiography. In the end, it is difficult to avoid the baleful conclusion that what remains both of Marxism and of his claim to be Marxist is in each case the same: almost nothing.

The approach of Banaji to Roman history has implications not just for the latter but also for Marxism itself, as is outlined in the following chapter.

55 See Banaji (2024: 654, 664, 682). On the many contradictions informing the case made by Breman about the connection between unfree production relations and capitalist development, see Brass (2024a: Chapter 8).

CHAPTER 3

Is Marx at Home in Ancient Rome, or Is the Eternal City the Locus of an Eternal Capitalism?

> One cannot observe events which have long passed and of which no memory has been preserved.
>
> An observation by EDWARD EVANS-PRITCHARD about the methodological difficulties faced by anthropologists conducting participant/observation fieldwork, which could just as well apply to social historians undertaking research into the economy, the grass-roots voices, and the society of ancient Rome.[1]

∴

Introduction: Deconstructing Rome (in a Day)?

Despite it seeming to be an unlikely place and time to address (and perhaps even resolve) questions about the origin, nature, and logics of the capitalist system, Marxists have in the past – and continue to do so now – found it necessary to intervene in the debate concerning the nature, structure, and reproduction of the economy in ancient Rome. There they have encountered the presence of strong disagreement over matters that are central to Marxism: not just about theory and methods, but also about the presence or absence of economic growth, together with obstacles to this; the characterization of the labour regime, property forms and rights, relations of production and the productive forces, together with conflicts generated by these structures and processes. At issue, therefore, are a number of interrelated issues: how to analyse the Roman economic system, did the empire decline, and if not what are the implications of this for Marxist historiography. Marx himself was always clear that ancient Rome was not – and could never be seen to be – a capitalist economy.[2]

---

1 Evans-Pritchard (1951: 90).

2 See, for example, Marx (1972: 497; and 1981: 444–45, n.46).

The significance of this disjuncture for Marxism cannot be underestimated. If it is conceded – as it is, not just by non-Marxists and anti-Marxists but even by some who still regard themselves as Marxists – that the economy of ancient Rome was capitalist, and further that rather than decline the empire flourished, to the advantage of all, then capitalism as a mode of production is indeed systemically eternal, and no reason exists as to why it could – or indeed should – be transcended. Moreover, if labour-power at that period was free and ubiquitous, and landlords were already de facto capitalists, employing not unfree tenants but free hired workers, and claims about the pervasiveness of multiculturalism are correct, little or no reason exists for conflict leading to crisis and systemic transformation. According to this paradigm, therefore, the economic dynamic and logic of first century Rome is in essence little different from that of nineteenth century Britain.

The presentation which follows is divided into two sections, the first of which considers the way in which historians of ancient society have come to rely on current theory and concepts taken directly from the social sciences (globalisation, multiculturalism), replacing earlier and more negative appraisals – including those by Marxists – of the trajectory followed by Roman history. Examined in the second part are the kinds of methodological problems encountered as a result, and resolved neither by new theory/concepts nor by new archaeological discoveries, as evidenced in attempts to discern reception in ancient society of grassroots meaning attached to images, coinage, and paintings.

I

A Huge Container

In what is a useful overview of the uneasy coexistence between Marxism and the historiography of ancient Roman society that earlier addressed the fall/flourishing debate, Giardina makes clear that he disagrees with those 'modernizing perspectives' which categorized the ancient Roman economy as capitalist.[3] Not considered by him on that occasion, however, are two important aspects of the debate where Marxism is concerned: the role of the 'new' populist postmodernism in the way Marxist influence on ancient historiography has diminished, and the deleterious implications of this process for

3 Giardina (2007: 18, 23).

Marxist theory as a whole. Both these aspects are central to the argument presented here, which goes well beyond that of Giardina.

Hence the view that what he terms 'Marxist and Marxist-inspired historiography [which] showed a considerable theoretical flexibility and opened up new research horizons' as positive, the combining of Marxist categories with non-Marxist ones as 'a sign of the vitality of Marxism, rather than of its weakening'.[4] These same 'anti-dogmatic' Marxists are commended by Giardina for regarding ancient Rome as in a sense 'modern', since by using analytical categories from current political economy they are consequently able to 'criticize capitalist exploitation'.[5] Observing that it was the study of material culture that particularly strengthened the influence exercised by Marxism on ancient historiography, since it was regarded 'as a decidedly Marxist method', he fails to note the downside of this process: namely, that it also helped to promote the idea of ancient Rome as a capitalist economy.[6]

Unmentioned by Giardina but lurking behind terms such as 'anti-dogmatic' Marxists deploying 'modernizing perspectives' is the impact on the study of ancient Roman society of postmodernism. Instead of being a sign of the vitality of Marxism, therefore, argued here is that it was much rather a negation of all that a Marxist approach upholds. This much is evident from the characteristics ascribed by him to 'the new advanced Marxist canon': not just 'a non-hierarchical relationship between structure and superstructure', and 'the rejection of economic determinism', but also 'a scepticism regarding the existence of laws of historical evolution'.[7] In short, the same epistemology as that espoused by the 'new' populist postmodernism.

Noting, rightly, that from the 1980s onwards Marxism ceased to be a feature of ancient historiography, due in part to 'an anti-Marxist bias that is not grounded in actual knowledge of Marx's work', and further that '[t]he rejection of the concept of crisis has been strengthened by the rise of another historiographical trend ... that is to say the "optimistic" interpretation of late antiquity', Giardina accepts that discarding crisis – a concept 'deeply rooted' in Marxist theory – has 'serious consequences' for any understanding of ancient

4 Giardina (2007: 15, 17).

5 Thus 'the rejection of dogmatic Marxism', notes Giardina (2007: 19), 'allowed scholars of antiquity with Marxist leanings to give a modern sense to their studies, because it offered more flexible and effective ways to historicize the modern categories of political economy and thus criticize capitalist exploitation'.

6 Giardina (2007: 21).

7 See Giardina (2007: 23) who notes that adherents of 'the new advanced Marxist canon' made little or no reference either to class or to class struggle, in contrast to the Marxist approach of de Ste Croix (1981).

Roman historiography.[8] Equally correct is his conclusion, one shared here, that '[t]he demolition of the concept of "crisis" has dragged down with it another important concept describing social change: that of "transition"'.[9] Without saying so, therefore, what is being referred to by him is the positive view (= 'optimistic interpretation') opposed to the decline thesis, as found in most postmodern-influenced revisionist versions of ancient Roman history.[10]

Decline and Fall?

The importance of the debate about ancient Rome, for Marxist and non-Marxist theory alike, is obvious.[11] On whether or not the Roman economy was capitalist, rival interpretations divide into two distinct camps. On the one side, therefore, are found those who subscribe to a materialist approach and maintain that decline occurred because the prevalence of unfree production relations discouraged labour-displacing technique. An effect of a plentiful supply of cheap labour-power, in the form of chattel slavery, meant that employers had no incentive to adopt or invest in more advanced productive forces, as a result of which at this conjuncture and in this context unfree labour-power was an obstacle to further economic development. The process of decline is itself an outcome of stagnation, ruralisation, over-taxation, famine, starvation, and oppression, a combination which sets the stage for the subsequent transition to a feudal mode of production. Broadly speaking, this negative view – the 'retardation' thesis as applied to the Roman economy – is

8 See Giardina (2007: 21–22, 27–28), for whom 'the rejection of the crisis paradigm has given rise to a new conformism marked especially by an insistence on the essential continuity of Roman history in the Imperial period. To deny that there was crisis in Italy in the second century AD, or a general crisis in the Roman world in the following century, is perceived as an expression of the same non-ideological, anti-dogmatic attitude – an attitude that is sensitive to empirical data and wary of general models. Continuism, by its very nature, tends to grow indefinitely. Thus it has expanded to embrace very long subsequent periods, transforming the late empire into a huge container extending well into the Middle Ages.'

9 Giardina (2007: 29).

10 Exponents of which, as will be seen below, include Banaji, Fowler, Brown, Beard, and Osgood.

11 This is acknowledged even by historians of ancient Rome. Observing that there 'are those who see the ancient economy in very modern terms', while others 'argue that Roman economic life was utterly different from our own', Beard (2008: 153–54) hedges her bets by observing merely that '[m]ost historians now come down judiciously between these two extremes', a view echoed subsequently by Scheidel (2012: 15) when observing that '[t]he story of the Roman economy is not a simple story of rise and fall'.

held not just by Marxists (Marx, Engels, Kautsky, Luxemburg, Walbank, and de Ste Croix) but also by some non-Marxists (Frank, Rostovtzeff, Oertel, A.H.M. Jones).[12]

In the same camp, therefore, are found non-Marxist historians of ancient society, writing and publishing during the first half of the twentieth century, who also support the idea of economic decline, albeit for different reasons. It was attributed by Rostovtzeff to the subjugation of aristocratic landowners by Roman armies composed of peasants and workers, while Oertel ascribed systemic demise to the destruction of a prosperous *laissez-faire* system by Roman 'state socialism'. For their part, Frank and Duff linked the end of the Roman Republic and the subsequent economic decline to the increased population of slaves from the east, who – never having known self-government – on becoming ex-slaves and citizens were not as opposed to religiously-sanctioned 'from-above' power exercised by a ruler-as-deity. Decline itself is characterized by a number of interrelated systemic processes: over-taxation, impoverishment, underconsumption, and economic retardation (non-development of the productive forces). This in turn led to decentralisation, de-urbanisation and ruralisation, together with the rise in religious belief, plus a return to peasant farming in the form of tenancy that prefigured the transition to feudalism.[13]

From the 1970s onwards, however, these sorts of views were increasingly opposed by those – among them self-proclaimed Marxists – who characterized the historical trajectory followed by ancient Roman society not as one of unfree labour, crisis, struggle, and economic decline but much rather as one of continuity, economic stability and growth, free wage labour and general prosperity, all evidence according to some for it being capitalist. Dismissing earlier interpretations by Marxist and non-Marxist alike as negative 'catastrophist' models, this revisionist approach replaced them with a positive view of what they termed Late Antiquity, a historiography that by contrast is a narrative

12 Details about all these interpretations, who holds them and why, together with the theory, concepts, and methods backing such views, are outlined by me elsewhere (Brass, 2021: Chapters 5 and 6: Brass, 2022a: Chapter 3).

13 'The history of the ancient centres of civilization becomes more and more a history of dissolution and decay', writes Rostovtzeff (1927: 352, 355, 356), noting that: 'One feature of the economic condition is especially remarkable – the complete change in agricultural methods throughout the empire. Scientific cultivation … disappears utterly and is replaced everywhere by a system which merely scratches the surface of the soil and sinks lower and lower into primitive routine. Though estates may be large and great tracts of land are owned by members of the new imperial aristocracy, yet agriculture is based on the tilling of the soil by small cultivators, either owners or tenants … Thus energy and power to work dried up, taste grew coarser, and a small privileged group kept on the surface of a sea of destitution … Christian literature alone was really alive.'

about an ever-present dynamic that is economically benign.[14] It is, in short, a framework purged of all the processes which generate what for Marxism leads to transition, among them crisis, struggle, and the non-development of the productive forces. No fundamental systemic transformation means in turn no transition, and thus also no distinguishing characteristics separating one mode of production from another. Exponents of this positive and ahistorical view include Brown, Veyne, Fowler, Beard, Osgood, and Banaji.[15]

Where this approach leads can be illustrated with reference to the step connecting Rome as an instance of dynamic capitalism to its being a prefigurative occurrence of globalisation. Thus Rome under Augustus is defined by Osgood as a 'world state' for two main reasons: not only did it 'encompass all the main centres of ancient Mediterranean civilization', but also because 'hundreds of thousands of men and women gained Roman citizenship' as did 'non-citizens [who] in the process started to become Roman too.'[16] This was a purely random process – 'just a series of more-or-less accidental events' – leading to the emergence of 'distinct new groups' consisting of financiers, urban dwellers, and a wealthy ruling class.[17] Osgood adheres to much the same kind of argument as Banaji, locating a capitalist economy ('commerce flourished as never before') in ancient Rome.[18]

---

14 This revisionism first took shape in the work of Brown (1971, 1978).

15 Restricting unfreedom to chattel slavery, and the term 'peasant' to a Chayanovian notion of smallholding proprietor engaged in subsistence cultivation, Banaji ignores that each of these concepts encompasses other categories: in the case of 'peasant', also non-owning tenants and sharecroppers; unfree production relations extend as well to attached or bonded labourers, and individual agricultural workers. Equally problematic is the assertion by him that workers in Late Antiquity were paid in gold, and that the ancient Roman economy was capitalist, in effect making the latter system historically ubiquitous. For his part, Brown challenges the presence of large rural estates, a 'black legend' of ancient Rome, forgetting that it was ownership by a single landlord of many small ones that conferred power on the large-scale size of landed property. Similarly downgrading both the fact and effect of power, Veyne presents the games merely as a form of reciprocity based on potlatch.

16 Osgood (2018: 2).

17 See Osgood (2018: 6).

18 Osgood (2018: 2). Claims made by Banaji (and others) about the presence in ancient Rome of capitalism are undermined by Garnsey and Saller (2014: 73) who observe: 'A prosperous merchant class, the source of whose wealth was not land, and whose success rested on enterprise and skill rather than traditional precepts and modes of behaviour, provides a potential threat to aristocratic values. But successful merchants fall easy prey to the dominant ideology: they buy or marry their way into the aristocracy and seek political office. Only the rise of a class of industrial owners, who possess social prestige and economic power independently as profit-makers and employers of labour, endangers the traditional social order. In ancient Rome there was no prospect of the emergence of such a class.

Moreover, Osgood – again like Banaji – objects to the decline thesis ('catastrophism') associated with Marxist and earlier non-Marxist historiography, a position justified by smuggling economic achievements into a list where non-economic ones predominate, avoiding the fact that the debate about decline focuses on economic issues and the capacity of Rome as a system of production to reproduce itself as such.[19] His opposition to the decline thesis is difficult to miss: 'So entrenched is the idea of the "fall of the Roman Republic" that it recurs in political debate and popular culture ... [a]ccounts like these resonate powerfully in an era of anxiety but they overlook a series of remarkable achievements'.[20]

It is certainly true that what happened before the coming of the principate must be explained with reference to occurrences in the preceding century, but interpretations differ as to the dynamic informing that process. Duff on freedmen, Frank on the economy, and Walbank on slavery all have a negative view of systemic developments, especially the impact of manumission and unfree production relations on labour market competition, politics and ideology. Osgood, by contrast, perceives developments throughout this period as either accidental, or largely positive and benign. Hence the Greek presence is presented simply as cultural, seen merely as a beneficial influence, without asking how it was regarded in terms of labour market competition and its attendant conflict, while analogously the status of Rome as 'world city' is linked not just to population 'diversity' (= 'multiculturalism') but also to 'integration', each of which is depicted as tension-free and thus also as unproblematically benign.[21]

As advanced by Osgood, the Rome-as-World-State thesis combines the view that on the one hand the population of Rome was 'diverse' (= 'multicultural') and that its economy was capitalist, with on the other that such processes were benign. This in turn is supported by a Panglossian interpretation the focus of which is on leisure. The latter, which is 'not just for aristocrats but also for

---

Moreover, economic realities, in particular the limitations of the market, virtually ruled out the possibility of the formation of a competing social hierarchy based on commercial wealth'.

19 'To focus obsessively on the "fall of the Roman Republic"', argues Osgood (2018: 3), 'not only minimizes ... political accomplishments and related innovations in literature, commerce, and religion [but also] obscures the fact that much of Rome's transformation into a world state happened in the century leading up to ... 44 BC.'

20 Osgood (2018: 1–2).

21 'Drawing new residents from ever farther away, Rome was becoming far less a city state and more a capital of a world empire' over the period 85–45 BC (Osgood, 2018: 161): 'The arrival of Greek experts transformed Roman education ... A surging interest in satisfying individual pleasures ... helped integrate the diverse population of the world city.'

ordinary Romans', licenses the categorization of ancient Rome as the 'city of love and laughter', a 'fun-loving city [of] special pleasures', and thus a context where 'joking could also unite the city'.[22] It comes as no surprise to find that the result of this combined approach to ancient society (caring economy + benign multiculturalism + widespread leisure) is accompanied by uncritical sweetness-and-light views such as '[t]he plebs were thrilled at the lavish feasts, gifts of money, and entertainments'.[23]

Sleepy British Positivists

Accordingly, the recent past has witnessed an epistemological shift in the way the ancient Roman economy and society are interpreted. In keeping with now fashionable paradigms encountered previously in the humanities and social sciences, therefore, current narratives about the nature of society in Antiquity are based on a number of claims reflecting these influences: not just about the presence in Rome of an economy akin to modern capitalism, but also a process of cultural 'decentring' whereby the Roman empire is perceived to be merely an effect of its margins, both of which processes are regarded as tension-free, benign, and essentially positive.[24] The most insidious and problematic of these influences, it could be argued, is the impact of the postmodern 'cultural turn', intent as it is on expounding what is said by the voice-from-below.[25]

22 Osgood (2018: 171, 173, 175).

23 Osgood (2018: 183).

24 Despite being unsure as to how it should be addressed, some historians of ancient society are nevertheless aware of this problem. Thus, for example, the warning sounded by Mouritsen (2005: 39): 'When faced with deceptively simple questions it is important to avoid "common sense" responses, which may be little more than unreflected projections of contemporary practices and assumptions'. In keeping with this another such historian (Murray, 2024: 419) confesses: 'What worries me ... is the rise of relativism [which] has become to my mind the crucial problem for the student of history; its aim is to neutralize the power of history, to subordinate it to the ideology of the present.'

25 Proclaiming the relevance of postmodern theory for the study of ancient society, Veyne (1990), Fowler (2000), and Brown (2012) turn to Foucault, Derrida, and Lyotard in the quest for extracting new meaning from what is contained in the written sources. In keeping with this sort of approach, a recent interview notes that Beard 'is far more than an advocate for the relevance of the ancient world. What has made her books and documentaries so refreshing is her scepticism: she is willing to demolish things long held as true about the ancients. She has also been part of the movement to expand Classics' boundaries, leading early courses on women and the body, for example, when women – along with slaves, migrants and regions outside Italy and Greece – were marginalised by the mainstream. The Roman empire is a "history of people of colour", she says. Another

A central question, therefore, is: can the theory, concepts, and methods of present-day social sciences, particularly those from social history and anthropology, be usefully translated to analyses of ancient history? Linked to this is why – when challenged by postmodernists – did historians of ancient society capitulate so easily, to the extent of accepting many of the criticisms made? One answer is that, unlike Marxism, they lacked a strongly entrenched theoretical approach enabling them not just to defend their practice as historians but also to launch a counterattack on behalf of their discipline. In the words of one historian of ancient Greece, they were found to be intellectually and politically weaponless when ambushed: 'I remember the fury with which this was greeted by Arnaldo Momigliano [the Italian historian of ancient society] who tried to persuade us sleepy British positivists that here was the greatest threat to history writing of the present age,' adding that in retrospect 'I think he was right …'[26]

Accepting both that 'using a term because it is currently fashionable will not suffice', and that consequently 'it has been severely criticized by other scholars … sometimes justifiably so', Pitts and Versluys nevertheless endorse the conceptual applicability of globalisation to antiquity ('it is methodologically sound to use globalisation theory in the study of Roman history and archaeology').[27] Dismissing the Rome-centric view of earlier historiography as Eurocentrism, Nederveen Pieterse endorses instead the approach of postmodern theory, in particular that of cultural studies, its conceptual apparatus of 'multiculturalism', and emphasis on 'connectedness' and identity.[28] All

example is her focus on Rome's evolving cosmopolitanism …' See 'The ancient world is a metaphor for us', *Financial Times* (London), 1–2 May 2021.

26 See Murray (2024: 419), who goes on to declare that '[i]t is not just Marxism then, but all belief systems that have been eroded. Where are the grand theories of history now? We can see how barren the landscape is by noting how it has become populated with massive books of historical entertainment which purport to present grand themes, all of them distinguished by their lack of any theoretical underpinning and their grasshopper methodology. Grand theory has become a sort of performing flea circus …'. Whilst rightly critical of postmodernism, and its deleterious effect on the historiography of ancient society, Murray nevertheless misreads the political nature of its epistemology, mistakenly imagining postmodernism to 'lack any theoretical underpinning'. Lacking, therefore, is an understanding of the conservative and populist roots of the 'cultural turn', a comprehension of which might have enabled a more effective counterattack directed at the theory, politics, and methodology of postmodernism itself.

27 Pitts and Versluys (2015: 3, 5, 16), who acknowledge that '[g]lobal history has become something of a new orthodoxy'.

28 Nederveen Pieterse (2015). In keeping with this sort of interpretation are the contributions to Umachandran and Ward (2024), a volume which – like many in the social sciences currently – not only endorses contingency, alterity, and cultural relativism, but

the latter aspects are regarded as positive, as is the effect on Roman society of migration from the periphery. Unsurprisingly, this, too, licenses a slide into claims about a flourishing Roman economy, labelled by some as capitalism.[29]

However, in the social sciences generally, and development studies in particular, the concept 'globalisation' indicates how/why industrial capitalism emerged from its European context and spread throughout the world. Accompanying the expansion and consolidation of market forces, this model of globalisation based on industrial production is in systemic and geographical terms a form of modernity which is not – and cannot be – the same as the 'connectivity' denoting nothing more than trade linkages, as depicted by supporters of pre-modern 'globalisation'. Whereas the concept Roman imperialism underlines both that and how the core of empire dominated the periphery, not least in terms of surplus extraction and other forms of economic appropriation, postmodernism reverses this epistemologically, maintaining that the core was much rather dominated by the periphery, the latter context being seen as a locus of empowerment. Replacing a disempowering 'Romanisation' with the empowering 'identity politics' encountered on the periphery, the transfer of 'otherness' from the margins of empire to its core is privileged analytically. This is very different from the earlier interpretation of Frank, who although using the same kind of core/periphery model, nevertheless regarded its cultural impact on ancient Rome as negative.

Where the historiography of antiquity is concerned, this epistemological shift has also involved a search for and finding of grassroots thought and action: what people then believed and did, and why. Asking why the study of classics is perceived negatively by many in academia, Beard appears at first to blame the influence of postmodern theory, but then takes the opposite view, advocating much rather that in order to survive the classics must take on board

---

also attacks classics as innately racist, Eurocentric and colonial. Such a view, the exponents of which seemingly regard anything 'Western' (for them a socio-economically undifferentiated concept) as having no validity whatsoever, contrasts with a brilliant analysis of the same questions by Hall and Stead (2020), whose non-exclusionary – and politically and intellectually progressive – approach examines the link between the classics and working-class history.

29 For examples of theoretically and methodologically problematic claims that the Roman economy was capitalist, see Banaji (2018), Maher (2021), and Erdkamp, Verboven, and Zuiderhoek (2020). Endorsing the New Institutional Economics as a suitable model for analysing the ancient Roman economy, at the centre of which is a capitalism based on rent-seeking state predation, Bang (2011) in effect replicates under another name the earlier neoclassical economic view of Oertel.

its ideas.[30] Addressing the meaning of the term 'civilization' as presented by Kenneth Clark, therefore, she insists his approach was symptomatically one that unfairly privileged artistic images in terms of Western aesthetics, thereby downgrading those of other cultures.[31] This contention, which is consistent with her positive view about multiculturalism, is for a number of reasons problematic.[32] Hence the preponderance of non-western images and art in the museums of metropolitan capitalist nations suggests, much rather, a parity between them aesthetically, not a hierarchical positioning with the western/classical at the top and the non-western/'other' below.[33] Furthermore, the

30 Observing that it is possible to 'lay the blame for the general demise of the subject firmly at the door of careerist Ivy League, and no doubt Oxbridge, academics who ... have wandered down some self-regarding postmodern cul-de-sac', Beard (2013: 6) then changes tack, and maintains instead that 'maybe it is precisely because professors of Classics have refused to engage with modern theory and persisted in viewing the ancient world through rose-tinted spectacles (as if it was a culture to be admired) that the subject is in imminent danger of turning into an antiquarian backwater.' Much the same view is advanced by her in an interview conducted at The British Academy on 26th July 2016, where she remarks that: 'There's a very important strand of the humanities, which is always taking that conversation afresh, it is renewing it. What I think I am doing is: I am talking to the Greeks and Romans; I am ventriloquizing the Greeks and Romans, because they can't talk to us. I am engaged in a conversation with them, and I am engaged in a conversation with the other people who have studied them over the centuries and, in a sense, have handed them down to me ... *But it is always essentially a process of making it new again, and making it for us.*' (emphasis added)

31 Invoking the relativistic approach of postmodernism, Beard (2018: 207) accuses Clark both of focussing on Europe and of ignoring the contribution of women, yet at the same time accepts the 'difficulties in escaping some of [his] constraints'. Missed is that the epistemological problem is not simply a question of 'escaping constraints', as she thinks, but rather one of conflicting politics. Clark had a particular view linked to his social background, while Beard has an equally specific view linked to the prevailing ideology of the present: that is, the privileging by postmodernism of 'otherness', an approach which she endorses.

32 Hence the contention (Beard, 2018: 102) that 'Winkelmann's legacy [about the hierarchical nature of civilisation] runs deeper. Even if we are often unaware of its effects, the inheritance of Winkelmann continues to offer western viewers a ready-made standard against which to judge the art of other cultures – sometimes a distorting and divisive lens that is hard to escape'. See also Beard (2018: 205).

33 Seemingly aware of this fact, Beard (2018: 208) nevertheless misrecognizes its implications, arguing that 'the problems of a European or western focus are not simply "solved" by including non-western art ... to cast a white western gaze over the art of the world ... risks becoming almost as ethnocentric a project as restricting that gaze to Europe.' For her, therefore, the issue is simply that a European perception – regardless of whether the gaze is positive or negative – of non-European art/culture is just another form of ethnocentrism, which is the view of postmodern theory. This contrasts with a different question: who – and why – is then to define meaning from the side of the 'other'? It, too, is an

influence that African images have had on painters like Modigliani and Picasso underline the positive reception within the artistic world of non-western aesthetic concepts. In making her claim Beard seems to be following the postmodern trope that maintains – wrongly – all aspects of western society are automatically privileged, while – correspondingly – all non-western ones are deprivileged.

The Imaginary World of Decoration

Another issue of interest to Marxism, therefore, is the recent application to society in ancient Rome of the term 'multiculturalism', which underlines the difficulty of importing concepts from modern social theory into the classics. As used by some classicists, the term conflates the presence in Roman society of ethnic 'otherness' with it being a non-antagonistic identity accepted unconditionally by those not belonging to the same category. Despite the fact that these two aspects of identity – presence and acceptance – are clearly not the same, those applying the term 'multiculturalism' to ancient Rome invariably omit to make this distinction. The misleading impression conveyed is of a culturally/ethnically/nationally diverse population at ease with this situation, an interpretation that is supportive of an equally mistaken view regarding the historical existence then of a benign economic system that was capitalism. As pointed out in earlier historiographical accounts, however, Roman society was indeed the site of conflict involving its ethnically specific components.[34]

Mimicking postmodern support for the culture of the migrant 'other', current historiography of ancient Rome reverses the earlier negative interpretation of Frank and recasts 'otherness' as positive. Hence the focus has shifted, both epistemologically and (thus) politically: away from a discourse about locals-as-victims to one about migrants-as-culturally-empowered. The

issue fraught with problems, in that the 'other' discourse is itself no less ideological/political than that by Clark about European art/culture, or about non-European equivalents by a European. In short, it can license in turn a nationalist/populist ideology by voices claiming to speak on behalf of (undifferentiated) non-western 'other'.

34 It is possible to argue that, just as Trotsky (1964) linked the prevalence of antisemitism in Russia to the historically predominant role of educated urban Jews in the Czarist bureaucracy who were tasked with formulating and implementing state policy (taxation, etc.) at village level, and seen therefore by peasants as directly responsible for such unpopular programmes, so too may imperial freedmen of Greek extraction carrying out analogous functions in ancient Rome have attracted similar hostility targeting their ethnic/national identity.

emphasis is no longer on the disadvantages to the (Italian) self, as argued long ago by Frank, but rather on the advantages of incorporation enjoyed by the (non-Italian) 'other'.[35] As in the case of so many other contexts, epochs, and issues, the historiography of ancient Rome has not escaped the desire by post-modern theory to find instances of culturally empowering 'otherness' involving identity politics.

This is itself part of a broader trend, away from materialist concepts positing the existence of an objective reality and towards an aporia, or the notion that historiography of ancient Rome is nothing more than literature.[36] Consistent with the latter approach is the privileging of culture at the expense of political economy, an epistemological break that moves the element of determination from the material base to superstructural phenomena. In what is an unmistakeably Panglossian view, one such analysis – by Beard – perceives the extension of citizenship and the consequent increasing ethnic/national 'otherness' of Rome's population as a positive development, evidence simply of success, without asking too closely either about the political implications of this or about its impact on the labour market and working conditions.[37]

Despite observations to the effect that the Roman population in Pompeii and elsewhere in the ancient world was 'decidedly multicultural', it is not

35 Although no mention is made of him by name, it is clear that Beard (2013: 179) has Frank in mind when she makes the following dismissive observation: "No writers today quite echo the strident complaints of early twentieth-century historians who … lamented the dilution of true Italian stock with the foreign blood of freedman, whose origins often lay in the East."

36 On this point, see Lendon (2009: 41-61), who observes that 'most contemporary writing in English about Latin historians slights these historians' concern for truth, [an] indifference to so important a part of what historians thought they were doing [that] constitutes a pervasive affliction in the scholarship ….'. Aporia is central to the 'new' populist postmodernism, since by questioning reality – *all* reality – it bolsters the view that nothing is (or ever can be) real, and consequently history is just competing opinions: epistemologically, no objective reality is possible, or indeed desirable.

37 Significantly, this positive interpretation (Beard, 2016: 330) regarding the 'widespread image of Rome as an open culture [which] made the Roman citizen body the most ethnically diverse that there ever was before the modern world' is itself structured by an idealized/benign view of slavery. The latter takes the form that no clear line separated the free from the unfree, and that slavery was anyway only a 'temporary status'. In short, the familiar revisionist trope to the effect the unfree were essentially no different from the free, a claim based on the observation that both worked together, alongside one another. Such a view overlooks a number of things. To begin with, substantial evidence confirms that in other contexts where free and unfree toiled together, differences did occur, in terms of hours worked and payment received. Moreover, unfreedom coincided largely with the productive life of a slave, and manumission occurred only when this ceased to be profitable.

always evident what precisely she understands by this term.[38] In short, Beard invokes the term in relation to ancient society – for example, 'many people in the multicultural world of empire' – without appearing to consider whether such a modern concept, drawn as it is from debate within the present-day social sciences, has – or, indeed, can have – the same meaning in the historical period and context to which she applies it.[39] This notwithstanding, the author of a nineteenth century novel about Pompeii is criticized by Beard for drawing aspects from his own time into the account, and in effect portraying the context as a form of modernity.[40] Ironically, this is exactly what she herself also does when attaching the modern label 'multicultural' to ancient Roman society in general and Pompeii in particular, with its twenty-first century meaning, depicting as unproblematically positive a cultural identity based on national/ethnic 'otherness'.

It is clear from the way 'multiculturalism' is coupled with the word 'benign' that Beard regards the former concept as embodying a positive view about identity, contrasted by her with the negative associations – 'aggressive humour', 'xenophobia' – in which 'otherness' is depicted in some images.[41] Subsequently 'multiculturalism' is linked also to 'multilingualism': the dual inference being not only that latter term constitutes evidence supportive of the former, but

38 See Beard (2013: 191). References to ancient society as 'multicultural' are scattered throughout publications by her. Symptomatic of this approach is the positive interpretation (Beard, 2016: 330) regarding the 'widespread image of Rome as an open culture [which] made the Roman citizen body the most ethnically diverse that there ever was before the modern world.'

39 Beard (2013: 176). Other references to 'multiculturalism' confirm that, in spite of a dearth of information, she views it in positive terms. Hence the assertion (Beard, 2009: 52, 80ff.) that 'Rome in due course would become the most successful multicultural society of the ancient world' is followed by the qualification that 'exactly what skin colours were represented [in Greco-Roman society], and in what numbers, in the multicultural population of the Roman empire is something of a puzzle'. In keeping with her positive conceptualization of the term, Beard takes issue with the view that racism was present in the Roman empire, suggesting that the accusation of 'touchy-feely view of Greco-Roman ecumenism' she (Beard, 2009: 67) aims at others might also be said of her.

40 The fictional account is by Bulwer-Lytton (1834), about whom Beard (2008: 88–89) complains that he 'emphasized the familiar modernity of the House of the Tragic Poet. Underneath the colourful Roman idiosyncrasies of painting, design and diet, he found a society and an architecture which was not so far away from his own, elite nineteenth-century London.'

41 'The imaginary world of decoration', observes Beard (2008: 150), 'embraced a galaxy of Graeco-Roman myth and literature [and] the cultural highlights of Egypt [including] satires and burlesques on its inhabitants and their weird customs. This is not, of course, all benign multiculturalism. The stereo-typed pygmies ... are portrayed with a mixture of aggressive humour and xenophobia.'

that a dynamic economic trade ('this was a bustling, commercial, market town') made it so.[42] Hence the construction of a relay in statement composed of mutually-dependent concepts: multiculturalism = multilingual = commerce = benign, a conflation that facilitates a discursive slide into – and epistemologically supportive of – the claim that the economic system of ancient Rome was capitalist.

A Good Measure of Cold Water

Because descriptive terms like 'an open culture' that was 'ethnically diverse' tell us little or nothing about how ethnic/national 'otherness' was perceived, by whom, and why, there are reasons for questioning the extent to which the presence in Rome of 'multiculturalism' was viewed as positively as the use of this postmodern concept implies. A version of the decline thesis which antagonizes postmodernists is that advanced by Tenney Frank.[43] His interpretation attributed the political and economic decay to the incidence of manumission, and the corresponding rise in the number of freedmen, ex-slaves whose cultural origins meant they were less committed than the native Italian populace to upholding the ideals of the Republic. Opposition within Rome to rule by an Emperor, the worship of the latter as deity, and the end of the Republic, argued Frank, were all processes connected to the increasing number of Roman inhabitants who had come from places that had never known self-government.

42 'All in all', contends Beard (2008: 162), 'there can hardly be any doubt that, whatever exactly it was, and however small by comparison with the great trading centres of Puteoli or Rome, Pompeii's port must have been a thriving, international and multilingual little place.' This is the reason, moreover, that Beard finds it necessary to depict Pompeii as economically 'thriving', a situation that requires the presence of many businessmen from foreign places, all speaking their own languages and – by extension – furnishing her with 'proof' for the conceptual efficacy of 'multiculturalism'. The result is little different from the similar attempt by Banaji to 'imagine' a thriving port scene in Antiquity, full of capitalists engaged in trade.

43 The case made by Frank about the decline of Rome is supported by Duff (1928) and – with some qualifications – by Chilver (1941: 84), but questioned by Treggiari (1969: 238) and Beard (2013: 179). An early attempt to shift the issue away from a question simply of race, and onto the wider one of the way in which ideology can and does change over time, Barker, Clark, and Vaucher (1954: 248–49) make the following point: 'But probably the vital matter was that the old Roman stock had been replaced by men of mixed blood; this does not mean the much discussed "inferior races", but means people who, whatever their potentialities, had not the Roman tradition or feeling for Rome's past. And this affected the west very much more than the east.'

Although it is easy to dismiss this argument as racist, it is important to note that, economically speaking, Frank did not denigrate the foreign 'other' involved in the change he describes.[44] Much rather the opposite is the case, in that he regarded such 'others' – Greek/Graeco-Syrian ex-slaves and their sons who originally came from the East – as extremely competent economic agents who deserved the success they achieved in the late republican era. Indeed, his criticism was directed not at these foreign 'others' but rather at the native Italians who – following the Punic wars – preferred to invest money in land instead of commerce and trade.[45] Framed in terms of cultural/national/ethnic identity, Frank nevertheless hints at an underlying presence of rivalry for employment, a theme taken up by other historians of ancient Rome.

Thus, for example, Duff hints at the intensification of rivalry in search for employment, pitting the Italian/Roman-born against the 'foreigner', the former free, the latter unfree.[46] For their part, freedmen competed with later incomers for jobs.[47] As Sherwin-White has shown, such resentment manifested itself as racism, a discourse that is familiar where labour market competition is both acute and involves workers of different national/ethnic identities.[48] Although

---

44 Duff attracts a similar level of opprobrium; his analysis of freedmen is accused by Mouritsen (2011: 1, 2, 84 n78, 86, 117) of being 'problematic', 'dubious', xenophobic', and 'snobbish' for looking down on ex-slaves.

45 For the large size and high value of rural holdings owned by Pliny, leased to and worked by tenants, see Chilver (1941: 150ff.).

46 Duff (1928: 107–108). Labour market rivalry, together with its effects, is overlooked by Mouritsen (2011: 7–8), who confesses bafflement as to the reason for antagonism towards freedmen, noting that 'a prominent section of Roman public opinion remained critical of freedmen, which is puzzling given the consistently high level of manumission [that was] not just remarkably common but also highly controversial.' Asking '[h]ow do we explain this contradiction?', he seeks non-economic answers ('the concerns about manumission were essentially moral and ideological rather than socio-economic.'). In other words, job competition is excluded from issues contributing to hostility aimed at freedmen.

47 Departing from the emphasis placed by Frank not on migration but on manumission as a source of labour market competition, Duff (1928: 118–19) argues that: 'A more promising field for the freedman was [the] liberal professions ... But in these occupations a new competitor appeared in the form of the free-born immigrant. *Peregrini* did not come to Rome in any great numbers for the purposes of the retail trade [which] had been captured by the slave-descended population of the city ...[However,] teachers, architects, artists and doctors ... came and settled in Rome and other towns of Italy in greater numbers ... Accordingly, natives of Athens, Pergamum, Rhodes, Antioch, Alexandria and other cities of the Hellenistic world came to Rome where higher remuneration and the Roman franchise awaited them.'

48 Sherwin-White (1966). Significantly, perhaps, not often considered in discussion (e.g. Mouritsen, 2005) about the meaning of freedman Roman epigraphy is its link to such conflict. The presence of the latter is hinted at in the mere fact of recording social position

objections by the Italian/Roman-born to the employment of 'foreign' slaves in agriculture are attributed by Duff to a question of status diminution, another explanation is also possible.[49] The issue of undercutting/displacement by a cheaper and easier to control form of labour-power would have been particularly important for peasant smallholders, since they depended frequently on earnings from seasonal/temporary off-farm employment on rural estates for a significant component of their economic livelihood.

Needless to say, theory depicting the negative side of ancient Rome, leading to its decline, is regarded now as controversial, not least because it directly contradicts the claim made by exponents of postmodernism that the extension throughout the empire of citizenship was – and could only ever be – considered as positive, as embodied in the term 'multiculturalism'. Of particular interest to Marxists is that such an interpretation shares with Marxism itself a focus on the deleterious economic impact of labour market competition, its attendant social antagonism and conflict, plus the contribution of the latter to the kinds of political and ideological crises prefiguring systemic transition. Unlike Frank, however, Marxism places the same kind of process in a world context, where accumulation requires access to an industrial reserve that is now global in scope, and the conflict it generates involving workers of different nationalities and/or ethnicities is correspondingly more acute.

As crucial for Marxist theory is the way such claims about 'multiculturalism' in ancient Rome also feed into and are supportive of additional contentions that its economy was a benign form of capitalism, undermining thereby the epistemological link between crisis, systemic decline, and the supplanting of one mode of production by another. This positive and ahistorical interpretation of capitalism, one that – in the absence of impoverishment and overtaxation characterizing the decline thesis – is crisis-free and seemingly benign, conceptualises this particular mode of production as systemically eternal. If capitalism has always existed, then it is difficult to see either the necessity or a historical space for feudalism, let alone an eventual transition to capitalism and then to socialism. As bourgeois political economy has always maintained is the case, capitalism is a 'natural' systemic form, and as such cannot be overcome or

---

and achievement, in that the object of such inscriptions is a freedman declaration along the lines of 'I am as much a part of this society as the native freeborn'.

49 Drawing attention to shortcomings in assessing evidence based on epigraphy, Duff (1928: 109) makes a useful methodological point. Because they were buried without an indication of the kind of work they did, nor were their names reproduced on items they manufactured, slaves are less well represented in the record than freedmen. Although the workforce was composed of slaves, therefore, 'epigraphical evidence tends to minimize their importance'.

abolished. Locating it in ancient Rome, therefore, boosts the latter interpretation and simultaneously weakens the very foundations of Marxist theory, and all that depends on this politically.

II

Turning to the question of sources, and what these enable one to say, following in the footsteps of social history, with its methodological and theoretical focus on revealing a hitherto silenced/ignored voice-from-below, archaeology and the classics more generally have shifted from uncovering material culture to examining and addressing the nature of 'the social', as embodied in those who inhabited the grassroots in ancient society. Such a project represents enormous methodological difficulties, not least how is one to access the views of people who for the most part left no detailed written record, either of what they thought and why, or of the reasons for doing what they did. More items of material culture are discovered over time, certainly, but do we – can we – as a result know more about what comes under the broad rubric of 'the social'?[50]

Remediable by New Discoveries?

If classicists argue that no one who has not undertaken an excavation of an ancient site can pronounce on what archaeology is and does, then equally it is legitimate for anthropologists to point out that, in the absence of a capacity to undertake participant/observation fieldwork, it is difficult – if not impossible – to access the kind of empirical data on which to construct theory about what inhabitants of such societies thought, and its connection with what they did.[51] Much the same methodological problem arises with regard to work arrangements, although here problems also stem from the faulty conceptualization of production relations, and consequently what sort of economic process was in place. This, of course, is one issue that is central to Marxist theory and methodology, in debates with non-Marxist ideas and within Marxism itself.

---

50 Observing that '[i]t is important to be specific about the limitations of the evidence', Scheidel (2012: 3, 4) accepts that – among other things – '[h]istorians are unable to establish Roman GDP without relying on exceedingly schematic extrapolation from select data for prices and wages.'

51 This is not to say that eliciting opinion from the present-day grassroots in the course of anthropological fieldwork is either straightforward or easy, far from it; which merely underlines the nature of the methodological problem facing historians of ancient society concerning access by them to the mass voice-from-below in the contexts they study.

Warnings about over-interpreting the sources on which the historiography of ancient society depends extend from a lament as to 'how hazardous a task is the reconstruction of early Roman history from what the Romans tell us and how inevitable it is that scholars must disagree in their evaluation of this evidence, and vary in the degree of scepticism with which they approach the statements of the authorities for each separate period', to a cautionary statement that 'when history rests on earlier narratives, its reliability reposes on the availability, often at many removes, of first-hand information. Very little of such information is directly accessible, especially to the historian of Greece or Rome ... In practice, however, the dearth of trustworthy evidence for the political history of Rome is hardly ever remediable by new discoveries.'[52] That much 'newness' derives not from what is discovered by archaeology but from reinterpreting what is already known – bringing to bear on the latter source of paradigms/concepts in the social sciences – is conceded by some who study the ancient Roman economy.[53]

Where Beard is concerned, methodological problems surface immediately with regard to the kind of historical context that she covers: ancient society in general, and that of Rome in particular. How can we know what the mass of people there and then understood by what they saw, let alone read or heard, since there is no evidence left by them about these subjects? Sure, there are written texts that have come down to us, but as to what 'those below' all actually thought, and why, and how this was formed, by what or whom, together with the way opinions changed when they did (and why), it is impossible to say with any certainty. Yet it is this very issue – 'how art works and how it should be explained' – that Beard intends to address, going even further, by locating this approach historiographically in 'the generations of humankind who have used, interpreted, argued over and given meaning to those images.'[54] Her object is

52 See, respectively, Jones (1928: 332) and, some six decades later, Brunt (1988: 509–510). Later still, Garnsey and Saller (2014: 71) make the following concession: 'We know little in detail about the economy of the Roman world. There are no government accounts, no official records of production, trade, occupational distribution ... A systematic account of the Roman economy is therefore beyond our reach. Economic historians, more even than those historians with traditional interests, must set themselves limited objectives and be imaginative and discriminating in their pursuit of them.'

53 Hence the acceptance by Scheidel (2012: 2) that although 'the scarcity of a potentially decisive type of documentation – that of ancient statistics – inevitably inhibits our efforts, on the whole the main challenge lies not so much in the amount of evidence ... as in its interpretation.'

54 Noting that '[t]his book is written in the conviction that what we *see* is as important to our understanding of civilization as what we read or hear', Beard (2018: 11–12, original emphasis) contextualizes this historically by announcing that 'it also prods at some of

nothing less than 'to expose the very long history of *how we look*', explicitly following the earlier approach of John Berger, 'whose priorities are much closer to my own'.[55] However, whereas he was talking about how art was interpreted principally in the modern era, she by contrast wants to trace how statues were seen by those in ancient society.

That it is the gaze in the latter sort of context which is to be addressed and given meaning is clear, both from locating images in 'conversations with the classical world', and also from the object being to explain how they were 'seen and understood by the men and women who lived with them'.[56] Underlined thereby is an intention to access 'the conversations of the classical world' methodologically, bringing into consideration what such populations contributed to the range of voices participating in the conversation. Apart from the few who left written records of their own views and opinions, what the rest of the masses composing ancient society thought and did, and why, remains unrecorded by these people themselves, and as an unmediated voice-from-below cannot be accessed as such.

Hence the central methodological problem faced by Beard is that the focus of her approach is on the reception of images by – and thus the meaning for – the grassroots in ancient society.[57] This kind of analysis depends on being able to retrieve both the mass voice-from-below and agency linked to it, or precisely that which is denied by the very nature of the historiography she practices. Whereas the present-day anthropologist conducting long-term fieldwork in a rural area, able as a result not just to ask questions of those inhabiting such contexts, but also to follow up answers with further clarification and intellectual probing throughout what is a lengthy stay, comparing what is said with what is done, the historian of ancient society by contrast is unable to obtain the same kind of detailed information garnered by participant/observation.

The kind of difficulties encountered can be illustrated with reference to the way Beard interprets the effect on the viewer in ancient Egypt of large statues

---

the certainties about how art works and how it should be explained ...[i]t is even more about the generations of humankind who have used, interpreted, argued over and given meaning to those images.'

55 See Berger (1972) and Beard (2018: 13, 211, original emphasis).

56 See Beard (2018: 13, 15, 22), who surmises thus: 'It is important to remember that plenty of ancient Egyptian viewers, or ancient Romans, may have been just as cynical about the colossal statues of their rulers as we are now about the parade of images of modern autocrats.'

57 Significantly, therefore, many of her publications (Beard, 2007, 2021, 2023) address the meaning of issues (power, rule) and images (statues, paintings), not just to us now but also to them, then.

featuring the body and face of the pharaoh.[58] Her argument is that their function as propaganda designed to intimidate does not work, since '[t]he more power flaunts itself in your face, the more it risks undermining its claims to be taken seriously', and consequently 'it is a fair guess that [onlookers then] would have walked by and laughed'. Such claims are themselves predicated on knowing how and why these images were perceived by 'ancient viewers', and what they thought about them; this information is lacking, and 'a fair guess' is methodologically not sufficient to sustain the case being made. Ridiculing power does not, unfortunately, alter the efficacy of power itself, especially when images are backed up by force (military, state), or draw upon a legitimizing ideology (religion).

Elsewhere, ironically, Beard is clearly aware that images are not always what they seem, and thus frequently open to misinterpretation. Accordingly, she notes that a consequence of cast in Pompeii composed of a woman with 'her skirt gathered around her hips giving the probably misleading impression that she was pregnant', a result of which *déshabillé* state Victorian scholars 'took her to be a prostitute'.[59] Methodological reservations notwithstanding, when questioning clashes with multiculturalism, doubts tend to be set aside. When considering one of the three mummy portraits from Roman Egypt, therefore, despite acknowledging that 'we know almost nothing about him', Beard nevertheless goes on to say that the image 'is a wonderful combination of the traditions of Egypt, Greece and Rome, and a brilliant example of the cultural mix of the ancient Mediterranean.'[60] As will be seen below, brushing aside doubts concerning multiculturalism is not, however, a procedure applied by her to holders of earlier views. Similar kinds of methodological difficulty face claims based on 'new' discoveries made by archaeology.[61]

Ancient History Rewritten?

Archaeology is faced with two interrelated questions: does evidence from new material findings add to the record aspects of ancient society about which one does not already know, and does it licence thereby a revision of existing models. Many claims about new discoveries by archaeology concern not what is dug up but rather two very different procedures: the application of

58 Beard (2018: 67).
59 Beard (2013: 243).
60 Beard (2018: 46).
61 For one such instance of this claim, see for example Banaji (2018: 62–63).

scientific technique to such items as are discovered, and the meaning consequently attributed to them.[62] To a large degree, this sort of claim to newness mimics the assertion by cliometric historiography during the 1970s that its scientific approach enabled a revision (from negative to positive) of the meaning applied to plantation slavery in the antebellum south. Then, too, it was argued that a new interpretation was driven by new methods, which turned out to be incorrect. Cliometric methods were shown to be faulty, to the extent that the claims purportedly based on them no longer held.[63]

References by exponents of Late Antiquity justifying the novelty of their views in terms of what archaeology has revealed usually omit to identify such evidence, let alone how it changes earlier interpretations.[64] That new archaeological finds do not in fact provide the justification sought is an issue that is rarely aired. Hence the utility of a study addressing the meaning of images on coinage in Late Iron Age Britain, a numismatical analysis by Creighton that underlines the methodological problem faced by archaeology as clearly as possible.[65] A case built on the idea of a common language is faced with evidence that 'the idea that there was a uniform language ... is inherently unlikely'.[66]

62 For claims about the pathbreaking nature of archaeology as a result of the application of scientific procedures, see Conticello (1992: 43ff., 55ff., 63ff.) and Medwid (2000: 9–11). This is not to say that science has nothing to contribute to the advance and elaboration of knowledge – far from it: however, it is crucial also to be aware of what scientific procedure cannot do, and this boundary is not always recognized by those conducting research into the socio-economic structure of ancient Roman society.

63 See the forensic dismantling by Sutch (1975) of the methods deployed by Fogel and Engerman (1974) in support of their revisionist claims about slavery.

64 Thus, for example, assertions by Banaji (2018: 62–63) that 'the archaeological revolution of ... the last three decades throws up a huge challenge for historians of late antiquity', and '[t]he explosion of survey archaeology since the late 1970s has shown ...' remain unaccompanied by explanations as to what precisely the 'archaeological revolution' demonstrates.

65 It should be emphasized that the arguments in the analysis by Creighton (2000) are examined here critically not because they are bad but much rather the opposite: because his is a serious and intellectually rigorous approach, pushing a theoretical and methodological case based on the interpretation of writings/images appearing on the coinage in ancient society as far as it is epistemologically possible to go. Of interest, therefore, is where the limits to such interpretation lie, and what are the consequences when an attempt is made to go beyond them.

66 Creighton (2000: 152), who acknowledges that a chapter outlining his approach 'has been full of speculation, though I hope warranted speculation'. He continues (Creighton, 2000: 145): 'We have here two worlds colliding with very different traditions. Sometimes "Romanisation" is portrayed as if it were simply an acceptance of new forms of material culture, such as new types of pottery, clothing and food. It is far more than that. It is a fundamental change in the way people think about and perceive their world. The lack

To talk about 'a fundamental change in the way people think about and perceive their world', it is not merely necessary but crucial to know what people actually thought. It is equally clear – and Creighton is honest about this – that such knowledge is lacking, and by its very nature methodologically inaccessible. Nevertheless, he expresses a wish to pursue this very end, in spite of the fact that 'analysing changes in thought patterns [are] very difficult'. It is one thing to argue, as Creighton does, that elite Britons raised in Rome as hostages saw and transmitted the numismatic iconography to Britain itself – a plausible argument; it is quite another, however, to maintain that this same iconography was received in the same way by those occupying plebeian situations in the wider British society, not least since there is no way of knowing if this was so.

Despite it being an issue highlighting the methodological difficulties facing archaeology, Creighton attempts to resolve it by focussing on meaning, which requires a model about reception, or what those at the grassroots of ancient society in Roman Britain understood by symbols.[67] Observing that 'the arrival of Latin and writing has to be placed in a linguistic context', a procedure which, he accepts, 'involves speculation and the construction of hypotheses about the nature of change'. The latter is qualified yet further, the 'fact that some members of the elite now had the ability to speak and write Latin is not a mechanism of wider societal change in itself', adding: 'We need to imagine how the different communities in Britain responded to these new developments'.[68]

The fact that in Late Iron Age Britain 'the elite learnt the art of writing, and however much Latin they learnt, the result was put into effect on the medium of coinage', prompts a crucial methodological question.[69] Asking, rightly, 'what would the reaction ... have been?', Creighton accepts both that '[a]n illiterate Briton would have noticed the writing but been unable to decipher it', and that '[m]uch of the visual language which [the Roman elite] used probably left a large proportion of the British audience completely mystified'. In short, not

of written sources ... makes analysing changes in thought patterns very difficult, but that does not mean it should not be done, if we are to achieve a feeling for what it was like to exist in the past.' In the key phrase 'a fundamental change in the way people think about and perceive their world' lies the clue to the methodological difficulty ahead.

67 Noting that 'written language on coin arrived in Britain fully developed ...[a] fully developed literacy, and this was by and large in Latin', Creighton (2000: 146, 165) accepts that 'we must then wonder how many people in Britain were able to read these inscriptions where proclamations of ancestry and titulature were made'.

68 See Creighton (2000: 146–47, 164), who notes subsequently: 'Exactly what happened with the arrival of Latin in Britain can probably not be known, but the kind of hypothesised scenarios ... are based upon fairly broad sociolinguistic principles ...[About] the oral forms of discourse ... we can only surmise'.

69 For this and what follows, see Creighton (2000: 165, 174).

only did the language of power have little impact on the population, but this form of ideological consciousness as a method of rule was itself anyway unnecessary to ensure the subordination of 'those below'.[70] Although it is possible to know the type of food consumed by individuals, what age they were, the occupation they carried out, and where they lived, therefore, without a record written by the subjects concerned about what they thought and why they did what they did, it is impossible with any certainty to discuss the grassroots meaning attached to these issues.

Sins of the (Academic) Ancestors?

Inescapable, therefore, is the extent to which theory and evidence contained in eighteenth and nineteenth century accounts of ancient Roman society tend to be written off in a somewhat peremptory fashion by many present-day classicists. Hence the plethora of asides by Beard to the lack of evidence supporting claims made by earlier researchers.[71] In her account of Pompeii, this dismissiveness is on full display: that a house there belonged to Cicero is 'almost certainly wrong'; 'that the [image of] a phallus on the street is a directional sign to the local brothel is certainly wrong': an argument is rejected as 'Bright ideas, but certainly wrong'; items in one house have been 'rightly or wrongly' identified; and 'spotting the [artistic] work of the same "hand"... is a seductive but dangerous business'.[72] Nevertheless, questions about the way she herself interprets evidence keep on surfacing.

Evidence for street life in Pompeii, contends Beard, can be accessed methodologically from what is depicted in paintings.[73] It is possible to know more about 'the people in the Pompeian streets', she declares, because '[w]e can in fact get one step closer to them, thanks to an extraordinary series of paintings

70 'The impact of the new language on common people would probably have been slight up until the Claudian annexation [in 43 AD]', agrees Creighton (2000: 163), adding: 'In many respects, so long as the common people knew what was expected of them from their overlords, it did not matter what language they spoke'.

71 About such methodological problems, she (Beard, 2013: 171–72) even goes so far as to acknowledge that 'historians of the ancient world have always [filled the pages of their books] by a combination of scholarship, conjecture and fiction.' It is unclear whether the latter term refers to made-up details/accounts written by someone else, or by the classicist in person.

72 For these observations, themselves a few instances among many such, see Beard (2008: 45, 59, 86, 90, 125–26).

73 Beard (2008: 54).

found in the Estate of Julia Felix'.[74] Having built her analysis of street life in Pompeii on evidence contained in what paintings depict, however, Beard effectively undermines this kind of approach, confessing that 'To be honest, this is all completely baffling, and no amount of modern scholarship has ever managed to unravel the meaning …'.[75] The full extent of this difficulty emerges when she allocates identities to those depicted on two ceramic pots decorated with human figures.

One of these is described by her as depicting a slave or servant girl handing the mother her child, 'part of the female domestic world … a template for how to be an Athenian wife'.[76] However, the identity of each figure is assumed; the slave or maid could just as well be a sister; the baby might be hers, not that of the other woman; and the latter might be being handed the baby in order to confer approbation on it. Any number of scenarios are possible, yet Beard has settled on one, privileging it despite not knowing the identities of those involved, or what they are doing and why. About the other, Beard notes similarly that 'when you find a slave depicted on an Athenian pot, they are often shown at literally half the size of an Athenian citizen,' attributing once again identities to the figures depicted, which might be that of a younger brother (hence smaller image) helping his elder sibling. Without knowing who/what the images represent, it is not possible to construct an argument as to who or what is being depicted.[77]

Among the issues championed by Beard is gender, especially the way classics and other kinds of historiography have downplayed or ignored both the presence and the important economic role of women in society, ancient or otherwise.[78] In light of this, it is indeed ironic that she appears uncurious as to the presence/role of women as workers, observing merely that they 'are not mentioned in very great numbers'. Asking '[h]ow were the mills turned? By men or animals?', she opts for animals (mules, donkeys, small horses).[79]

---

74 See Beard (2008: 72–73, 77), who elaborates: 'One large room in this establishment … was decorated with a painted frieze … apparently showing scenes of life in the Pompeian Forum [which] offers all kinds of hints about how we might begin to repopulate the Pompeian cityscape: and not just with men in white togas … It prompts us to imagine children at their lessons, beggars plying for cash, traders and hucksters of all kinds, or local officials at their business.'

75 Beard (2008: 131).

76 Beard (2018: 35–37).

77 Beard (2018: 40).

78 See, for example, Beard (2017), who also indicts modern accounts which underestimate the role of women in the early Roman empire (2008: 181).

79 Beard (2008: 168–69, 174–75).

Overlooked is the answer – neither – provided by a nineteenth century source: they were turned by women, in Pompeii as elsewhere in the ancient (and not so ancient) world.[80] It is odd that Beard should have missed this, not least in view of her complaint that the absence of women as workers is due to male oversight, particularly that by nineteenth century classicists who attached little or no significance to gender issues, a criticism that is itself contradicted by what one such has observed.

Much the same kind of problem informs the way slavery has been reinterpreted by Beard, a shift in meaning from the coercion and oppressiveness of an unfree work relation as depicted in other, earlier analyses to a more benign relational variant based on kinship.[81] 'In Rome', she declares, 'the Latin word *familia* does not mean "family" in our sense, but the wider household *including* the slaves and ex-slaves'.[82] Reproduced thereby is the old canard found in modern literature on slavery equating this with kinship or even free labour and downplaying its involuntary element of compulsion.[83] Not only does this fail to take into account the differences in hours/conditions of work done by those in each category (free, unfree), but it also overlooks the dissimilar work/conditions operating within slavery itself; between those undertaking household duties in the house of their master and those working long hours and in onerous conditions as his field hands or in mines owned by him.[84]

---

80 'Originally mills were turned by hand,' comments Dyer (1867: 357–58), 'and this severe labour seems [in Pompeii and elsewhere] to have been conducted by women. It was so in Egypt; it was so in Greece in the time of Homer, who employs fifty females in the house of Alcinous upon this service. It was so in Palestine at the time of the Evangelists, and in England in the fourteenth and sixteenth centuries.'

81 Among those who regard slavery merely as a form of kinship are Miers and Kopytoff (1977), while those who see no difference between free and unfree labour include revisionists like Banaji (2001) and neoclassical economic historians such as Fogel and Engerman (1974).

82 See Beard (2008: 99, original emphasis); for a similarly benign view of slavery, see also Beard (2016: 330). However, she does hint at a less benign view of this unfree production relation, presenting what is a contradictory picture of slavery (Beard, 2008: 156): 'Vivid evidence for the use of a slave workforce on these farms [in the vicinity of Pompeii] comes from a distinctive type of metal contraption, almost certainly stocks, or leg irons (one big enough to shackle fourteen people) found at a number of out-of-town properties'.

83 On the basis that a house in Pompeii contained among its occupants ex-slaves, Beard (2008: 117–118) argues '[t]hese are all nice indication of the permeable boundary between slave and free in Roman society.'

84 The plight of slave existence, in house and field alike, is underlined thus by nineteenth century accounts (Dyer 1867: 345, 358): 'Below this second story [of a house in Pompeii] there is yet a third, in part underground ... the lodging of slaves. This was divided into little cells, scarcely the length of a man, dark and damp; we cannot enter it without a lively feeling of the wretched state to which these beings were reduced ... Among the Romans

When considering graffiti and other literary forms encountered in Pompeii as evidence for the voice-from-below, Beard notes that it 'raises the question of the levels and uses of literacy', and consequently it 'is very easy to get the impression that the city was a highly literate, even cultured place.' Despite initially doubting this, she nevertheless concludes 'it is clear that for many people well below the level of wealthy inhabitants reading and writing must have been integral to the way they organized their lives, and to their ability to do their jobs and earn their living.'[85] Since the very same point is found in a pre-war account, it seems that the latter was right on this point, which emphasizes that such earlier sources (among them nineteenth century ones) cannot – and should not – be dismissed as no longer having anything of interest to say about the historiography of ancient society.[86]

Conclusion: Back to Basics

To the question posed in the title, about the relevance of a Marxist approach to an understanding of ancient Rome, the answer presented here is yes, but not in the revisionist way depicted by exponents of Late Antiquity. Instead of systemic decline characterised by economic retardation, impoverishment, ruralisation, and crisis, leading eventually to feudalism, which is the view shared by Marxism and earlier non-Marxist historiography alike, current interpretations influenced by postmodernism maintain that not only was the economy of ancient Rome capitalist, but its workforce consisted of free and ethnically/nationally diverse hired labour unaffected by market competition, struggle, and racism. If the latter version is correct, it negates the very idea of systemic

poor freemen used sometimes to hire themselves out to the service of the mill when all other resources failed … This labour, however, fell chiefly upon slaves, and is represented as being the severest drudgery which they had to undergo. Those who had been guilty of any offence were sent to the mill as punishment, and sometimes forced to work in chains.'

85 See Beard (2008: 182ff.), who then notes: 'The recent fashion among historians and archaeologists has been to pour a good measure of cold water on the idea that, appealing and evocative though this material is, it demonstrates widespread literacy and high cultural aspirations among the populace in Pompeii …[t]here have also been doubts about quite how far below the elite the ability to read and write extended …[However] it is clear that for many people well below the level of wealthy inhabitants reading and writing must have been integral to the way they organized their lives, and to their ability to do their jobs and earn their living.'

86 'One of the unexpected things we learn about these Pompeians', remarks Tanzer (1939: 83), 'is that their standard of literacy was so high'.

transformation, based on a succession of modes of production, that underwrites Marxist theory and historiography.

Generally hidden, the reason for reinterpretation within the classics and ancient history is said to be necessary because new material requires this, not just adding to knowledge but challenging existing interpretation. Instead of causation lying within the domain of the material, however, reinterpretation is currently determined externally, by new theory now fashionable outside the discipline. Hence 'discoveries', 'recent sources' are in the end nothing more than a changed paradigm, to a theory that currently enjoys a high profile elsewhere. Simply put, looking at old evidence in a new way, which merely underlines the difficulty when data necessary for this reinterpretation are absent.

To some degree, the inability on the part of classics to respond adequately and robustly to the postmodern onslaught appears to derive from an absence of a strong theoretical foundation to defend, a problem that Marxism does not have. Confronted with a critique aimed at the epistemological underpinnings of their discipline, historians of ancient society (= 'sleepy British positivists') were as a result ill-equipped to resist effectively, not least by questioning in turn the claims made by postmodern critics. Having nothing of theoretical substance from which to mount a counter-attack, thereby not just challenging but also rebutting the criticisms made, such as it was the defence by some exponents of the practice of ancient historiography buckled under pressure. Others simply took on board postmodern ideas, attempting unsuccessfully to apply them to an understanding of the way ancient society operated.

Consequently, for Beard and similarly postmodern-influenced historians the spread of citizenship and multiculturalism was nothing other than positive. Seen from a Marxist point of view, however, it could be argued that, where the education in the classics is concerned, workers have been disempowered twice. First, by the exclusionary nature of classics as a topic of study. And second, they have been short-changed yet again, but now in a different form: the story about ancient society, they learn, is no longer about them as plebeians, and how this entails oppression, exploitation, and subordination, but rather about other sorts of non-class identities and issues, declared to be the only sort of empowerment appropriate for those like themselves. A familiar conservative trope, along the lines of 'be satisfied with what you are, and don't aspire to anything more'.

Attempts to elicit hidden meaning both from ancient texts about Roman history and from the latest archaeological finds are faced with the same methodological problem: the endeavour to arrive at society-wide meaning, by re-examining the written record and sources or by attributing new significance to recently uncovered components of material culture, is fraught with difficulty, since it rests centrally on the capacity to retrieve information or data that cannot be accessed – what the mass of the population thought, and how this fed into what they did. Each new artifact is claimed to redefine the historical record. Artefacts excavated are invariably labelled by archaeologists in a number of contradictory ways: not just straightforwardly in terms of what the item consists of and was used for, but also – and more problematically – what sort of individual owned/operated it, why, and to what effect. Coinage similarly comes with stories attached, moving into areas of knowledge for which there is neither information nor evidence, not least concerning the meaning/reception of its iconography.

However, no evidence to this effect is presented, nor is reference made to what assumptions underlie the way archaeological finds themselves are interpreted. Moreover, as Brown and other adherents of postmodernism indicate, their new views are based not on archaeology but on re-interpreting those sources which survive, attempting to find therein evidence for the case they wish to make. In epistemological terms, therefore, the issue prompts the following question: which theory – theirs or that of Marxism and earlier non-Marxism – is better at explaining what these texts mean? Postmodernism looks on the bright side of life, in the filmic spirit of *Monty Python's Life of Brian*, taking a positive view about the economy (slavery benign, market extensive, freedom and capitalism widespread) and culture (religion benevolent, life easy), while – in order to account for the systemic logic, its dynamics and contradictions – Marxism and earlier non-Marxist approaches look at the negative elements (the fact and causes of economic decline and resulting transformation).

Nor is it accurate to categorize its economy as capitalist; significantly, those who claim that it was are not themselves Marxists. Arguing that the economy of ancient Rome was capitalist, and that rather than decline the empire flourished, current historiography reifies the accumulation process as systemically eternal. In this way capitalism becomes what bourgeois economic theory has always claimed it is: an innate economic form that is systemically ever-present, and as such is one that cannot be transcended. Abolished at a stroke, therefore, are the fundamentals of Marxist theory based on crisis and conflict in one mode of production generating a dynamic leading to its supplanting by another and different mode, or the very logic informing the historiography based on Marxism. For this reason, chipping away at what a Marxist approach has to say regarding ancient Rome cannot but have profound implications for all its historiography to follow.

A variant of the combined Rome-as-capitalist-economy and Rome-as-global-empire is the Rome-as-World-State thesis. The latter produces a sweetness-

and-light impression of Roman society, a narrative the focus of which is on a version of 'sin city', an all-singing, all-dancing image of positivity, reproducing the stereotypical Hollywood film trope of ancient Rome as a place essentially of leisure, orgies, licentiousness, fun, and laughter. This is consistent with the historiographical revision that has taken place, one that accentuates the positive and downgrades or ignores the negative, depicting Rome as a largely tension-free capitalist economy, able to satisfy the wants of aristocracy and plebeian alike. Methodologically, such claims to new interpretations are said to be based either on a re-reading of the existing sources, or on what recent archaeology has revealed.

Rather obviously, Marxist theory is not – and never should be seen as – immune to criticism. Nevertheless, the insistence by non- and anti-Marxists that it is passé, and consequently has nothing of interest or relevance to say about the historiography of ancient society cannot be permitted to pass unchallenged, as is so often the case today. That the political agenda behind these kinds of indictments is itself frequently hidden underscores the importance of scrutinizing the epistemology of those making them. For Marxism, this has involved questioning the arguments opposed to the decline thesis, among them the following interrelated claims: that processes such as the consolidation of large estates, ruralisation, decentralisation, stagnation, retardation, overtaxation, poverty, and crisis, were either insignificant or absent; that the workforce was not unfree, and consisted not of tenants but rather of hired labour that was free; that multiculturalism was tension-free because of an absence of labour market competition; and, of course, that ancient Rome was a flourishing capitalist economy, making the latter mode an eternal systemic form.

The methodological and theoretical problems raised by these interpretations, looking at the history from the view of ancient Rome, re-emerge when examined from the reverse angle – from the perspective of the capitalist present. Hence the difficulties comparing ancient Rome and the modern West are outlined in the following chapter.

CHAPTER 4

Ancient Rome and the Modern West: Death or Resurrection?

> There are those in our own country today, too, who speak of the protection of the country. Of survival. The answer to that is: *Survival as what*?
>
> Part of the summing up speech delivered by Judge Haywood, played by Spencer Tracy, in the film *Judgment at Nuremberg* (1961), directed and produced by Stanley Kramer, and written by ABBY MANN.[1] A question that is not asked as often as it should be – let alone answered – these days.

∴

Introduction: Woe Is Me

Each episode of *Up Pompeii*, a 1970s television sitcom comedy set in the ancient Roman city lying in the shadow of Vesuvius, began with its main character, the slave Lurcio, trying to compose a Prologue, only to be interrupted by a soothsayer prophesying imminent disaster, crying 'woe, woe is me'. Half a century later one is witnessing the proliferation of an historiography that shades imperceptibly into what might be termed 'doomology', or invoking the causes of past civilizational decline in order to find – and if possible pre-empt – current parallels.[2] This sort of analysis entails a twofold approach, juxtaposing what happened to an ancient social system, and why it came to

1 Mann (1961: 171, original emphasis).

2 Among the more recent exponents of 'doomology' who – with different approaches and conclusions – seek to explain the historical dynamic and logic structuring the appearance/dominance/survival/disappearance of empires, social systems, cultures, or civilizations, are Toynbee (1965), Hanson (2001), Diamond (2003), Miles (2014), Kennedy (2017), Virga (2023), Cooper (2024), and Furedi (2024). Speculative variants of this kind of historiography, projecting a greater or less pessimistic outlook, include Judt (2010) and Shaw (2019). It goes without saying that 'doomology' informs much environmental discourse about climate change and global warming. Terrestrial 'doomology' also has a direct link with the realm of science fiction (Stapledon, 1930).

a violent end, with events and processes unfolding in an equivalent context during the present, the former serving as a warning about what might occur in the latter.[3] Implicitly or explicitly, therefore, much 'doomology' entails not just a comparative approach of historical trajectories, along the lines of 'look what happened to them, the same could befall us', but also the search for ways of avoiding such a fate. Reversing the order of Marx's famous dictum, it appears that civilizational decline is being depicted first time (by comedy sitcom) as farce, and the second (by 'doomology') as tragedy.[4]

The most recent example of this genre, and in many ways the most interesting, takes the form of a comparative analysis of two kinds of systemic decline: that of imperial Rome, and that of the modern West (Europe, the United States). It is undertaken by an historian of ancient Rome, Peter Heather, jointly with a political economist, John Rapley, whose focus is on 'globalization as experienced on the ground in the modern developing world.'[5] Upholding the concept of long-term systemic decay as applied both to the Roman Empire and to the modern West, they maintain that decline is neither automatic, nor the effect solely of internal causes. Common to each of the two instances compared, therefore, is a single external process: an imperial core that over time gives rise to an economically developing periphery which ultimately supplants it.[6] In their words, it is an approach which 'contends that Rome's demise still has important lessons for the present, using the Roman Empire, and the wider world that it spawned, to think again about the unfolding history and current situation of the contemporary West.'[7]

---

3 For obvious reasons, such kinds of analysis tend to be written by those currently inhabiting a society deemed to be under threat. See, for example, Stoddard (1922) and Huntington (1996).

4 See Marx (1979: 103).

5 Heather and Rapley (2023: 4). For an earlier analysis comparing ancient Rome with the West, see Syme (1958).

6 'Rather than having their own future entirely determined by choices and events unfolding within their own domains', observe Heather and Rapley (2023: 4–5), 'we both [argue] that "our" empires fundamentally began to generate the end of their own dominion because of the kind of transformations they unleashed in the world around them'. This, they continue, is because 'Empires come into being to generate new flows of wealth in both conquered provinces and some more peripheral territories too ... Any concentration or flow of wealth is the potential building block of new political power [and] large-scale economic development in the periphery kick-starts a political process which will eventually challenge the domination of the imperial power that initiated the original cycle.'

7 See Heather and Rapley (2023: 3), who go on to elaborate (Heather and Rapley, 2023: 75, 81): 'Like fourth-century Rome, the post-1945 West still largely managed to control the more robust clients in its inner periphery, while its own internal prosperity blossomed as never before ... It is ... self-evidently the case that the modern Western Empire has not fallen, will not fall anytime soon, and in fact need never fall in the same way as its ancient predecessor'.

Broadly speaking, their approach to 'doomology', combining ancient history and development studies, offers a useful way of comparing the then/there with the now/here; rather than leaving the whole coverage down to a single author, it draws instead on complementary strengths and skill sets of two. Where the historiography of imperial Rome is concerned, the Heather and Rapley combination provides a salutary if qualified counter to the currently fashionable interpretation which, because Roman commercial activity is perceived as dynamic and flourishing, claims to see no difference between the economic system of ancient Rome and that of the modern West, dismissing any talk of decline as unwarranted 'catastrophism'. Much of their focus is on migration, unsurprisingly so given its centrality to the decline narrative in both ancient Rome and the modern West. They alight thereby in the midst of current political debate about the interrelated nature of capitalism, its economic dependence on yet more labour market competition, the role of migration as part of what is now a global industrial reserve of labour-power, and more broadly narratives addressing systemic survival or decline.

Its usefulness notwithstanding, one obvious difficulty facing a comparative approach such as this, covering widely separate historical conjunctures, is methodological.[8] Because it is better documented empirically, the case about the modern West, globalization and migration appears as the more familiar side of the equation. As Heather and Rapley accept, there is a major problem in the case of the comparative study they wish to undertake: for Rome, data about what went on beyond the frontiers of Empire is scarce, whereas for the modern West this kind of information is far more abundant.[9] Even when the comparison is restricted to different contexts within the same time frame, therefore, methodological difficulties can arise, a point noted in an earlier

8 The sorts of methodological problems raised by the focus of some sources are identified succinctly by Heather (2000: xiii) in his introduction to the eight volumes covering the barbarian invasions of the Roman Empire written during the late nineteenth century by Thomas Hodgkin (2000) who, as Heather agrees, 'wrote a very particular kind of history. What he did not write was social and economic history of the kind dictated by the broadly Marxist or Weberian agendas shared by most historians of the late twentieth century. Modes of production and social bonds did not interest him. Nor did he write a history focused on the administrative institutions of government ... What he wrote *par excellence* was narrative history of the old school.'

9 'The limitations of our available sources', concede Heather and Rapley (2023: 38–39, 40–41), 'make it difficult to explore the effects of the Empire's economic stimulus through the lives of those who lived beyond its borders, as we can for the more recent past in the case of the modern West.' Thus: 'Behind this macro-economic transformation stood myriads of small-scale innovators and entrepreneurs ...[b]ecause individual transactions were mainly recorded on perishable materials like wood or papyrus, these individual success stories can't be told ...'

and even more wide-ranging historical synthesis.[10] Hence the importance of what constraints this issue places on any theory comparing the two contexts examined.

The chapter which follows consists of three sections, the first of which traces the similarity between the comparative analysis and 1960s development theory about modernisation. The role of migration is considered in the second, while the third examines the link between on the one hand the process of decline and on the other labour market competition, class struggle, the rise of populism, and the crisis of capitalism.

I

Decline, Development, Modernisation

Inevitably, it is necessary for Heather and Rapley to position their arguments about the decline of the Roman Empire in relation to the continuing influence exercised over this historiography by Gibbon.[11] For the latter, evidence of systemic decay took multiple forms: deserted fields (*agri deserti*), which simultaneously reduced output and the tax base on each of which the continuing prosperity of the Roman state depended; disengaged elites, who withdrew from urban life; hyper-inflation, leading to the debasement of the currency; and the rise of Christianity, the pacifist teachings of which undermined the moral fibre of Roman ideology, while the proliferation of clergy increased the amount of unproductive labour.[12]

10 See Eisenstadt (1963: viii), who cautions: 'Any such comparative work poses a series of problems. The first is due to the fact that no single worker can master all the primary sources of all the societies on which the comparative analysis must depend. Hence, he must rely largely on secondary sources. He must be fully acquainted with historical research in these fields, and know the different controversies among historians, so that he can evaluate them, can beware of too facile use of any data or view, and can explore the extent to which such data can be analyzed according to the problems he analyses and the categories he uses.'

11 Heather and Rapley (2023: 12ff.).

12 Gibbon (1995). A similar emphasis about the cause of decline, based on the deleterious impact of religion, was advanced by Frank (1920). Slaves acquired from the East as a result of conquest or purchase eventually became freedmen, and – as citizens of Rome – increased in numbers. This transformation, he maintained, underwrote the trend licensing political absolutism based on Emperor-worship and deification, as such components of the Roman population who 'had never known self-government' did not object to the anti-democratic rule of an Emperor. An important aspect of this transformation was the change in religious belief, towards what Frank termed the 'emotional and mystical religions of the East' which privileged 'faith' and 'intuition'.

Against this view, Heather and Rapley deploy a number of arguments, one of which consists of evidence from northern Syria about the presence there of 'prosperous late-Roman peasants'.[13] This, they argue, in effect negates the decline thesis of Gibbon, since 'such well-off late-Roman peasants should not have been there', as over-taxation left 'no space for this kind of rural prosperity.' In keeping with this, the 'charge-sheet against Christian religion' is questioned on the grounds that it was neither pacifist, as Gibbon thought, nor did it undermine the culture of Roman society and its state. The model applied by Heather and Rapley to the actual/potential decline trajectory followed by ancient Rome and the modern West, by contrast, is in many ways similar to that used by the modernization framework to explain the growth path that Third World nations were expected to pursue during the 1960s 'development decade'. Among the concepts deployed by the latter that find echoes in their approach are take-off, multiplier effect, import substitution, and world systems theory.

Take-off is a concept that underwrote the orthodoxies of 1960s development theory. According to Rostow it applies to a process whereby '[t]he forces making for economic progress, which yielded limited bursts and enclaves … expand and come to dominate the society', when a 'new class of entrepreneurs expands [and] the economy exploits hitherto unused natural resources and methods of production', a situation in which '[t]he revolutionary changes in agricultural production are an essential condition for successful take-off'.[14] Compare, for example, Rostow, for whom '[i]n non-economic terms, the take-off usually witnesses a definitive social, political, and cultural victory of those who would modernize the economy over those who would … cling to the traditional society [but] the victory can assume forms of mutual accommodation …', with the following by Heather and Rapley: 'Over the long term … enough new wealth was collected in the hands of particular groups in both the ancient and modern inner peripheries to generate an irresistible change in prevailing patterns of political power'.[15] Similarly, the 'mutual accommodation' of Rostow corresponds in turn to the 'negotiated outcomes' of Heather

13 See Heather and Rapley (2023: 14–15, 17–18), who describe this as 'a staggering discovery [which] has demonstrated that the trajectory of Roman macro-economic development was exactly the opposite of what the narrative of decline had supposed.'

14 See Rostow (1960: 7–8). The parallel with the latter is expressed thus (Heather and Rapley, 2023: 44–45): 'As European empires spread across the planet, from the early modern period onwards, economic opportunities followed in their wake, to be seized by a great many individuals and families like the Tata's [whose] success story echoes those of non-Romans in the periphery of that earlier Empire'.

15 Cf. Rostow (1960: 58) and Heather and Rapley (2023: 66).

and Rapley, for whom the process of negotiation with barbarian kings enabled Roman landowners to preserve their rural property.[16]

Of additional interest is that the approach of Heather and Rapley is a reverse variant of Wallerstein's world systems theory, a dualism also based largely on geography. Instead of underdeveloped-periphery and developed core, however, they replace this with a developing-periphery and underdeveloping-core, a binary whereby the latter is eventually supplanted by the former.[17] The resistance framework of Scott is likewise structured by a core/periphery geographical model, with the former area seen by him as a site of disempowerment and latter of empowerment.[18] In this respect, it is similar not just to the pattern identified by Heather and Rapley but also to the claims made by subaltern studies.[19]

Core, Periphery, Migration

Insofar as they follow a development model akin to the 1960s modernisation thesis, Heather and Rapley come close to arguing that what existed in the regions on and beyond the frontier of the Roman Empire was a form of accumulation.[20] This is because their view – in keeping with that of Prakash and the subaltern studies framework – is that the margins were places of economic growth and empowerment, linked to a process of import substitution.[21]

16 On 'negotiated outcomes', see Heather and Rapley (2023: 104, 135, 141–42, 144–150).

17 For references to a core/periphery duality, see Heather and Rapley (2023: 23).

18 See Scott (2009), who applies his model not just to present-day Asia but also to the Roman Empire.

19 Not the least of the many ironies is that, having been criticized for an approach that runs counter to postmodern endorsements of multiculturalism, Heather (2006: 536, note 35) invokes favourably the unambiguously postmodern approach of Prakash (1994), indicating that the latter's post-colonialism is similar to his own interpretation (subalterns rise up against empire).

20 Hence the view (Heather and Rapley, 2023: 32): 'But whether they had migrated voluntarily or been forced to do so, it was these great masses of humanity on the move [slaves, colonists] which meant that the former provincial fringes of the Empire finally surpassed its original heartlands in prosperity.' On the pattern of economic development at the northern periphery of the Roman Empire, see Heather and Rapley (2023: 40, 58, 83).

21 Whereas Heather and Rapley see economic development on the margins as a result of colonisation and conquest, others (such as Banaji) regard the same process as preceding or prefiguring contacts with the West. The decline experienced at the core of Empire is explained (Heather and Rapley, 2023: 25–26) thus: 'If we return to Rome, the rise of the modern West helps explain the initially mysterious decline of the Empire's original Italian heartlands. Here, too, straightforward economic logic dictated a shift in economic

This in turn is linked to a multiplier effect, in which trade begets trade, and generates further economic growth.[22] Trade with the barbarian periphery during the first three centuries after the end of the Republic generated wealth in such contexts from which eyes were cast on the wealth of Rome itself.[23] From this emerged what is now generally recognized as a familiar historical pattern of imperial decline.

Hence the 'foreign military muscle behind … the Visigothic and Vandal/Alan realms … was already established on Roman soil by AD 410', and by AD 500 'the vast majority of the territories of the old Western Empire had passed under the control of militarized groups of barbarians'.[24] In an attempt to protect its frontier and stem further encroachment, Rome increased military expenditure, which required in turn a combination of higher taxation and hyper-inflation. Hence 'all serious modern discussions' about the fall of Rome agree that, in order to resist competition from the periphery, it was necessary to allocate more resources to this. However, according to Heather and Rapley hitherto 'modern political discourse' has addressed only one aspect of the decline narrative: migration, in the form of barbarian invasions, a process which epistemologically underwrites any comparison of the Roman Empire with the modern West.[25]

In terms of the decline thesis, therefore, although the modern West 'has not fallen', it has nevertheless 'reached a major tipping point' in terms of a declining share of global output, a situation which licenses 'a sustained comparison

---

dominance away from an original imperial centre … [o]ver time, the agricultural resources of the rest of Empire, in the macro-economic conditions created by the Pax Romana, were developed much more fully and entirely eclipsed this early Italian dominance … as conquered lands began their own intensive production, local and therefore inherently cheaper products were bound to drive out Italian exports.'

22 'The crucial variable which really shifted the epicentre of prosperity', note Heather and Rapley (2023: 25), 'was the extra wealth created by the export trades in the different areas'

23 'During the first three centuries AD', explain Heather and Rapley (2023: 55–56), 'the Roman economy, despite all the expansion beyond the frontier, remained significantly more developed than its barbarian peripheries [and] provided highly attractive targets for acquisitive eyes …[b]y the fourth century these wealth-generating contacts with the Roman World … had been growing in intensity for three hundred years, and their revolutionary effect upon Rome's neighbours became only too visible.'

24 Heather and Rapley (2023: 79).

25 Heather and Rapley (2023: 97–98). Earlier they (Heather and Rapley, 2023: 10–11) observe that: 'For some Western commentators, Gibbon's diagnosis of Rome's fall offers an obvious solution. The West is losing its identity in a tide of foreign, especially Muslim, migration, it must shore up its defences, and reaffirm core cultural values, or it is destined to tread the same path to imperial Armageddon. Roman history as it is understood in the twenty-first century, however, offers some startlingly different lessons for the modern West.'

with the unravelling of the Roman system'.[26] A central aspect of this concerns the how to interpret – as negative or positive – the current migration into the modern West. On this point Heather and Rapley adopt a resolutely pro-migration position, contending that, unlike the barbarian invasions of the late Roman period, the object of which was the acquisition of land, post-1945 immigration into the West, by contrast, 'has involved many more economic gains' for receiving nations. For this reason, including an ageing population and the need for social care, 'halting migration absolutely … seems to be a recipe for absolute economic decline'.[27] For Heather and Rapley, therefore, the effects of migration underline what for them is the main difference between ancient Rome and the modern West.

Pointing to the establishment in AD 420s of permanent settlements on Roman territory, they argue it was this, not immigration to the modern West, that posed a threat, since '[t]oday's immigrants generally support rather than threaten the economies and societies of the developed world'.[28] The problem lies elsewhere, in the fact that land, the source of wealth in ancient Rome, was occupied by barbarian settlements, deprived the state of a wealth-generating resource, thereby posing fiscal difficulties for an ability to generate taxable income. Currently, argue Heather and Rapley, the modern periphery does not have to occupy the core, since the same end is achieved by bringing industry and production – the modern wealth-creating assets – under its own control. In short, whereas the imperial Rome experience of migration was negative,

26 'Nonetheless', caution Heather and Rapley (2023: 81–82), 'there is every reason to suppose that the modern West's imperial life cycle has at the very least reached a major tipping point. In what is clearly far more than a blip, its share of global GDP has fallen by more than a quarter in less than two decades. Against this backdrop, sustained comparison with the unravelling of the Roman system, despite many differences in context and precise detail, continues – we would argue – to possess great explanatory power [and] a set of unfolding patterns is already clear enough in the modern world to make it possible to use Roman history to show … that the West is currently experiencing only the beginnings of what will be an … existential crisis [which] is revolving around the same key components which undermined its ancient Roman counterpart'.

27 See Heather and Rapley (2023: 112). 'If the large-scale "barbarian" invasions of the late-Roman period in the end provide no kind of analogy for current immigration into the modern West', the same source continues (Heather and Rapley, 2023: 114), 'they can nonetheless be mobilized as an effective counterpoint through which to understand why not. The late Roman Empire saw a particular form of migration which quickly turned into an armed struggle for the control of a fixed stock of landed assets. Immigration into the West since 1945, in stark contrast, has involved many more economic gains than losses for recipient countries, and the overall benefit has only increased as native Western populations age …'

28 Heather and Rapley (2023: 128).

and contributed to its decline, for the modern West the equivalent process is positive, and offsets – if not prevents the realisation of – decline. Given the centrality of migration to the case about the presence or absence of decline, how the former is interpreted by Heather and Rapley merits a closer look.

II

Open Doors, Disgruntled Corners

In keeping with the positive way in which they interpret migration, Heather and Rapley identify two key features, as they see it, characterizing this process.[29] First, people have always moved in search of better prospects, a population 'flow from poorer to richer areas'; and second, migration is traumatic for the migrant. Both license a discourse combining individual resilience and initiative in the face of suffering. Not much consideration is given to a third, economically less benign, aspect: the impact of migration on the receiving context. It is this aspect that has become such an important issue in present-day capitalist societies, not least because the enhanced labour market competition that results generates in turn a rising populist backlash, with its attendant ideologies (nationalism, racism). Instead, they maintain that migrants 'may better themselves, but also the imperial structure as a whole': that is, immigration benefits both its subject and society.

Addressing the migration/empire model of colonization/reverse-colonization, they note its link to 'Great Replacement' ideology of the far-right in the West, and how its imagery of 'marauding vandals' and Islamic state fuel the claim that '[t]oday's immigrants are the modern-day barbarians at the gate', leading to a 'population replacement' that will undermine the West. Such views are dismissed by Heather and Rapley, describing them as emanating from 'disgruntled corners' of Western societies, a 'kind of metaphor [that] relies on a false equation' based on a 'highly questionable value judgement'.[30] Nevertheless, they agree that nowadays there is strong opposition to immigration in Western countries, and that it is linked to concerns – by these same 'disgruntled corners' – about living standards, resulting in 'striking electoral

29 Heather and Rapley (2023: 105–106).

30 That Heather and Rapley (2023: 139) disapprove of hostility expressed against open-door migration is evident from the description of 'from below' protest as due to nothing more than 'resentment' and 'manifest bitterness', terms which – like 'envy' – avoid having to understand antagonism and conflict as the product of serious underlying socio-economic causes.

successes' for those against open-door policies.[31] This is followed by the usual warning against regulating migration ('any substantial reduction in immigration will necessarily have consequences for economic prosperity').

However, this overlooks the fact that currently in the modern West it is only some categories that gain – mostly employers who want cheap labour. Workers already in jobs are faced with the possibility of having to compete with incomers, taking pay cuts in order to remain in post, or risk losing the latter to migrants. Accepting that immigration has had an 'uneven impact' compared with 'past celebrations of its unmitigated benefits', Heather and Rapley concede that 'a supply of immigrant labour does constrain wages that would otherwise rise in a more restricted labour market.' Nevertheless, they then double down on their original and positive claim, insisting once again that 'immigration delivers a net gain to the entire economy.'[32] Circumventing or downplaying the problem of labour market competition, Heather and Rapley insist that 'the modern world offers not the remotest parallel to the mass, organized, military confederations which forced their way across the frontier and seized substantial chunks of Roman real estate'.[33]

Who Is Empowered, and Why?

Accordingly, there are a number of difficulties with their views about migration. To begin with, the claim that stopping or regulating migration will necessarily result in a deleterious economic impact on the modern West fails to consider two things. That it is not nations or societies but capitalists who benefit; and that, with decent pay and conditions, locals would be attracted to do the work that cheap migrant labour is recruited to do. Both these points involve focussing on the logic, the dynamic, and the reproduction of the capitalist system itself, which Heather and Rapley do not do. Thus discussion by

---

31 'Substantial portions of different Western electorates have become hostile to immigration', acknowledge Heather and Rapley (2023: 111–112): 'Worried about jobs, incomes and cultural cohesion [their] antipathy has proved strong enough to effect some striking electoral successes ... prompting even some more mainstream politicians to seek ways to reduce their countries' dependence on foreign workers', then adding immediately the usual caveat: 'however, any substantial reduction in immigration will necessarily have consequences for economic prosperity'.

32 Heather and Rapley (2023: 109).

33 Heather and Rapley (2023: 107–108, 148), whose disdain for the view that immigrants 'were supposedly taking jobs and lowering wages' suggests a downplaying of labour market competition as an issue.

them of *laissez-faire* deregulation attributes causation simply to states, without mentioning the role in this process of class formation and struggle: the pursuit, specifically, of outsourcing and restructuring by capital in order to remain competitive, and perhaps even to survive, in the process cutting the cost of labour (deployed either in Third World nations themselves, or drawn from there for work in metropolitan contexts). It was this as much as anything else that was behind the power in the periphery, as many companies and workers from there joined the economies at the core.

Focusing on the modern-day advantages migration confers on Western nations, Heather and Rapley contend that 'even unskilled immigrants provide more economic benefit than cost', declaring that in the United States 'illegal immigrants comprise a higher share of the workforce than they do of the overall population, suggesting that a disproportionately high number of them are actively engaged in the productive economy.' This is the same error as made by others who maintain that the majority of immigrants in the European Union are wrongly classified, since they are no longer part of the industrial reserve but much rather in the active army of labour. As is argued elsewhere, what this demonstrates is the opposite of such interpretations: not the conceptual inefficacy of the industrial reserve, but much rather the operationalisation of its main purpose, a transformation whereby migrants have displaced locals who were either previously employed in the active army, or else hoped to enter the latter.[34]

Although the issue of cheap labour is referenced in passing, therefore, two of its most important aspects – its origin and purpose – are not fully explored in relation to the future political and economic prospects of the modern West.[35] First, the reason why a 'vast pool of labour' exists was that the Green Revolution in developing countries drove many peasants off the land, and – by turning them into workers – made them available to international capital as cheap labour. And second, this enlarged the industrial reserve went from being a regional or national economic resource for capital to a global one, available either in its own country or as immigrants to the West. In the case of the latter, their entry into the labour market at the core enhanced competition, enabling producers to lower labour costs and work conditions, undermining gains made by the working class over the years, and eventually generating the rise and consolidation there of a populist reaction.[36] The crucial point is that each of these

34 On this point, see Brass (2024a: 75).
35 Heather and Rapley (2023; 120–121).
36 On the reserve army of labour, the economic and political advantages it hands to capitalists, and why it is so central to the continuation of the accumulation process, see Beveridge (1931), Kalecki (1943), Dobb (1955), Sweezy (1946), Glyn (2006), and Brass (2024c).

aspects empowered producers, and helped shift the global balance in the class struggle away from labour and towards capital.

III

Crisis and Ruralisation

In light of their own argument that the process of decline was determined by external developments on the periphery of empire, it is perhaps unsurprising that Heather and Rapley take issue with Gibbon, because his 'emphasis is consistently on internal factors as fundamentally responsible for imperial collapse'. Unlike some, their view concerns not the fact of decline itself as of its suddenness: it is not that decline did not occur, or take place gradually, but rather that it happened so quickly – and seemingly unexpectedly – at the height of Roman economic power.[37] On the basis of pottery finds, argue Heather and Rapley, rural settlement in the Roman Empire was at its peak in the fourth century, 'right on the eve of its political collapse'.[38]

In the case of Italy itself, a different explanation is possible: such a development – pottery in rural settlements – points to de-urbanization, giving rise to ruralisation as the urban better-off abandoned Rome and moved to the countryside where they owned estates. Consistent with evidence of increased settlement, ruralisation can also be seen as evidence not so much of well-being as of economic crisis.[39] That political collapse followed shortly after is, accordingly, less of a surprise. Additionally, the presence outside Italy of prosperous peasants can be seen as an indicator both of ruralisation and of socio-economic differentiation, although the latter raises all sorts of questions about the evidence.[40]

37 'What used to be taken as clear evidence of economic decline, isn't', maintain Heather and Rapley (2023: 19), because in their view '[t]he Roman Empire did not endure a long, slow decay from its second-century Golden Age, until its fall became inevitable in the fifth. Imperial prosperity peaked right on the eve of collapse.'

38 Heather and Rapley (2023: 16–17).

39 On this see Walbank (1946), who argued that a result of the prevalence of slave gangs used by landowners in Roman agriculture was that wages generally remained low, the consequent cheapness of labour meaning there was little or no incentive to install productivity-enhancing technique on which further economic growth depended. This in turn led to a process of economic decentralisation, a retreat to the countryside and more emphasis put on subsistence cultivation.

40 Among these questions are: what kind of peasant was categorized as 'prosperous', and why? Were they sharecroppers, tenants of some sort, or proprietors of the land they cultivated? Moreover, what proportion of the rural population was composed of 'prosperous peasants'? Insofar as the latter may well have existed alongside – and even employed/

Both in the Roman Empire and in the modern West, the trajectory followed by the development model involves a dual pattern: the decline of the imperial core accompanies and is an effect of the rise of the periphery. The question posed here is to what extent is this consistent with Marxist theory, and to what extent does it depart from the latter. It is, of course, possible to categorize Marxism as yet another epistemological approach subscribing to a variant of 'doomology', and insofar as it maintains that development based on capitalism is indeed destined to decline and give way to socialism, this is an accurate description. An important difference exists, however; unlike Marxists, who take issue with the existing system, many exponents of 'doomology' by contrast are defending this same system from what they perceive to be an undesirable internal or external threat. Whereas 'doomology' narrative generally presents change as being for the worse, Marxism, by contrast, argues that change is for the better.

Class Struggle or Negotiation?

In an important sense, the core-in-decline and periphery-on-the-rise pattern of development is somewhat different from Marxist theory about imperialism, which maintains that economic resources flowed from the periphery to the core, as a result of the latter exploiting the former.[41] Staying with a unidirectional framework, Heather and Rapley reverse this, arguing that as the core declines while the periphery rises the resource flow goes in the opposite direction, from the core to the periphery. This is a useful corrective to prevailing Thirdworldist interpretations that stem not from Marxism but from nationalism, which tend to regard current patterns of surplus extraction merely as a continuation of an historically long-established, one-way appropriation, nowadays effected unproblematically by ex-colonial nations from their erstwhile colonies.[42]

exploited – other peasants who were poor and/or landless is in keeping with how Marxist theory interprets rural society.

41 Diverging from recent attempts by Pitts and Versluys (2015) and Osgood (2018) to conceptualise the Roman Empire as a case of globalisation, Heather and Rapley (2023: 45–46) correctly point out that 'modern Western imperialism was literally global, bringing much of the planet under its direct rule [whereas] Roman imperialism, on the other hand, was regional …' For the view that Roman imperialism was hegemonic, not aggressive, see Badian (1968).

42 An example of this kind of Thirdworldism is Patnaik and Patnaik (2017). For a different view, see Brass (2024b).

Rather than class struggle, entailing as it does conflict between protagonists with irreconcilable economic positions and political interests, Heather and Rapley tend to depict interaction between historical and contemporary opponents as less antagonistic. Emphasized is the 'negotiated' nature of outcomes, which gives the process they describe a more benign aura, largely devoid of competition and conflict.[43] Hence their argument that, unlike ancient Rome, a consequence of the spread of democracy is that 'labouring classes [have] acquired a sustained political leverage' and modern Western states have as a result to please a 'much larger political base'.[44] This highlights the difficulty with the term 'negotiation', in that acquiring leverage obscures the fact that historically such gains as have been achieved had to be fought for, in the course of prolonged class struggle conducted against employers and the state.

In the lesson taught by the past, to be learned by those in the present, the element of 'negotiation' is explicit ('the continuation of Roman civilization was only made possible through negotiation ... For western states today to negotiate successfully, it will also be crucial for them to adopt a nuanced position towards China itself').[45] Instead of contradiction leading to disagreement, discord, and resulting necessarily in hostile action, therefore, they see agency instead in terms of 'negotiation', a concept indicating that the issue in question can be settled amicably, and is thus resolvable without resort to force, the outcome of which involves neither expropriation nor appropriation by one set of interests at the expense of another but rather mutually-advantageous conciliation and compromise.

Populism and Its Contradictions

Lacking also is a sustained consideration of populism, what it is ideologically, why its discourse is so effective politically, and the reason for its current hegemony among working class voters.[46] Ostensibly, populism corresponds to

43 Thus the end of the Roman Empire 'in southern Britain had root causes which were not at all about "barbarian" violence [but] negotiated outcomes which transferred significant features of the old imperial culture into the new world order', note Heather and Rapley (2023: 104): 'What actually brought about Britain's post-Roman civilization collapse into an entirely pagan and Latin-free Dark Ages was not barbarian migration, but its voluntary severance from the Roman world: the original Brexit'.

44 Heather and Rapley (2023: 141).

45 Heather and Rapley (2023: 135).

46 It is only late in the analysis that populism is mentioned (Heather and Rapley, 2023: 148), the inference being that it is little more than a manifestation of the 'disgruntled corners' in Western societies.

a form of 'negotiation' between capital and its plebeian adherents, all of whom unite around a discourse about the sameness of non-class identity (nationality, ethnicity). However, the contradictions structuring populism illustrate all too clearly the limits posed by the term 'negotiation', and in particular its inability to explain zero-sum situations. In the modern West, right-wing governments pursuing a *laissez-faire* agenda, but wanting to keep the electoral support of working class for this cannot at the same time operate an open-door policy where immigration is concerned. Yet it is precisely the latter which their capitalist supporters most want: that is, continued access to a global industrial reserve in order to stay in business. Two examples illustrate the nature of the problem.

In 2015 the UK conservative administration proposed to curb immigration, hoping thereby to regain those of its electoral base lost to UK Independence Party. What happened next is significant. First, the backlash from many business organizations and thinktanks (Institute of Economic Affairs, Confederation of British Industry, Institute of Directors, the British Chamber of Commerce), all of which complained of the adverse economic impact that would result from no longer having access to cheap migrant labour.[47] And second, the hasty backtracking by government, which assured them post-Brexit exemptions would, in fact, allow continued recruitment/employment of migrant workers.[48] A decade on, much the same kind of episode surfaced in the United States, where a split emerged between the two kinds of support given to the populist Trump: on the one hand large sections of the working class who elected him President because he undertook to curb immigration; and on the other, a billionaire such as Musk who wants continued access to foreign workers, in the form of an extension of the H-1B visa scheme. These two examples underline the contradictory aspects of capitalism: a disjuncture between a political

47 Although in the UK it was a conservative administration of Theresa May that faced this dilemma, the origin of the issue can be traced back to the 'New Labour' government of Tony Blair who – against the advice of cabinet members with a trade union background – authorized an open-door policy in 2004. It was the 'decision that year to allow migrants from 10 mostly eastern and central European nations, including Hungary and the Czech Republic, to work in the UK with very few limits [which] led to a sharp rise in immigration'. See 'Blair was urged to delay free movement from EU that fired immigration anger', *The Financial Times* (London), 31st December 2024.

48 The full extent of the issue facing successive governments became evident when by 2023 migration to the UK had reached almost one million, only eight percent of which corresponded to asylum seekers. See 'Net migration hit record 900,000 last year', *The Financial Times* (London), 29th November 2024.

objective (anti-immigration to attract working class voters) and an economic one (pro-immigration to ensure capitalist profitability).

These are issues that pose difficulties for the kinds of solutions envisaged by Heather and Rapley for avoiding the decline and fall of the modern West. Their view extends from learning to accept immigration as a fact of life, to putting in place a raft of measures such as a universal basic income, a minimum standard of living, affordable housing, and higher taxes on wealth.[49] Whilst all the latter are indeed desirable, how precisely this sort of programme can be realized within the capitalist system itself remains problematic. In short, as long as producers have access to the industrial reserve, attempts to rein in the accumulation process with the object of moving beyond capitalism will not succeed. For this reason, those who argue, as do I, that without at the same time challenging the continuation of capitalism, by advocating and working towards a transition to socialism, the laudable objective of Heather and Rapley designed to pre-empt the sort of decline that befell ancient Rome is destined to fail.[50]

Conclusion

A prevailing cliché is that in times of crisis people tend to call up examples from the past in an attempt better to comprehend what the future has in store for them. Revisiting the decline and fall of the Roman Empire has been – and is still – the preferred way of searching for such parallels that might provide lessons for the present trajectory unfolding in the modern West. In what is a useful and timely analysis, Heather and Rapley examine the fate of the Roman empire in terms of what this portends for the modern West. Taking issue with the interpretation of Gibbon, for whom imperial decay was an effect of internal causes, their comparative approach by contrast stresses external determinants: economic growth at the imperial core stimulates a similar development at the margins of empire, a process whereby the latter eventually supplants the former.

The same kind of pattern is evident in the modern West, argue Heather and Rapley, where erstwhile colonies are in the process of gaining a foothold in the economies of past colonial nations. Highlighting not just the presence

49 See Heather and Rapley (2023: 163–165).

50 The reference (Heather and Rapley, 2023: 53) to the early 1970s Popular Unity government of Salvador Allende as 'a Chilean socialist utopia' suggests that the latter is perceived as an unrealisable (or perhaps even an undesirable) political objective.

of a core/periphery link, but also – and more importantly – that it empowers the margins, they provide a useful counter to prevailing arguments that depict peripheries simply as sites of economic disempowerment. Much of the approach followed by Heather and Rapley overlaps epistemologically with the way the development pattern would unfold during the 1960s, a geographical model structured by concepts such as take-off, multiplier effect, import substitution, and world systems theory.

At the centre of this story is migration, perceived to be crucial for economic growth in and thus the survival of the modern West. Unlike ancient Rome, where this process took the form of the barbarian invasions which necessitated additional military expenditure by the imperial core in the form of taxation so as to defend the frontiers, present-day migration is seen by Heather and Rapley as a positive contribution to the economies of the modern West. For this reason, they contend that it cannot – and should not – be stopped. Ironically, whilst analytically privileging economic competition between the core and the periphery, Heather and Rapley downplay the significance of labour market competition in the modern West, migration from the periphery to the core exerting downward pressure on wage levels, work conditions, and thus also working class livelihoods in metropolitan capitalist nations.

The connection between migration, the crucial role of the industrial reserve in the reproduction of the capitalist system, and the contribution of populism to political crisis in the modern West, are as a result largely absent from the way Heather and Rapley interpret the issue of systemic decline. By privileging negotiation over class struggle, they miss how populism exposes the contradictions driving apart the two different components forming the current electoral support on which conservativism relies: on the one hand capitalists who want an open-door immigration policy, to which on the other the working class is strongly opposed.

PART 2

Histories: Personal, Political

CHAPTER 5

The (Not-So-Hidden) Politics of Populism

> For schools, the teaching of forgetting was the most important mission ... Stupefaction thus advanced in all comfort, and even a little boastfully, adorning itself in all the masks of virtue and justice ... In this way, the reality of entertainment came to substitute for the other reality, and all citizens became children.
>
> The future of Europe as seen from the political right, a fable set in the fictional locale of Ørop where, since time and history no longer exist, lost also is a sense of selfhood.[1]

∴

Introduction

Unsurprisingly, perhaps, now that Trump has been re-elected US President, with the help of strong backing from blacks and Latinos who usually vote for the Democratic Party, arguments often encountered hitherto in academic circles (and to a lesser extent in the media) that populism and identity politics are innately progressive – and consequently should be supported by leftists – have responded in a number of entirely predictable ways. Either they have gone silent, claimed that they foresaw this outcome all along, or conversely excoriated the advance of populism without recognizing the underlying affinity between the views condemned and their own espousal of identity politics.

Lamenting the silence that has characterized both domestic and foreign response to the second Trump presidency, press comment notes the 'muted response Trump's return has elicited from the US left', as 'his first inauguration triggered outrage, uproar, and a wave of resistance, now there is barely a whimper', concluding that his opponents 'appear cowed into submission'.[2] It could be argued that this was a battle lost a long time ago, when the identity politics championed by 'new' populist postmodernism, about the innateness of

---

1 Camus (2024b: 8, 10, 16).

2 See 'Outrage turns to silence as Trump protests fail to materialise', *The Financial Times* (London), 25–26 January, 2025.

nation and ethnicity, in effect gifted him an oppositional discourse (not least the undecidability of aporia), thereby conferring legitimacy on his *approach* to politics (*not* the politics itself), and with it his current agenda. This has prompted some academic devotees either of populism or of identity politics, and usually of both, at least to reconsider the whole question of these ideologies, albeit rather late in the day.

Hence the acknowledgment that mobilization of single issue social movements on the basis of non-class identity possessed their 'foundations [of the new activism] lay in the post-structuralism of Michel Foucault [and] in post-colonial studies', and further that when 'diversity programmes focused on race and gender, conversations on class were often lacking', a belated recognition which overlooks and unknowingly repeats the long-standing critique by Marxism that such discourses are conservative, nationalist, not to say reactionary. Tardy realization notwithstanding, it is then implied that what was wrong with these movements was organization, not the views some of them held about the desirability of open-door migration, on the grounds that it empowered 'otherness', supportive as this was both of the industrial reserve and yet more labour market competition that benefits capital.[3]

Seemingly unaware of prefiguring debate, an exponent of identity politics takes issue with the populism of Trump, little realizing the underlying epistemological connection between her own position and his.[4] She interprets the electoral support received by him largely in terms of gender, and the insecurity resulting from the loss of male authority, downplaying thereby the contribution to his success of the combined issues of unregulated migration, increased labour market competition, and declining livelihood prospects. Avoiding the issue of class, therefore, each protagonist engages in the reciprocal deprivileging of the populist view held by the other. Similarly unaware of prefiguring debate, another commentary declares that American and European populisms are distinct and antagonistic, again repeating but misconstruing the issue.[5] Insofar as populism licences and empowers specific forms of nationalism and ethnic identity, therefore, it will at some point engage in conflict with those

3 See 'Where "woke" went wrong', *The Financial Times* (London), 1–2 February, 2025, a long article spread over two pages which makes no reference to the connection between immigration and 'identity' politics, together with the its role in fuelling the populist backlash in metropolitan capitalist nations.

4 See Judith Butler, 'Trump is unleashing sadism upon the world. But we cannot get overwhelmed', *The Guardian* (London), 6th February, 2025.

5 See 'European and US populism don't mix', *The Financial Times* (London), 30th January, 2025.

populists who support different nationalisms and ethnicities, both at home and abroad.

This chapter is divided into five sections, the first of which examines the prefiguring role of identity politics in the rise and consolidation of populism. The second and third consider two different sorts of popular culture response – each pessimistic – to a seemingly unstoppable capitalism, one of which maintains that opposition to this economic system is now impossible while the other advocates an opting out, and a retreat into earlier non-class selfhoods. However, that consciousness and struggle based on class still operate at grassroots levels, unexpectedly among 'white trash' and 'the left behind', is outlined in the fourth section, despite which – as is shown in the fifth – social science continues to regard populism as empowering and progressive.

I

For the most part, earlier analyses, rarely cited by those currently writing about populism, not only examined this ideology with the object of identifying components specific to it, but also tried to account for the presence of all these characteristics by locating the discourse in a historical context and process from whence it emerged.[6] Its longevity is evident from the fact that the roots of populism can be traced back to the conservative reaction against both the Enlightenment and the 1879 French revolution, when the political survival of the ruling classes and their property base made it necessary for them not just to seek but also – and more importantly – to obtain the support of plebeian elements in society. With the emergence of a working class that was urban and industrial, landowners emphasized the only mutual characteristic open to them: the sameness of a distinctively rural selfhood uniting them with their tenants and agricultural labourers. The resulting identity stressed the uniqueness and eternal character of tradition and culture all had in common as a result of inhabiting the countryside, but nevertheless retained the notion of hierarchical 'difference' based on class.[7]

6 These earlier and still valuable analyses of populism, ones published before the rise of postmodern theory, include those by Marxists, non-Marxists, and populists together with those sympathetic to this approach. Extending from Europe to Russia and America, important case-studies and histories of populism include those not just by Lenin (1960) and Trotsky (1969b), but also by Buck (1920), Hicks (1931), Hecker (1934), Normano (1949), Mitrany (1951; 1968), Venturi (1960), Lampert (1965), Wortman (1967), Ionescu and Gellner (1969), Jasny (1972), Parsons (1973), Walicki (1969; 1975; 1980), and Goodwyn (1976).

7 'The maintenance of "organic" relations between landowner and peasant', notes Lampert (1965: 14), 'would somehow preserve the Russian soul from being corrupted by the disruptive,

Becoming and remaining 'popular' in this manner entailed searching for and finding an identity that both rulers and the ruled could be said to share, and for populist discourse this took the form of nationalism, the ideological focus of which turned outwards and onto the foreign 'other'. Conflict with the latter reinforced and consolidated this perception, licencing in turn the extension of a nation-as-rural combination into a discourse about peasants-as-backbone-of-the-nation. Any process of separating the peasantry – supporters of private property ownership – from their means of production, mainly land (= depeasantisation), was equated by populism with a process of cultural erosion, and with it the loss of an innate and enduring tradition on which depended national identity.[8] Established over time, therefore, were the binaries underwriting the agrarian myth.[9] On the one hand elements constituted as positive: 'natural'/harmonious rural-based small-scale economic activity (peasant family farming, handicrafts) and culture (religious, ethnic, national, regional, village, family identities derived from Nature). On the other, by contrast, were the elements deemed negative: urban-based large-scale economic activity (industrialization, finance capital, manufacturing collectivization, planning, massification) and its institutional/systemic effects (class formation, struggle, revolution, socialism, bureaucracy, the state).[10]

---

constricting, and formalizing spirit so powerful in the bourgeois society of western Europe. A closer examination of the facts, however, shows that paternalistically-minded Russian landowners had very little natural affinity with the people whom they ruled ...' Similarly, in late nineteenth-century America the object of farmer antagonism was mainly the urban 'plutocrat' – the industrial manufacturer, the railroad owner, the banker, the middle-man (Hicks, 1931: 405).

8 Ionescu and Gellner (1969: 108) point out that in Eastern Europe during the early twentieth century, 'Most peasant parties were also adamant in their belief that the right of private ownership of the land and of other goods was one of the foundations of the good society. To encourage the small peasant owner to make a success of his enterprise was one of the tenets of their programme.'

9 For the centrality to populism of agrarian myth discourse, see Brass (2000b; 2014).

10 Hence the following view (Ionescu and Gellner, 1969: 4, original emphasis): 'Populism could be characterized by a peculiar negativism – it was *anti*: anti-capitalistic, anti-urban, as well as xenophobic and anti-semitic. In contrast ... populism worshipped the *people* ... The fact is that the people were more often than not identified in the peasants who were and are, in underdeveloped societies especially, the most miserable of the lot ...' In a similar vein, Walicki (1980: 96, original emphasis) reports that 'the Slavophile interpretation of Russian history ... had nothing in common with "republican liberty" [which] presupposed the people's active participation in political affairs; ancient Russian freedom, on the other hand, meant *freedom from politics* – the right to live according to the unwritten laws of faith and tradition, and the right to full self-realization in a moral sphere on which the state would not impinge.'

The first highpoint of populism can be said to have taken place during the first decades of the twentieth century, when it featured prominently in the political debates about the nature of peasant society before, during, and after the 1917 Russian revolution.[11] A hiatus occurred after 1945, when both it and nationalism were tainted as a result of their complicity with fascism. From the 1980s onwards, however, marked a second highpoint, when populism and nationalism fused once again to re-emerge as a much broader 'from below' response to the deleterious impacts of economic liberalisation on a world scale: deregulation, outsourcing, downsizing, an expanding industrial reserve, and the intensification of labour market competition in the metropolitan capitalist heartland. In the absence of socialist ideas/practice, and as capitalism spread across the globe, this form of nationalist discourse has been deployed effectively by populists who claim it is the only way to safeguard/retain workers' jobs and living standards.

Currently, however, and in contrast to the earlier approach, much academic writing about populism simply declares it to be a concept that can be applied indiscriminately to all sorts of different contexts, parties, policies, or individuals, without indicating why this is so. Lacking in many of these instances is an attempt to place it in terms of theory and political economy. Thus, for example, the link between populism and nationalism is either not addressed, or – if addressed – presented as an ideology devoid of history. The trend today is to divide populism into what is claimed are two distinct and opposed forms: a good variant, and a bad variant, each of which is incessantly asserted to exist. However, little or no attempt is made by holders of this view to outline the characteristics of the supposed distinction, and the ones that do inadvertently and quickly reveal the falsity of this claim.[12]

This is due in part to the increasing academic dominance of postmodern theory, which has shifted debate towards a position championing non-class identities (nationality, ethnicity) as empowering. In doing so, it has merged with – and become supportive of – both a populist and nationalist approach to politics more generally, with palpable outcomes in the real world. Endorsing the culture of the 'other', the 'new' populist postmodernism in effect legitimizes open-door migration from which accumulation benefits, privileging the nationality/ethnicity of the 'other' from the sending country, enabling thereby the far right in turn to deploy a similarly populist discourse but now in defence of the worker in the receiving nation.

---

11 These debates, involving Marxists and populists, are covered in the important analysis by Solomon (1977).

12 See the critique by Brass (2022b: 269–299) of just such an agrarian populist argument.

While it is untrue that populism and its grassroots support have remained exactly the same throughout history, the difference that does exist does not correspond – as some argue – to a good and bad variant. Comparing broadly the populisms of the early and late twentieth century, that of the first period was located in the economically underdeveloped countries of Eastern Europe where societies were largely rural, and as such relied mainly on peasant backing. In the second phase, by contrast, it was now also found in the core nations of metropolitan capitalism, drawing followers from urban as well as rural areas and occupations, consisting not just of farmers but also workers. In certain respects, populism has indeed changed, but in others not, and it is important to distinguish between them. Across both periods, therefore, the fundamentals of populist ideology have remained constant.

At each historical period the enemy targeted by populism was the same: peasant opposition in the early part of the twentieth century was to the penetration of capitalism into the countryside, while that in the later era was by peasants and workers to the effects of a well-established capitalist competition, arising from intense market rivalry both as producers of agricultural commodities and as sellers of the commodity labour-power. Retained over both periods, moreover, was a discourse opposed to an internal enemy (the state) and an external one (the foreign 'other'), whether financier or immigrant labour, both from abroad. What changed was not intrinsic to populism itself, but rather the expanded range of those social forces drawn into its ranks by appeals to non-class identity politics: that is to say, as a result of it being the anti-capitalist discourse of the right operating where accumulation was now on a world scale and taking place in the absence of a socialist alternative.

Present-day populists – rather like their 1905 Russian precursors, the Social Revolutionaries – aspire to nothing more than 'democracy', but of what kind and for whom is never specified. Mistakenly regarding themselves as little different from Marxism, the policies of the Social Revolutionaries were described by Trotsky as 'reflecting the contradictory life-conditions of the peasantry in a country rapidly becoming capitalistic.'[13] In this respect, populists – then and now – are much of a muchness. Considered in the rest of this chapter,

13 In the words of Trotsky (1934: 239): 'The Social Revolutionaries ... struggled theoretically against Marxism – although sometimes surrendering to it. They considered themselves a party which realised the union of the intelligentsia, the workers and the peasants – under the leadership, it goes without saying, of the Critical Reason. In the economic sphere their ideas were an indigestible mess of various historical accumulations, reflecting the contradictory life-conditions of the peasantry in a country rapidly becoming capitalistic. The coming revolution presented itself to the Social Revolutionaries as neither bourgeois nor socialistic, but "democratic"...'

therefore, are views held by some of those who either do not recognize or else simply ignore the populist roots – and consequently the political character – of their arguments.

II

A prevailing discourse in the domain of popular culture now proclaims the impossibility of resistance to capitalism, as the agency of the state has shifted from an earlier optimism to current pessimism. In this counsel of despair, oligarch money has bought up everything, and is now entrenched and too powerful to be opposed. No politician, government, or institution is going to oppose this.[14] Emblematic of this discourse of despair is the hopelessness expressed by Houellebecq in his most recent writing about the future in store for modern European societies, and in particular how the very idea of progress now seems to have been abandoned.[15] Failing to make a political distinction between Marxism and the 'new' populist postmodernism, Houellebecq conflates these two opposed and antagonistic theories, and consequently ends up blaming them both for the inability to transcend the current discourse of despair.[16] This melancholia permeates the narrative of his most recent fiction, about the

14 It is a view expressed in spy fiction by Beaumont (2023: 286–88, original emphasis), whose protagonist comments: 'Listen. Your people, the Whitehall crowd [are] idiots. You're all playing the little game. Left, Right, Labour, Conservatives ... We are living in a world where people of high intelligence, people who have *real* expertise, need sovereignty [and] need to be able to to operate with *extreme freedom*. These people actually know what the goal is, and how to achieve that goal ... Smart people have to do things that the masses *don't* understand', concluding: 'I believe in maximum freedom. Radical deregulation. Hyper-mobile finance. The sovereignty of the individual. Shrink the State.' Whereas for the earlier fictional equivalent – James Bond – the State was a virtuous institution, capable and willing to defend the nation against a foreign power, now the State is seen as part of the problem, either unable to discharge any longer such a role or, indeed, as having already been purchased by oligarch money.

15 An interviewer points out to Houellebecq (2022: 102–103) that whereas 'his ancestors had a project, believed in progress, in civilization [Houellebecq's] characters faithfully reflect the abandonment of all this.' Later in the same interview (Houellebecq, 2022: 105, 107) he is asked whether indeed '[p]eople have lost heart', to which Houellebecq replies: 'I don't think the West really wants to live', adding that: 'The terrible thing is the extent to which you can't say anything anymore ... Nietzsche, Schopenhauer and Spinoza wouldn't be accepted today, political correctness, in its current form, makes almost all of Western philosophy unacceptable. More and more things are becoming impossible to think. It's scary.'

16 Declaring that 'the leftist scum who monopolized intellectual debate throughout the twentieth century' were responsible for 'the misdeeds of the "left intellectuals"', composed of 'Marxists, existentialists, anarchists and leftists of all kinds [who] have been able

terminal physical decline of its main character, a metaphor for what is happening to France itself. Symptomatically entitled *Annihilation*, his pessimism is very much on show.[17]

A civil servant based in Paris, Paul Raison – the main protagonist, who works for the finance minister Bruno – is like his father before him employed in the service of the French state in 2027. It could be argued that the annihilation process refers not just to Paul as an individual but also to France itself, and perhaps also to Western civilization.[18] In a sense, therefore, he represents a sort of everyman, caught between two politically antithetical positions. On the one hand, the ideas and values of Bruno, a modernizing technocrat and finance minister under a Macron-type President and subsequently the power-behind the throne in the case of his successor. On the other, the deep ecology eco-fascists who wish to obliterate all progress, and return to the stone-age.[19] Bruno is the embodiment of the technocrat, for whom progress/economic growth is all; the eco-fascists, by contrast are against everything that Bruno represents.[20]

to prosper and infect the world', Houellebecq (2022: 115) asks: 'Did they at least contribute an idea, a new thought ...[n]ot in the least.'

17 In many ways, this narrative by Houellebecq is part of the same 'doomology' genre considered in Chapter 4 of this volume.

18 Nothing can be done about capitalism, infers Houellebecq (2024: 26) when describing French presidential policy as leading 'only to the creation of some precarious and underpaid jobs, on the edge of slavery, within uncontrollable multinationals.' Later on he draws the following conclusion (Houellebecq, 2024: 164): 'For some decades France had been transformed into a random juxtaposition of conurbations and rural deserts, it was more or less the same thing everywhere in the world, except that in poor countries the conurbations were metropolises and the suburbs shanty towns.'

19 Describing nihilistic anarcho-primitivists opposed to environmental destruction as 'an essentially American movement, distantly inspired by the Luddites although much more extreme [which] wanted not only to destroy industry, trade and modern technology, but also to abolish agriculture, religions, the arts and even articulated language', Houellebecq (2024: 265) indicates that their object is 'to bring humanity back to the level of the middle Palaeolithic era.'

20 'Bruno Juge, more than anyone else', notes Houellebecq (2024: 268), 'embodies revival through industry, technological modernity, progress ...', somebody who (Houellebecq, 2024: 430) 'still tended to some degree to see the economy as a sub-product of technology'. By contrast, '[t]here was an eco-fascist movement that saw the human race, as well as other social species, as being made up of naturally hostile tribes, constantly fighting,' explains Houellebecq (2024: 390), adding that in order to offset declining fertility rates '[m]odern countries like Japan and Korea inclined toward artificial reproduction, while technically less advanced counties, such as those of Western Europe, resorted to immigration. Both instances achieved the goal sought by capitalism: a slow but continuous growth in the world population, which meant that growth objectives could be fulfilled and investments were guaranteed a suitable yield. The only alternative was an eco-fascist ideology ... or one that was openly primitivist and anti-growth ... a synthesis between the

The latter part of the narrative concerns Paul's health decline: faced with the prospect of losing his tongue as a result of mouth cancer, and with it an ability to speak, even to live, the predicament confronting Paul symbolises the political neutralisation of the French people forfeiting their ability to speak in – and thus influence the direction taken by – an increasingly meaningless bourgeois democracy.[21] It's no use, Houellebecq seems to be saying, opposing what is happening today in France (in Europe, and perhaps even the world), since between them – *laissez-faire* capitalism on the one hand, a primitivist and conservative form of anti-capitalism on the other – these two antagonistic forces will destroy civilisation as we have known it.[22] Hence the element of annihilation, not just of Paul but also of French society, a process which (Houellebecq hints) is furthered by immigration, a view that replicates to some degree that of the Great Replacement argument.[23] Significant, therefore, is the immigrant-as-threat narrative that features in a dream had by Paul, in which

---

two being entirely imaginable.' The result, according to Houellebecq (2024: 392), is '[a] strategic alliance between people who want to cause chaos, and who have the technical know-how to achieve it, and others who stand to benefit from it, and who can supply the finance to make it happen.

21 This inability any longer to speak about crucial issues is depicted also in a dystopian fictional account of Ørop, a supposedly unpublished Hans Christian Andersen fairy tale written by Camus (2024b) about the future of Europe, where a refusal to address the issue of borders is presented as akin to *omertà*. Hence the stifling of debate is portrayed as follows (Camus, 2024b: 19–20, original emphasis): 'Those wishing to make a career for themselves in public affairs or the press had to take as their motto: *I would say even less*. And whatever office they might set their sights on in Ørop, they had to give the guarantee that they would see nothing of what was happening, that they would hear nothing of what was taking place, and above all, above all, that they would never put words to things ... If, despite all the precautions that had been taken, some rumblings were nevertheless heard, if the country was shaken by a dreadful cracking which the authorities were unable to completely smother or immediately sweep under the rug, the ambitious and the prudent, the true men of state, those who were going to make great careers for themselves in the official hierarchy or in the organizations that controlled and shaped opinion, stood out by their talent for translating this unpleasant noise that had pierced the silence into soothing nothingness, by their talent for reducing it to columns of numbers, elaborate excuses.'

22 Myths of the golden age, writes Houellebecq (2024: 266), 'have always had an incredible mobilizing power, and that's even more true today with all the programmes about the wisdom of traditional civilizations ...', a position informing his expressed desire for just such a golden age. 'I'd like to escape the obsessive presence of the modern world', declares Houellebecq (2022: 32), and 'move to a *Mary Poppins*-type world, where everything's fine'.

23 For an exponent of the Great Replacement, see Camus (2018; 2023; 2024a; 2024b, 2024c), whose approach – like that of Houellebecq – also belongs to the 'doomology' genre discussed in Chapter 4 above. After the sinking of a boat full of immigrants, resulting in some 500 deaths, Bruno observes (Houellebecq, 2024: 401) 'it's a horrible thing to say, but

the latter is followed by immigrants, two of whom pretend to be his friend but plan to kill, torture and dismember him.[24]

His analysis of the unspoken compact between the 'from below' agency of deep ecologists on the one hand, and the 'from above' objectives of finance capitalism on the other fits closely with the binaries of Great Replacement thesis, which argues for a similar overlap uniting financiers (= 'Davocracy') with progressives (= 'social justice warriors').[25] In short, pro-capitalists and supporters of what is a conservative form of anti-capitalism, opposed not to capitalism as system but only to its large-scale variants. This emphasis on non-class 'otherness' as the way forward where political mobilization is concerned has not been lost on the far right, which has quickly joined battle on this terrain (challenging the status quo because 'people's concerns are deemed invalid or even worse not worth being considered'), its own in historical terms, a move gifted it by 'new' populist postmodern belief that it is a terrain on which any ideological and political battle should be fought.[26]

---

immigration is going to come to a halt, and in electoral terms that's entirely in our favour. Economically, I'm not sure that it's good news … but electorally it's perfect'.

24 On this dream, see Houellebecq (2024: 432–33). 'People have started to say', writes (Houellebecq, 2022: 100), that 'what I thought for a long time, which is that Islamic fundamentalism is not really a deviation from the Islam of the Qur'an. It's just an interpretation of the Qur'an, one that's perfectly consistent. What fascinates me is to see that a large majority of people in the media keep repeating that the underlying message of Islam is a message of tolerance, one that forbids murder, is full of respect for other believers …'

25 In this discourse, progressives act as 'useful idiots', providing the ideological justification for open-door borders sought by commercial producers wanting additional consumers for their commodities. The historical trajectory leading to Great Replacement is outlined by Camus (2024b: 24): 'Ørop was thus well and truly invaded. And how could it have gone otherwise? The other nations and other peoples would have considered it too stupid to not profit from their opportunity and not conquer any part of this vacant empire, which had resisted them for centuries, which had indeed often subjugated them, and which now, by its inexplicable absence from itself, invited them to subjugate it.' For a critique of the Great Replacement narrative, pointing out its similarities with and – crucially – differences from Marxism, see Brass (2021: Chapter 8).

26 Nowhere is the latter position more evident than in the speech made by the US Vice-President, J.D. Vance, to the Munich Security Conference on 14th February, 2025, where the unwillingness of European governments to address the issue of immigration was interpreted by him as a denial of democracy. 'Of all the pressing challenges that the nations represented here face', he said, 'I believe there is nothing more urgent than mass migration. No voter went to the ballot box to open the floodgates to millions of unvetted immigrants. Democracy will not survive if their people's concerns are deemed invalid or even worse not worth being considered. And more and more all over Europe, they're voting for political leaders who promised to put an end to out-of-control migration'.

Despite recognizing employer advantage from open-door access to workers, exponents of Great Replacement are nevertheless unwilling to blame capitalism (= 'Davocracy') for this, regarding it almost as an unintended or accidental effect of the migration process.[27] Significantly, therefore, Great Replacement perceives the economic benefit to employers solely in terms of the need of producers for additional consumers. This, of course, is very different from the way Marxism interprets what the capitalist gains: hence the latter approach sees access to ever-cheaper forms of labour-power not as a fortuitous but inadvertent bonus conferred on commercial producers but rather as the object of the accumulation project itself, and thus as a much sought-after outcome. In short, as the enhancement of the industrial reserve, with all that it implies for the nature of the class struggle.

Issues that Marxism discusses in terms of political economy and class, therefore, populism – like conservatives and the far-right – addresses within a discourse principally about culture and non-economic identity, as rival kinds of national or ethnic belonging. Accordingly, framing the issue of borders largely in a narrative about the innateness of culture, one set of populists claim that open-door policy is an empowering contribution to ethnic/national diversity, while another insists that it leads inexorably to ethnic or national erosion. If Houellebecq is an instance of the latter, then Louisa Yousfi is an example of the former.

III

A Border Crossed

Unlike Houellebecq, who sees in the 'other' a threat to French society and values, Yousfi celebrates this same kind of opposition to what she terms 'the Empire'. In an important sense, therefore, her perception of France is the mirror image of his. Yet the underlying pessimism of the views held by Yousfi about modern French society are in the end no different from those of Houellebecq, albeit for very different reasons. This is because what she champions is an innate form of 'otherness', conceptualized by her as 'barbarianism', an identity

27 'Most managers', argues Camus (2024c: 42, original emphasis), 'know all too well which side their bread is buttered on, and how to secure an inexhaustible source of cheap labour. Incidentally, concern for the country and its dignity has not always been, in the course of history, their major preoccupation. And yet, despite the obvious links between replacist ideology, and its lies on the one hand, [and] business globalism on the other, one is reluctant to point to *self-interest* as the main driving force behind the doctrinal dogmas *against* their own, and often their most immediate interests ...'

counterposed to the established order. The latter is portrayed in negative terms, associated with an undifferentiated 'Western civilization' and linked closely to what she terms 'the Empire'; against this is projected a largely positive image of 'otherness', because for her 'Barbarianism is a primitive vitality'.[28] Endorsing barbarian 'otherness', Yousfi also alters its meaning in a significant way, shifting this from 'a barbarian I am, and a barbarian I shall remain' to 'a barbarian I am, and a barbarian I *wish* to remain'.[29] In an argument which is simultaneously a desire to be accepted by 'the Empire', Yousfi supports open-door migration, and maintains that borders have to be destroyed so as to enable those 'behind us' to pass unhindered.[30]

Because she is strongly opposed to attempts by 'the Empire' to integrate the barbarian, of concern to Yousfi is how the barbarian in its midst can be bought off by means of integration, regarded by her as a betrayal of barbarian selfhood.[31] In contrast to her wish for acceptance by 'the Empire', therefore, she urges resistance to the process of integration that recognizes her privileged status as a writer, one she fears decouples her from what she sees as an innate barbarian identity.[32] The latter is the object of a combined assimilation undertaken by 'the Empire', a process that entails integration = acculturation = disintegration, all of which in her view must be resisted. Although she is aware of the pitfalls accompanying this idealization of roots in a distant time and place, Yousfi nevertheless doubles down on her endorsement of such a discourse.

---

28 Yousfi (2025: 1–2).

29 Yousfi (2025: 4, original emphasis).

30 'Simply crossing a border is not enough to eradicate it', she contends (Yousfi, 2025: 6), since in her opinion 'to cross a border without destroying it is to perpetuate it and block the path of other randomly designated barbarians behind us.'

31 See Yousfi (2025: 4), who writes: 'There's a long history of domesticating barbarians. In the language of Empire, this is called integration'. As is well-known, fearing integration-as-betrayal of those 'we've left behind' is historically an anxiety expressed by postcolonial exponents fulfilling the role of representing an 'other' voice in a distant country, someone who privileges the migrancy of exile as part of a diaspora, and either projects him/herself or is depicted publicly as the spokesperson of a particular national or ethnic category, putting forward the ideology and politics said to be part of such an identity in discussion and debate.

32 Referring once again to the border as symbol and physical barrier the validity of which she does not recognize, Yousfi (2025: 7–8, original emphasis) comments: 'The potential for betrayal is inherent in the border ... We'll soon be saying at *our* gates, at *our* borders. That's what called successful integration: when their barbarians become ours too ... "I know where I'm from" is the phrase of a defector that expresses a border crossed and the process of going up in the world ... it means that once I'm up there, I won't forget my lowly origins. It's an oath of loyalty to those we've left behind'.

Hence the dilemma confronting the 'other', as she sees it, out of context in a foreign place: mourning an 'authenticity' that never existed, yet is deemed lost. Its supporters, Yousfi accepts, are faced with the critique that they should not succumb to identity politics, a nostalgia for a non-existent existence. This, she accepts, is a feeling that haunts every immigrant, and takes the form of 'something is slowly leaving them forever as they become more integrated.'[33] Recognizing this critique, and also its source in Marxist theory, Yousfi distances herself from it.[34] Notwithstanding the shortcomings inherent in such a project – emblematic of and encouraged by postmodernism – she privileges just such an identity, dismissing the argument that 'self-proclaimed barbarians' are attempting not to eliminate the concept of 'otherness' so much as reframe it 'but this time in their favour'.[35]

Against this her contention is that the issue concerns not reinstating a past – which she rightly labels 'a fantasy golden age', and 'a fabricated precolonial authenticity' – as a rejection of the present. The barbarism to be retained, Yousfi then maintains, is not that of the past, in another country, but one that has not been 'contaminated' by 'integration'. It is unclear what precisely is meant be this, not least because the identity in question necessarily draws on aspects said to have existed previously and elsewhere.[36] That is to say, a discourse about a different cultural being, 'someone else', in 'another place', at

33 'How do we mourn an authenticity that we have never known and yet genuinely lost?', asks Yousfi (2025: 8), adding: 'People nudge us and whisper: it's identity politics and we shouldn't give in to it. It's an evanescent and paradoxical feeling: a nostalgia for something that never took place. Doesn't everyone from an immigrant background feel this, deep down? Feel that something is slowly leaving them forever as they become more integrated?'

34 'In the political arena', concedes Yousfi (2025: 8–9, emphasis added), 'such questions would *seem* absurd; they would be sacrificed on the altar of historical materialism and condemned for encouraging people to idolize a fantasy golden age, to erect into a dogma a fabricated precolonial authenticity'. The insertion into this description of the word 'seem' indicates a distancing from the sentiments expressed.

35 'There is a similar panic', Yousfi (2025: 9, original emphasis) maintains, 'when it is claimed that these decolonizing types, these self-proclaimed barbarians are trying to recast race relations, but this time in their favour.' She continues: 'They fail to understand that our question [what we could have been] does not call for an answer ... it's less a question of rediscovering what we *were* than resisting what we are in the process of *becoming*. From this perspective, the "certain barbarism" that we wish to hold on to is precisely that which has not been affected – contaminated – by our integration into the Empire.'

36 In her words (Yousfi, 2025: 9), 'it's not about becoming a barbarian, but remaining one and accepting the political truth contained in the term ... our history, our culture, and our soul'. This suggests that what she wants is indeed to be considered part of 'a fantasy golden age' composed of 'a fabricated precolonial authenticity', a discourse she accepts is absurd.

'another time'. Equally problematic is the term 'contaminated'. To begin with, being looked down upon is not generally an experience applied to writers from erstwhile colonies, who much rather are regarded by many in bourgeois academia as an 'authentic' voice with things of value to express, to be learned from and heard with attention and respect. Consequently, this cannot be characterized as a negative response from – a contamination by – 'the Empire'.

Unsurprisingly, perhaps, culpability for any 'regression into savagery' on the part of the 'other' is that of 'the Empire' itself, and its misguided pursuit of integration.[37] In keeping with her view about 'contamination', Yousfi attaches blame for any barbarian 'savagery' to contact with white civilization, a view which amongst other things exculpates warfare, slave raiding, and oppressive practices encountered in the precolonial social formation. If she is saying that all our ills are down to capitalism, then one cannot but agree. But if the claim is that such troubles and the suffering caused are simply an effect of the denial by white society of an innate barbarian selfhood, then one has to disagree. Is it really the case, as Yousfi seems to think, that modernity/progress/development is a negation of barbarian selfhood to the degree that what she terms derogatively 'civilization' has nothing to offer the 'other'? If so, then not only is this incorrect, but it also confirms that she is in the end trying to reinstate a past identity from another place, or the very project dismissed earlier.

Another and more concerning interpretation of what she means by 'contamination' links it to learning anything on offer from 'the Empire', portrayed as coming from the trope of 'white saviour'.[38] In effect, this appears to be the astonishing claim that there is nothing to be learned from anyone else (along the lines of 'we are not here to learn from those who – in terms of nationality and ethnicity – are not like us'). Hence the claim that 'redemption' through integration cannot benefit the barbarian, since the latter benefits from nothing in modern society.[39] The self-serving epistemology informing her position, however, is conceded: 'But already I can hear their objections: "So when

37 'Asserting that the "regression into savagery is a process of integration"', avers Yousfi (2025: 21–22), 'is not to advance sociological explanations for our inner monsters by tracing the genealogy of all our civilizational shortcomings; rather, it is to state that our monsters are engendered not by too little contact with you but too much – too much France, too much Empire'.

38 Rejected by Yousfi (2025: 10) is what she terms 'a master's attitude ... to educate the good savages – the eternal victims – ... the line taken by our many unwelcome advocates and false allies.'

39 'That's why you, and all your talk of redeeming indigenous types through integration, can never really save us', insists Yousfi (2025: 22), 'In fact, nothing from that world can save us ... because we're not the ones who need saving.'

you're ugly, it's a reflection of our ugliness, whereas when you're beautiful, it's down to your own beauty"', a riposte acknowledged as valid ('In a way, they're correct …').[40]

Accordingly, no political unity between the barbarian self and anyone in 'the Empire' is possible, a view supportive of the innateness of national/ethnic difference and encapsulated in the words '[t]he community of tears will never materialize'.[41] Such an opinion, privileging as it does the barbarian (= beauty) while simultaneously deprivileging anything connected with 'the Empire' (= ugly), once again highlights the contradiction at the heart of her argument. Set alongside utterances like 'The Americans are the worst thing to have happened on Earth', and 'We were *not* all Charlie …', plus a hostility towards development, and then combined both with a defence of 'otherness' as innate, and thus also with an adherence to the agrarian myth, what remains can be seen as ideologically symptomatic.[42] In short, the discourse of populism.

IV

Unmentioned by Yousfi is the link between on the one hand the assertion of the innate 'otherness' of the immigrant, an identity she champions as positive and empowering, and on the other migration, the industrial reserve (composed of labour-power that is unfree as well as free), and the survival of capitalism as a system. In short, how employers and their state use such an identity to delegitimize working class opposition to the intensification of labour market competition, enabling them to lower wage costs and reduce working conditions.[43] This is achieved by extending the domain of identity politics from one addressing the culture of the 'other' and inserting it into the debate about the industrial reserve.

Hence cultural identity coupled in a generally positive sense with ethnic/national 'otherness' slides imperceptibly into – and becomes associated with – questions of political economy, and state policy to do with regulation of the border. Forbidden as a result is the ability – by worker organizations and representatives – to criticize the open-door policy operated by the bourgeois state at the behest of capital, since to do so necessarily invites opprobrium on the

---

40 Yousfi (2025: 23).

41 For this see Yousfi (2025: 32).

42 Yousfi (2025: 27, 33, original emphasis). The reference is to *Je suis Charlie* that emerged from the attack on the satirical magazine *Charlie Hebdo* in January 2015. It must be emphasized most strongly there is no suggestion that Yousfi *approved* of the attack.

43 Together with supporting evidence, this argument can be found in all published work by me that has appeared over the past four decades.

grounds of racism. It is this slide, with all that it signifies for the emergence and consolidation of populism – unity between employer and worker based on non-class identity – that is so damaging to any consciousness, any solidarity, and any struggle based on class.

There is a noticeable divergence between the pro-'otherness' of Yousfi and the approaches to the combined issues of self/'other', identity politics, and immigration, on the part of those such as Kapuściński and Goad. Departing from the way the issue is framed by most commentators, Kapuściński is aware that discourse around race-as-difference is a two-way street, as is the ideology of 'otherness' itself, and just as whites can perceive non-whites as 'other', so too can the latter view the former as 'other'.[44] This second aspect is not usually mentioned, or – if noted – is deemed unimportant. Moreover, such 'otherness' can be conceptualized in opposed ways, in either negative or positive terms.[45] Kapuściński points out that 'Herodotus himself wrote about Others without contempt or hatred, he tried to get to know and understand them, and often directly demonstrated the many ways in which they were superior to the Greeks.'[46] Currently, however, even for someone who is not him/herself 'other' to speak positively of the 'other' is considered by the latter demeaning, suggesting that any discussion of what this identity means is of necessity confined to those possessing it.

Rednecks, *Policières*

Significantly, a defence of the views held by 'rednecks' in America, those dismissed as 'white trash', by Goad, who not only describes himself as one but is also located politically on the right of the spectrum, yet insists – contrary to the prevailing trope – that the true divide is not race but class.[47] Taking issue with immigration as a method whereby capital undermines working class solidarity, leading to a reframing of the identity emerging from the operationalization

---

44 About how he defines 'otherness' Kapuściński (2008: 13) states: 'In my case I use these terms mainly to distinguish Europeans, people from the West, whites, from those whom I call "Others" – that is, non-Europeans, or non-whites, while fully aware that for the latter, the former are just as much "Others"'.

45 As the debate about Orientalism (Said, 1978) underlines all too clearly, it is just as possible for white Europeans to idealize the 'other' as the embodiment of prelapsarian virtue, as a 'natural' identity living fruitfully and happily in a state of Nature, untainted by the corrupting effects of progress and modernity.

46 Kapuściński (2008: 18–19).

47 Goad (1998).

of the industrial reserve as a difference based on race, not class, the target of his argument is 'corporate policies', not the migrant.[48] It is – or it should be – impossible to miss the irony of a Marx-quoting 'redneck' giving voice to a position that most leftists and progressives have long ago discarded.

In the case of the UK, contrary to prognostications by media and other commentators, who insisted that hostility to immigration was on the decline as people had become more sympathetic to the idea of multiculturalism, opposition has now risen again.[49] In response to record increases in the scale of legal – that is, government approved – migration, electoral support given to the Labour Party is shifting towards the populist Reform UK precisely on account of the latter being seen as consistent in its campaigning against open-door policy.[50] This political development notwithstanding, liberal opinion counsels

---

48 Speaking of force used by employers against workers throughout American history, Goad (1998: 114–115) comments: 'Subtler methods of worker control have proved more effective. Immigration has historically been one of these methods. I realize that that ... anyone who questions our spread-eagle immigration policy is automatically tagged as a racist ... If anti-immigration sentiments were strictly racist, black leaders such as Frederick Douglass and W.E.B. Du Bois wouldn't have pleaded with capitalist management to staunch the flow of European immigrants and give the jobs to native-born blacks instead. And if all the anti-immigration forces today were merely redneck bigots, opinion polls wouldn't show native-born blacks and Hispanics consistently outscoring whites in their resistance to further immigration. The working class, regardless of color, knows keenly that we aren't suffering from a labor shortage. Look how the special-interest groups skew on the topic, and a clearer picture might emerge: Monstro-corporations are funding pro-immigration causes, while labor unions and workers' organizations oppose them. Polls repeatedly demonstrate that three of every four Americans disapprove of further immigration. Ignoring the public's wishes, George Bush in 1990 conjured an imaginary "labor shortage" and pushed through legislation that cracked open the floodgates a further forty percent. More immigrants have entered this country legally over the past ten years [the 1990s] than in Ellis Island's heyday.' Crucially, the quote ends with the following observation: 'I want to make it clear that I'm objecting to corporate policies and am not placing a molecule of blame on the immigrants.'

49 According to a press report, not only is Reform UK 'now neck and neck with Labour largely because its stance on immigration is proving attractive to floating voters', but '[a]mong those who are backing Reform, the poll found that 37% say they do so because of its hard line policies on immigration and border controls', and further, 'among people who are "Reform considerers" (thinking about backing the party), about 72% said they were doing so because of the party's immigration and borders policies.' See 'Reform UK bearing down on Labour as voters back harder line on immigration', *The Observer* (London), 9th February 2025.

50 In the UK, revised figures indicate that in 2023 net annual migration into the country almost reached one million, of which only 8 per cent were asylum seekers from outside the EU, while the majority came via legal routes on work visas. In the words of the Labour Prime Minister, the figure was 'shocking', and 'happened by design, not accident',

against further border regulation, stressing that it is livelihoods and not immigration that concerns voters.[51] Ignored thereby is the connection between them: that increased labour market competition has implications for wage levels, work conditions, and standards of living is, however, not lost sight of by members of the working class.

What this underlines is two things. On the one hand, that class identity continues to lurk within the ranks of 'white trash' or 'the left behind', notwithstanding the support of the latter for the populist agenda of the far right, which now owns the discourse about the industrial reserve, a discourse that once belonged to the left. On the other, the folly of two interconnected political errors made by those who continue to regard themselves as positioned on the left of the political spectrum. First, downgrading or abandoning the concept of the industrial reserve, deprivileging thereby the deleterious labour market competition on the struggle about class. And second, consequently the setting aside of organization/mobilization based on class for that based on non-class identity – that is to say, on the nationality or ethnicity of the 'other'. Even the *policière*, that most conservative element of popular culture, now addresses such issues.

Thus, a conversation between Fazio and Montalbano, fictional Sicilian detectives, inadvertently reveals why migration is a political safety-valve. The issue of unemployment and overqualified youth, which features in the demonstration, the lockout of strikers, and the reason why the two main characters are unable to marry, is central to the detective story, and forms an ever-present backdrop to the narrative.[52] Inspector Montalbano is told by another character that 'Margherita and I have been together for two years. We wanted to get

---

since the previous conservative government 'policies were reformed to liberalise immigration ... Brexit was used to turn Britain into a one-nation experiment in open borders'. See 'Net migration hit record 900,000 last year', *The Financial Times* (London), 29th November, 2024.

51 See 'The surge in support for Reform is making Labour nervous. Now it needs a plan', *The Observer* (London), 9th February, 2025. That some 72% of voters support a ban on zero-hours contracts suggests that, as noted by Goad with regard to the US, the population of the UK is more receptive to radical policies than those currently on offer from the Labour Party. See 'Labour urged to defend workers' rights bill as poll shows huge public support', *The Guardian* (London), 9th February, 2025.

52 When the workers at the cement factory are all sacked, a riot ensues, and they are attacked by the carabineri (Camilleri, 2020: 141–43). One worker says 'I'm out of a job ... who's going to feed my kids?', prompting Inspector Montalbano to observe: 'What kind of world was this that took away a person's right to work and earn an honest living? So the state's answer, when these poor bastards dared to protest, was to greet them with clubs, tear gas, arrests, and convictions?'

married right away, but we were never able to find even the smallest jobs that might allow us to raise a family. I have a university degree and earn a little cash unloading crates of fish at the dock. Margherita also quickly got a degree, but she's in the same fix as me. How are we going to get on in life if there's no work? It's getting harder and harder for me to bring home the little we need to eat and still have the strength to start over again the next day.'[53] Faced with the prospect of a jobless life, with all that it entails, youth either moves elsewhere in search of employment or stays at home and causes political problems for those who rule.[54] A case, perhaps, of *tertium non datur*, or the impossibility of a third way advocated by populists.

V

In a recent contribution to the social science journal *Polity*, Urs Geiser endorsed Critical Agrarian Studies (CAS), an approach he wishes to apply to the study of rural society in Sri Lanka.[55] To this end, he draws a contrast between on the one hand earlier Marxist debates about the peasantry, those of the 1970s and 1980s, and on the other 'new challenges to the field of agrarian studies' said to be provided by CAS. The latter is positioned by Geiser as the 'other' of – and, indeed, the only feasible alternative to – market-based development theory lacking 'a critical perspective that would address power relations [and] normatively … continued to be embedded in the modernisation project'.[56] This, he suggests, CAS would do in three ways: first, by reinterpreting theory about class; second, by refocussing methodology away from household heads and onto its kinship components; and third, by seeking out politically radical/progressive policies.

In what follows, therefore, the efficacy of this approach is questioned. Despite accepting that '[c]ontemporary agrarian studies need critical introspection to clarify their own ideological position', this is not considered further

53 Camilleri (2020: 233).

54 Fazio tells Inspector Montalbano (Camilleri, 2020: 36–37): 'You know, at the [trade union] demonstration there weren't just workers from the factories that are being closed, there were just regular people, and that's the real tragedy. There were kids with no hope of ever finding a job. I even recognized some of my son's former schoolmates who're now married with kids, clerks and university graduates who've lost their jobs with no chance of getting them back. If things go on this way, their only choice will be to emigrate, like they used to.' To this Montalbano replies: 'I know, Fazio. And that's the least of it, because if these people suddenly decide to let out all the rage they've got inside, the whole thing could end very badly. If you're in no position to feed your children, you're ready to do just about anything.'

55 Geiser (2023).

56 Geiser (2023: 43–44).

in terms of what it might reveal.[57] Although the issue is presented by Geiser merely as an assessment of what insights might be obtained from the application of CAS, it is clear that he is broadly sympathetic to this approach, regarding it as progressive, and thus also as having much to offer both analytically and politically.[58] It is, in short, an option that in his words 'invites attention'.[59]

Populism, or the Identity That Dares Not Speak Its Name

As clear is that, while the apparent faults of Marxist theory are set out in some detail, far less evident is the kind of alternative on offer from CAS.[60] It is almost as if all of a sudden the latter had sprung from nowhere, untainted by any political agenda, and was thus just a matter of common sense only remaining to be recognized as such by everyone. For this reason it is important to enquire what precise ideas and meanings lie behind its description by Geiser in vague, apolitical and unhistorical terms like 'more nuanced theoretical approaches', 'this broader field of nuanced studies', and 'these [older] debates need to be critically reflected upon, and made more nuanced'.[61] The sole clue as to what CAS advocates merely repeats the equally vague and unhelpful description found in the recent *Handbook* edited by Akram-Lodhi and others.[62]

It is argued here that under these various disguises ('nuanced' alternatives), however, lies a very different story, a political one that Geiser does not tell. Consequently, it is impossible to understand his arguments without the additional knowledge of three things: the political background, consisting of

57 Geiser (2023: 46).

58 Hence the view (Geiser, 2023: 43) that 'a contemporary re-engaging with agrarian studies ... requires a critical reflection on such concepts and notions that informed the [earlier, Marxist] debates'.

59 Geiser (2023: 47).

60 Geiser (2023: 40–43).

61 For these descriptions, see Geiser (2023: 1, 3, 5). Other, similarly general terms that reveal little about the politics involved, but are nevertheless deployed by Geiser (2023: 41, 42, 44) in distancing himself from Marxism include 'diverse theoretical approaches within [the] social sciences', 'alternative approaches to understand agrarian structure and change', 'a broader range of theoretical approaches [corresponding to] what I call critical social science approaches', and 'a broad interdisciplinary framework, inspired by theory'.

62 See Akram-Lodhi *et al.* (2021) for this definition: 'Critical agrarian studies represents a field of research that unites critical scholars from various disciplines concerned with understanding agrarian life, livelihoods, formations and their processes of change. It is 'critical' in the sense that it seeks to challenge dominant frameworks and ideas in order to reveal and challenge power structures and thus open up the possibilities for change.'

a debate between Marxists and populists; its historical longevity, going back well beyond the 1970s; and what lies behind the current rise to academic prominence of populism, together with its implications for development theory.[63] Missing from the account by Geiser, therefore, is that far from being untainted by a political agenda, CAS is much rather an exemplar of what is termed the 'new' populist postmodernism, the object of which is to establish and consolidate an agrarian populist hegemony over the way peasant economy and society is interpreted.[64] The negative outcomes of this, it is claimed here, have serious political implications for the study of development and the role in this of peasants.

Comprising a number of currently fashionable paradigms in the social sciences – among them not just CAS but also subaltern studies, everyday-forms-of-resistance, empire, multitudes, and global labour history – a longstanding agrarian populism fuses with recent postmodern theory to form a mutually supportive discourse, that of the 'new' populist postmodernism.[65] The latter combines the agrarian populist espousal of 'natural'/harmonious rural-based/small-scale economic activity (peasant family farming, handicrafts) and culture (religious, ethnic, national, regional, village, family identities derived from Nature) with the championing by postmodern theory of what it categorizes as innate and 'authentic' cultural identities (nationality, ethnicity) encountered

63 Significantly, populist discourse emerged historically from opposition by conservative politics to the Enlightenment, and the consequent need to gain popular support among the masses for nationalist ideology. It flourished in the late nineteenth and early twentieth century when peasant movements throughout Europe mobilized against either capitalist development in the countryside or the transition to socialism. Prior to the 1939–45 war, most peasant parties throughout Europe and Asia were strongly nationalist, and agrarian populist organizations generated much rural grassroots support for right wing (as in the United States, India, Bulgaria and France) or fascist movements (as in Japan, Spain, Italy, Germany, Slovakia, Hungary, Croatia and Romania). This was because for populism a 'pure' (or middle) peasantry engaged in smallholding cultivation within the context of an equally 'pure' village community (that is, unsullied by an external capitalism or socialism) was presented as embodying all the culturally-specific attributes – timeless/sacred 'natural' and ancient bonds such as ethnicity, language, religion, customs, dress, songs, traditions – that were constitutive of a 'pure' national identity.

64 Reticence about the political identity of CAS as upholder of agrarian populism is a characteristic Geiser shares with Akram-Lodhi et al. (2021). Marxists, by contrast, do not attempt to hide their political allegiance. For an extended critique of CAS, see Brass (2023a).

65 Since details about the 'new' populist postmodernism, what it stands for and why, are contained in everything I have written over the past four decades, there is no point referencing just one publication as distinct from any another. The nearest Geiser (2023: 43) comes to acknowledging the presence of postmodern influence is the brief observation that in Sri Lanka 'most researchers applied more cultural theories to engage with nationalism, identity politics, processes of othering', without enquiring further into this process.

at the rural grassroots (traditional community, indigenous culture and organization), all of which are deemed empowering, historically eternal, and thus non-transcendent.[66]

Equally significant is the antipathy towards Marxist political economy shared by populism and postmodern theory. The development approach of Marxist theory is dismissed as no longer relevant to an understanding of rural society for a series of interconnected reasons. As noted earlier in this chapter, first, its objection to the continued efficacy of peasant economy, and its form of smallholding private property.[67] Second, its opposition to mobilization based on non-class 'otherness'. Third, for imposing an inappropriate Eurocentric development model on non-metropolitan (= Third World) contexts. And fourth, for supporting urban-based large-scale economic activity (industrialization, manufacturing, collectivization, planning, massification) and its accompanying institutional/relational/systemic effects (class formation/struggle, revolution, socialism, bureaucracy, the state).

Perils of Misunderstanding Populism

A sign of the difficulties faced by Geiser in his 'search for progressive policies [based on] normative thoughts' derived from CAS is a double misrecognition,

66 Historically – and currently – populism has sought neither a modern going beyond capitalism to socialism, nor the capture/control of the State, but rather a process of State 'avoidance' combined with a return to a 'natural' village-level social order. Restored thereby is smallholding agriculture based on individual peasant proprietorship that capitalism or socialism had threatened to erode or destroy, the object of populist resistance being simply to re-establish the 'eternal' family farming system as envisaged by Chayanov (1966). In contrast to Marxist theory, populism maintained both that undifferentiated peasant economy was an innate organizational form, and that it would continue to exist despite 'external' systemic transformations (from feudalism to capitalism, and from the latter to socialism). Since in this discourse 'peasant-ness' is equated not just with smallholding agriculture but also with culture and national identity, depeasantization becomes synonymous with deculturalization and the erosion (or loss) of national identity.

67 Marxist theory has always insisted that in the course of capitalist development the peasantry was differentiated along class lines, its top stratum (= rich peasants) consolidating means of production and becoming small capitalists, while its increasingly landless bottom stratum (= poor peasants) joined the ranks of the proletariat. For this reason, to regard peasants as a uniform category – as did populism – was mistaken, since these distinct rural strata possessed economic and political interests that were not just different but antagonistic. Instead of private property – the individualist smallholding economy – supported/advocated by populists, a Marxist programme of agrarian reform was based on collective agriculture, where rural property was owned/controlled by the State. Among the reasons for this was that the latter approach facilitated central planning.

as a result of not addressing its political identity. On the one hand endorsing as a way forward the agrarian populist views of Henry Bernstein; and on the other missing the fact that the importance of internally differentiating peasant households had already been undertaken by Marxism in the pre-CAS era. Citing the work of Bernstein as an indication of the theoretical path to be followed, therefore, Geiser omits to ask what kind of politics informs this approach.[68] Overlooked thereby is that Bernstein is himself an exponent of agrarian populism, as has been demonstrated by others on numerous previous occasions.[69]

Recommending also that CAS query a 'methodological focus on the head of the household [which] does not suffice', Geiser suggests that it adopt '[i]nstead an understanding of family or household internal dynamics [because these are] crucial'.[70] This, he continues, is because such a methodology 'raises questions on how we understand and generalise, rural life.' What is missed is that precisely such a methodology has been in place for many decades now, and is practiced by the very approach that has itself been deemed wanting: hence this same emphasis on how kinship and quasi-kinship relations in the peasant family are themselves transected by class, and thus have of necessity to be seen not simply as united on ties of affectivity but rather as divided in terms of property (land, means of production, labour-power) is found in research undertaken by a Marxist anthropologist.[71] In short, that the peasant family is composed of those who do not always possess the same economic position and interests has long been known about.

More broadly, the negative political consequences of replacing Marxism with the 'new' populist postmodernism as a development model are not difficult to discern. Unlike Marxism, for which struggle between capital and labour generates the necessary consciousness of class that prefigures and makes possible a transition to socialism, the agency pursued by 'new' populist postmodernism consists only of everyday forms of (peasant) resistance designed to achieve nothing more than a return either to a pre-capitalist systemic order or a more benign version of capitalism. Both these steady-state objectives are chimeras, since the accumulation trajectory, once established, necessarily becomes global and leads inevitably to neoliberalism. What capital wants from the peasantry in these circumstances is its labour-power, which – when reconstituted as part of a burgeoning global industrial reserve army on

68 Geiser (2023: 40–41, 44).

69 See, for example, Gibbon and Neocosmos (1985) and Brass (2022b).

70 Geiser (2023: 45).

71 On the need to internally differentiate peasant family and kinship in this manner, see Brass (1980: 440ff.; 1983; 1986a).

which producers everywhere can draw – serves to police and force down the wages/conditions gained over years of struggle and organization by the existing workforce in metropolitan nations, adding thereby to the intensity of labour market competition in such contexts which in turn fuels the populist backlash in these places.

By deprivileging struggle based on class and instead privileging non-class identity, therefore, the 'new' populist postmodernism merely throws petrol onto these flames, playing directly into the hands of conservatism and the far right. It makes difficult, if not impossible, the formation and reproduction of a solidarity based not on ethnic or national identity but on class. Moreover, where the industrial reserve takes the form of immigration, it permits populists in the receiving country to advocate unity between capital and labour of the same nationality, fracturing the possibility of a common mobilization involving migrant and local aimed at transcending the kind of economic advantage producers enjoy from continuing access to the industrial reserve. To the postmodern argument emphasizing the cultural identity of the migrant-as-'other'-nationality, populists counterpose an argument similarly emphasizing cultural identity, only this time the nationality of the non-migrant worker. Each component of the workforce is encouraged to see any ensuring conflict not as an issue about the economic sameness of class but rather as one based on national cultural difference.

What Marxism Does …

Turning, finally, to an inaccurate, not to say a mildly derogatory, reference by Geiser to my role as editor of *The Journal of Peasant Studies* (*JPS*). I am accused by him of adhering to a 'strict Marxist political economy, disqualifying all other research on the peasantry as "a-historical, cultural essentialism of postmodern theory"', which conveys the impression that I refused either to engage with this approach or to publish anything informed by it, both of which are false.[72] That the accusation is quite simply untrue would be clear from the part of that quote not mentioned by Geiser, which pointed out that postmodernism 'has been permitted to colonize non-economic discourse, more or less unchallenged. The effect on the study of development and the role in this of peasants and workers has been deleterious, leading in some instances to the denial of the desirability/possibility of economic development itself', concluding that

72 For this accusation, see Geiser (2023: 40).

'peasantries will be studied [by *JPS*] within the wider systems and historical situations in which they exist.'

As misplaced is the dual inference that, as a Marxist, I did not engage with postmodern theory and that consequently, as editor, I published nothing containing such views. To take but one example, after having criticized postmodern theory about Latin American peasants in a special issue of *JPS* edited by me, I invited an influential advocate of such an approach to compose a reply, which was published soon after.[73] To this I myself responded a while later, pointing out in what was an amicable conclusion that 'we on the political left have to be aware of both the epistemological lineage and theoretical direction of any discourse which we endorse, and in particular the vexatious issue of ideological proximity. (Both here and above the term "we" is used deliberately and in comradely fashion, expressing the view that Beverley is not perceived as being irretrievably lost to the socialist cause)'.[74] Despite my disagreement with the Subaltern Studies approach, moreover, I contributed a piece to a memorial volume celebrating Ranajit Guha, acknowledging both the influence and the importance of the series he edited.[75]

So much for the view that when I edited the *JPS* it adopted an exclusionary policy towards postmodern theory on account of my having 'disqualified all other [non-Marxist] research on the peasantry'.

Conclusion

Traced in this chapter is the connection between the abandonment by the left of most concepts belonging to its historical critique of capitalism, and replacing them – in some instances unknowingly – with a populist discourse. Thus, much contemporary writing about populism decontextualises it politically, adopting as a result the mistaken view as to it progressive character. Overlooked is that, in cases where the left has discarded or watered down the critique of the accumulation process, abandoning core political elements such as class and socialism, the resulting discourse supportive of non-class

73 The special issue on Latin American Peasants edited by me is Brass (2003), while the invited reply to it is Beverley (2004).

74 For this response, see Brass (2006). In a similar vein, not only did I publish other endorsements of agrarian populism and postmodernism during my time as JPS editor (e.g., Sivakumar, 2001: Desmarais, 2002; Nugent, 2003; Assies, 2005), but for my part I have also continued to engage thereafter with the neopopulist theory of Chayanov (Brass, 2022c).

75 For this tribute to Ranajit Guha, see Brass (2025b).

identities favoured by populism quickly cedes ground in any ideological struggle to conservatism and the far right.

Having abandoned the politics of class, endorsed open-door policies that fuel labour market competition by advantaging capitalism, and privileged instead the same kind of non-class discourse as that belonging historically to conservatism, is it any wonder that progressives campaigning on this analogous ideological terrain lose out to populists. Creating a space for identity politics, and empowering the concept of 'otherness' based on nationalism or ethnicity, invites reaction along the same lines, invoking a different selfhood that privileges not class but these same kinds of non-class ideology. In effect, it is a project that hands to the far right not just the weapons for struggle but also – and, one might add, inevitably – the victory, thereby confirming the old trope that a battle is won or lost before it takes place.

In keeping with this, popular culture sees capitalism in two distinct ways, split between on the one hand a discourse of despair and on the other the promotion instead of 'barbarian'/'otherness' as the only feasible objective. Despite this difference, both approaches are informed conceptually by the same discourse, positing the decline of Western civilization. Mimicking this retreat into the realm of pre- or non-capitalist alternatives, currently fashionable agrarian populism similarly attempts to resuscitate an age-old and long discredited concept of peasant economy, mistakenly declaring that because it is innate, eternal, and non-transcendent, it continues to be viable social form.

Those populists who deny the relevance to understanding the peasantry of concepts such as class and its related Marxist theoretical framework, claiming that it is a category which cannot be sub-divided along these lines, overlook the extent to which ethnographies do indeed reveal the presence in rural society not just of class division, but also struggle based on consciousness of this identity. All these aspects can be seen at play in the following chapter, based as it is on an anthropological participant/observation fieldwork study of beer drinking groups in a Peruvian agrarian cooperative during the mid-1970s.

CHAPTER 6

Drink, Work and Class in Rural Peru (Being There, Doing That)

'The kulak
from dawn to dusk unceasing
the very last puttee
from the poor peasant
is fleecing
Says he:
"The priest will absolve me
from grievous sin
and once more
I'll be
as pure as a lambkin"'

From the poem *Quacks and Priests* (1922), by VLADIMIR MAYAKOVSKY. Replace 'priest' with 'populist academics', and it has contemporary resonance.[1]

Introduction

Broadly speaking, the historical role in rural society of alcohol consumption is a matter of record, even though subject to disagreement concerning how to interpret drinking activity itself. Under the apartheid system in South Africa, for example, it was customary for agricultural workers to receive a portion of their wages in the form of wine as payment, the 'dop' system.[2] It enabled commercial farmers and planters to exercise control over their workforce via indebtedness, as is well documented. Significantly, the 'dop' system has

1 Marshall (1965: 152).

2 On the 'dop' system, and in particular its role as a form of labour control, see Wilson, Kooy, and Hendrie (1977), London (1999), and Williams (2016). Ethnographic accounts of migrant labour drinking groups in South Africa are found in Mayer (1980).

continued into the post-apartheid era, albeit framed nowadays mainly in terms of a health issue. For its part, the Peruvian case study depicted below is clearly of a historical kind, recounting events from the mid-1970s, but other research conducted recently suggests that – like the South African 'dop' system – much of the drinking structure and practices, along with their objectives, remain in place.[3]

Although hidden, it is the case that the information on which the ethnographic account that follows was collected as a result of participation in person in each of the two main contexts that feature in the analysis. Hence the first arena in which I participated alongside peasants and labourers was the drinking group, the source of much data concerning who took part, why, and with what object. The second case was as a worker, also alongside peasants and labourers, on plots of cooperative land privatised and cultivated jointly by groups composed of *socios*. Both contexts are related, in that privatisation itself was the outcome of decisions arrived at in drinking sessions, and much of the drink-derived ideology was also on display in the course of work conducted on privatised land.

Amongst other things, this chapter questions the now oft-heard political shibboleth that class differences have never had any place in analyses seeking to understand the way peasant economy operates, historically and contemporaneously. Thus, the ethnographic account presented here traces the connection between drinking ideology in a Peruvian agrarian cooperative and the formation and reproduction of class, together with discourse, consciousness, and struggle based on this socio-economic position. Indicated thereby is that peasant society is indeed transected by this sort of identity, the insistence to the contrary by populists notwithstanding.

The ethnographic analysis which follows consists of four sections, the first of which outlines the way drinking practices in rural Peru and elsewhere in Latin America have been interpreted. The economics and patterns of drinking are examined in the second, while the third considers its ideology and politics, with particular reference to gender identity and work. Section four connects the foregoing to the combined processes of class consciousness and struggle.

---

3 A study of drinking patterns in rural communities in the Ayacucho region by Yamaguchi, Lencucha, and Brown (2021) found that 'alcohol is seen as an enhancer of achieving a certain objective in negotiations … of important issues in business'. Asked who drank more, and why, the answer was '"The one who has more money: men"', a practice explained in terms of machismo: 'During a bout of drinking, men show not only physical toughness by the amount of consumption but also by their ability to purchase drinks for others.' Equally, '[f]emale intoxication is largely frowned upon'.

I

It is a truism that in Andean rural communities the drinking of alcoholic beverages is ubiquitous, generally unconnected with religious ceremonial, and structured by unresolved social contradiction.[4] Yet much of the anthropological literature on the Andes continues to focus on drinking either only or largely in so far as it is connected with religious ceremony in rural areas, with the result that alcohol consumption is analysed principally in terms of social activity which transmits or reproduces ideological forms that are generated in other institutional contexts.[5] Apart from the obvious – and thus generally unproblematised – category of 'drunk', little allowance is made for the possibility that the activity of drinking might itself confer identity which in turn affects the way its subject is viewed in other social and economic arenas.

Symptomatic of this same framework is the corresponding tendency – either implicit or explicit – to regard drinking as an obstacle to economic development, in the sense that resources spent on the consumption of alcohol are perceived as fulfilling non-economic objectives connected with ceremonial generally, and in particular the conspicuous consumption associated with the celebration of religious festivals, the *cargo* system (religious officeholding), or the acquisition of prestige.[6] Any surpluses generated by production within the

4 One of the contradictions referred to here concerns a dislike of, yet a social necessity to, drink, an element of structural ambiguity embodied in the inability to refuse an invitation to (or the offer of yet another) drink regardless of any personal preferences to the contrary. As Heath comments on this issue, 'most studies of alcohol use by anthropologists concerned tribal or peasant societies [where] drinking was examined in its natural context, with no expectation that great revelations would be forthcoming about ... why some people feel compelled to drink in ways that hurt themselves and others' (Heath, 1987a: 105; see also Heath, 1987b: 43). Another element of ambiguity concerns the extent to which (together with the reasons why) drinking is a context for the expression of solidarity as distinct from hostility. For example, the study by Simmons (1959: 105, 110) of a rural area south of Lima over the years 1949–1952, where conflict between landlords and sharecroppers over property rights was endemic, reveals that in drinking sessions the relations between these subjects were nevertheless positive and affective.

5 See, for example, Marzal (1971: 153–186), Conlin (1974), Valderrama and Escalante (1976), Brush (1977: 10, 67, 166), and Isbell (1978).

6 See, for example, Stein (1961: 101), Doughty (1971: 191, 195), Holmberg (1971: 200–201), Gifford and Hogarth (1976: 6ff.), and Harris (1978: 33–34). The characterisation by Doughty of drinking expenditure as part of what Wolf (1966: 7–9) designates the 'ceremonial fund' is in keeping with this approach, since money spent on drinking is viewed not as capital investment which generates further surpluses but as an economically unproductive disbursement that consumes existing surpluses. Harris (1978: 34) also subscribes to this view, writing

rural community are thereby dissipated, so this argument goes, consequently depriving agriculture in these contexts of requisite capital investment.

When problematised, socio-economic difference mediated through non-ritual drinking is seen as occurring between urban and rural contexts. In the case of Peru, this usually gives rise to a symbolic opposition between the binaries urban/beer and rural/*chicha*.[7] A corollary is that little attempt is made to identify – or account for – changes either in the form/content or the pattern/object of drinking within the rural community itself. By contrast, those texts which do analyse the socio-economic differentiation taking place among the peasantry in Peru during the post-reform era make no mention of the way in which drinking influences this process.[8]

Departing from these kinds of approaches, the results from participant/observation research conducted in the rural eastern lowlands of Peru during the mid-1970s revealed that class differentiation and conflict taking place inside an agrarian cooperative was itself reflected in the separation of peasants and workers in terms of the form, content, and pattern of drinking.[9] Significantly, fieldwork took place at a crucial moment in the post-reform era, when different peasant strata on the cooperative were engaged in a twofold

that 'drinking [is] also the form in which the communal surplus, or ceremonial fund ... is consumed'. However, examining alcohol consumption in a Mexican agrarian reform unit, DeWalt found that, contrary to initial expectations, 'drinking behaviour does not inhibit investment in the new adaptive strategies', adding: 'This point is surprising in the light of the complaints by development agents and others that most *ejidatarios* drink so much that they are not interested in the new opportunities now available' (DeWalt, 1979a: 185; see also DeWalt, 1979b). Nevertheless, drinking is perceived as a manifestation of, rather than a contribution to, wealth.

7 See, for example, Doughty (1971: 192).

8 See, for example, Van den Berghe and Primov (1971), Long and Roberts (1978), Guillet (1979), and McClintock (1981). An exception is Bunker (1987), who examines drinking behaviour in an agrarian cooperative in the Cusco region. An interesting study by Heath (1971) compares changes in drinking patterns in two areas of Bolivia before and after the agrarian reform of the early 1950s. In the mountain jungle region, where labour-intensive cash-drops such as cocoa and coffee were grown, landlords fled their estates and became urban traders and middlemen. Whereas in the pre-reform era they rarely used to drink with peasants, it was necessary for them to do so in the post-reform era in order to obtain access to crops which were then sold at a profit. By contrast, in the eastern lowlands of Bolivia, where landlords remained on their estates and became commercial producers of sugarcane and rice, there was no requirement for them to continue drinking with their tenants, as they had done in the past.

9 Fieldwork on which this chapter is based was carried out in Peru between January 1974 and April 1975. All prices are expressed in terms of 1975 Peruvian *Soles* (S/.), and at the time of fieldwork the exchange rate was approximately S/.100 = £1.

struggle: for control over newly acquired means of production, and to establish authority over various components of their workforce (young male agricultural labourers, and women).

In this context and at this time, a symbolic opposition between workers/*chicha* and peasants/beer existed within the rural community, and not between the latter and the town. Alcohol consumption can be viewed, moreover, as an important contribution to the accumulation process and the retention of wealth, in the sense that money spent on beer drinking group participation in the agrarian cooperative enabled access to an informal – though crucial – arena of political decision-making concerning disposition of, and thus control over, the economic resources available on this unit.[10] Within the co-owning membership, rich peasants were able to shift a portion of drinking costs (incurred by their wage labourers being invited to take part of beer drinking groups as non-paying individuals) onto middle and poor peasant participants.[11] Consequently, the latter paid an economic price for such access.

Furthermore, the beer drinking group not only reflected but itself generated social identity that was transmitted to – and had effects in – other institutional contexts on the cooperative. It was in ideological terms the very essence of masculinity, and therefore gender differentiation, as women were not permitted to participate unaccompanied by males. This exclusion, which also extended to agricultural labourers, gave rise to a multiple politico-ideological signification that reinforced subordination across a whole range of activities on the cooperative, since for peasants, beer drinking was equated with hard work, landholding, and adulthood, while non-participation denoted idleness, landlessness, and junior status. Nonetheless, this was challenged, at least in part, by agricultural labourers and women, for whom drinking was associated with physical violence, maltreatment, and laziness in both domestic and work situations.

---

10 The economic resources on the cooperative available to its membership included private plots of land; subsidised tomato seeds, fertiliser, irrigation, and tractor-time, all for use on such holdings; low-cost loans, and subsistence goods (milk, meat).

11 Each proprietor in the agrarian cooperative was classified as a rich, middle, or poor peasant on the basis of ex-tenant or ex-sub-tenant status together with the quantity, quality, and productivity of land owned. This last element was significant in differentiating the peasantry because of its crucial role in the production of coffee, the most profitable cash-crop grown on the peasant enterprise in the province (Brass, 1983).

La Convención, Peru

Located on the semi-tropical eastern slope of the Peruvian Andes, La Convención is the northernmost province in the Department of Cusco. Although its inaccessible geographical situation prevented extensive colonisation and settlement until the early twentieth century, the province has since the sixteenth century formed part of the rural estate system imposed at the Spanish conquest. The area is ideal for the cultivation of valuable cash-crops like sugar, cocoa, tea, and – in particular – coffee.[12] As the world market price for the latter commodity rose during the 1950s, estate tenants possessing large holdings began to cultivate this crop and accumulate capital through its sale to local merchants (*rescatistas*). Pre-reform La Convención was accordingly characterised by the socio-economic differentiation of the peasantry, as rich tenants extended the sown area devoted of coffee. This period was also marked by an increasingly acute struggle between the latter and their landlords over the ownership and control of land and labour on the estate system. Conflict fuelled the emergence over the years 1958–1962 of a peasant movement, as attempts by landlords to raise labour-rent or evict tenants was met with land invasions, the formation of peasant unions, a general strike throughout the province, the organization and repression of *guerrilla* activity, and finally the expropriation of the landlord class in the 1969 agrarian reform.[13]

Situated a few kilometres outside the provincial capital, Quillabamba, the estate of Pintobamba Grande covered an area of 946 hectares divided into two distinct but interrelated sectors of production. On the one hand, the landlord (later the cooperative) enterprise, consisting of 54 hectares of the best irrigated flat land (*pampa* or *playa*), on which were located infrastructural development (irrigation canals, two estate houses, milking and cattle sheds, storage facilities), livestock, and machinery.[14] On the other, the 717 hectares of hilly and less fertile land (*terreno accidentado*) sublet to peasant smallholders, who as tenants (*arrendires*) or sub-tenants (*allegados*) paid the landlord various forms of rent in the period before the agrarian reforms of the 1960s. After the peasant movement of 1958–1962, tenants and sub-tenants throughout the estates of La Convención became owners of their landholdings on the peasant enterprise.

---

12 Cuadros (1949).

13 Accounts of this struggle are contained in Villanueva (1967), Neira (1968), Craig (1969), Blanco (1972), Fioravanti (1974), and Brass (1989).

14 The presence of a disused distillery in the old estate house on Pintobamba Grande suggests that the production of alcohol used to be an important component of the landlord enterprise.

In the case of Pintobamba Grande, the landlord enterprise was expropriated by the agrarian reform legislation of the Peruvian state and in 1972 converted into a production cooperative (*comité de producción*). Of the 150 proprietors who had previously been tenants or sub-tenants, and who now owned land varying between 0.12 of a hectare and 36 hectares in size, one-third became members (*socios*) of the cooperative. Those in the latter category not only had their own individual smallholdings on the peasant sector of the ex-estate, but now also co-owned means of production on the cooperative. In exchange for these co-ownership rights, however, each *socio* was contractually obliged to contribute personally two days of unpaid work (*aportación*) per week on the cooperative, failure to do so resulting in expulsion from the membership. So as to avoid this sanction, and also to profit from the intersectoral wage difference, many *socios* began to employ substitute labour.[15]

Accordingly, the 1973–75 period was characterized by conflict within a membership composed of rich, middle, and poor peasant *socios* for access to and control over male agricultural labour, since this meant a corresponding ability to fulfil work obligations owed to the cooperative, the reproduction of member status, and thus continuing access to the economic resources it conferred. The labour-power of females was equally important in economic terms, but only in the context of production carried out on individual smallholdings in the peasant sector of the ex-estate.[16]

It was precisely in this situation, where on the one hand fierce competition among the *socios* was linked to the internally divisive political issue of non-completion (*incumplimiento*) of the statutory labour requirement, and where on the other it was equally necessary for the *socios* to maintain a united front against their workforce, that the practices, symbolism, and opposed meanings associated with beer drinking assume significance. Because of this, it is necessary to ask who drank what with whom, how often, for what reason, and at what economic cost; and conversely, who did not – or was not permitted – to drink with whom, the reason for this, and its socio-economic effects. It is also necessary to examine the way in which drinking ideology reproduced – or,

15 The ability of *socios* to appropriate a portion of the wage paid to the agricultural workers they used as substitute labour stemmed from the wage difference between the peasant sector and the cooperative. Hence *socios* redeployed labourers from their own private landholdings, where daily payment was less than half that received on the cooperative sector, onto the latter. When payment for every unit of labour-power supplied by each *socio* was made at the end of the year, those who had redeployed their own workers in this manner reaped the benefits of the intersectoral wage difference.

16 For more details on both these points, see Brass (1983; 1986a)

indeed, constructed – identity in a manner that had repercussions in other socio-economic contexts, not least that to do with work itself.

II

Drinking Costs and Patterns

Given that the production of alcohol has been historically important in the La Convención region, it is surprising that none of the analyses dealing with the emergence of a rich peasantry mention – let alone attribute significance to – its consumption in the estate system. During the seventeenth century cane alcohol (*aguardiente*) was manufactured in the valley on the sugar plantations owned by the Jesuits, and continued to be commercially central to the economy of the landlord enterprise until its expropriation in the 1960s.[17] In 1915 *aguardiente* produced in La Convención for sale in the Peruvian highlands was the most valuable commodity exported from the province, and second only to coca in terms of quantity.[18] During the mid-nineteenth century, it was said that rural inhabitants 'were inclined to drink ... and the weekly income was spent getting drunk on Sunday'.[19]

Another source reports that in 1911 much of the *aguardiente* produced in the valleys was retained for consumption by the estate workforce, particularly in the form of payment-in-kind received for labour-rent carried out on the landlord enterprise.[20] It also notes that landowners in the valley complained that their tenants drank too much *aguardiente* and *chicha*. The first brewery in Cusco was founded in 1872 by Gustavo von Mangelsdorff, a landowner of German origin, and by 1897 there were seven breweries operating in this region.[21] Although the account presented in this chapter refers to the economics and ideology of beer drinking and work activity as practiced on one particular ex-estate in La Convención during the immediate post-reform period, there is no evidence to suggest that claims made here cannot be extended to the rest of the cooperative structure based on ex-estates in the valley.[22]

17 On this history, see Fioravanti (1974: 41–54), and Brisseau (1981: 233).

18 See Tupayachi (1959: 224–225), Hobsbawm (1969: 35, Tables 1 and 2).

19 See Paz Soldán (1862; 377) who writes that they were '*inclinados á la bebida ... y la ganacia de la semana la gastan en embriagarse los Domingos*'.

20 Bowman (1920: 75, 84, 860). Landlord provision to their workforce of alcohol as payment-in-kind was also a feature of the 'dop' system in South Africa.

21 Kaerger (1979: 14, 28), Mörner (1979: 16).

22 Both peasants and workers in Pintobamba Grande who provided information about drinking and work activity emphasized that its practices and ideology were common

In Pintobamba Grande the cost of drinking was determined by four interrelated elements: the type of drink consumed, the frequency of consumption, the form and lastly the context in which drinking took place. Whereas labourers purchased and consumed maize beer (*chicha*) infrequently, and generally on an individual basis, peasant *socios* by contrast purchased and consumed bottled (larger-type) beer frequently and in groups, an arrangement facilitated by the easy availability of this commodity on both the peasant sector and the cooperative sector of the ex-estate. While a pint mug of *chicha* cost only S/.2, a litre bottle of beer cost S/.12, an economic difference which is magnified considerably once the drinking practices are taken into account.

Unlike the case of a wage labourer, who drinks alone, participation in a beer drinking group on the part of an individual peasant socio was also generally a commitment both to purchase a bottle of beer for – and to consume one from – each of the other participants. A single drinking session involving an average of six participants thus required a minimum expenditure of S/.72 per person.[23] In 1975 expenditure on *chicha* amounted to between two and eight percent of the daily wage received by an adult male labourer working in either the cooperative or the peasant sector. By contrast, evaluated solely in economic terms, consumption of beer in the context of a drinking group would entail expenditure amounting to 120 percent of the cooperative wage and three times the daily payment received by workers employed in the peasant sector.[24] Since the frequency of drinking was an additional determinant of cost, this also functioned as a differentiating mechanism between peasant *socios* and labourers; while the latter consumed a mug of *chicha* once or twice

---

throughout the rest of La Convención, a point sustained by the fact that many of them had friendship, kinship and fictive kin links to other inhabitants throughout the province.

23 Although extending in range from two to eight participants, drinking groups in Pintobamba Grande during the period of fieldwork were composed on average of six persons. This is similar in size to drinking crews in the Caribbean Island of Providencia (Wilson, 1973: 168). With regard to the formation, composition, and reproduction of specific drinking groups over time, one cannot but agree with Wilson (1973: 169) that 'my information about [drinking groups] is incomplete simply because at the time of fieldwork I did not fully appreciate their importance.'

24 In 1975 the daily wage of an adult male labourer employed on the cooperative sector was S/.60, while that for agricultural workers on the peasant sector was S/.25. Doughty (1971: 192) notes similarly that in the northern central highlands of Peru the 'low consumption of beer is apparently attributable to its expensiveness ... [during 1960–1961] a one litre bottle of beer cost between thirty and forty percent ... of a day labourer's average daily wage'. Wilkie (1971: 115) suggests that much the same kind of differentiation existed on the Mexican ejido between co-owning peasants and non-owning labourers, and comments that 'the *ejidatarios* drank more than the *libres*, but only because they had more money'.

a day, individual peasant *socios* participated in as many as three drinking group sessions daily.

The importance of the cost factor in the formation of, and participation in, beer drinking groups is underlined when considering four interrelated elements structuring these processes: the social composition of beer drinking groups themselves, their work/non-work context, plus the different politico-ideological ('free'/'non-free') and economic (paying/non-paying) modes of participation. Beer drinking group social composition for which data were recorded during 1974–75 indicates the presence in this particular arena of six categories: rich, middle, and poor peasant *socios*, agrarian reform agency (*Oficina Nacional de Reforma Agraria* or ONRA) personnel, wage labourers, and a residual category of 'others', consisting of male kin and spouses of the core participants.[25] Both the context in which the beer drinking groups occurred and its core constituents further determined the presence/absence of additional elements of this social composition.

Hence the formation of a beer drinking group during the intervals of work activity on the cooperative might licence participation by wage labourers employed in this context; although the latter also took part in non-work beer drinking groups, such participation was very infrequent. The opposite applies with regard to the equally context-specific presence of spouses of core participants, which was confined largely to non-work beer drinking groups. Since access by these two categories – wage labourers and spouses – to beer drinking groups was conditional on the additional presence in such contexts of an employer or husband, both these categories are identified as ideologically 'non-free' with respect to this particular activity, and contrasted thereby with the economically 'free' presence of peasant *socios* or ONRA personnel.

---

25 Data presented in Tables 1–6 were compiled as a result of participation in ten beer drinking groups which took place in the course of a one-year period. Since drinking sessions constituted an important arena for the collection of other types of fieldwork information, the social composition of those in which I took part reflected an obvious bias with regard to the preponderance of peasant *socios* in general and specific informants in particular. Two points should be noted, however, about the limited effect of this bias. First, it would prove impossible to operate beer drinking groups in the immediate context of the agrarian cooperative that wholly excluded its co-owning peasant membership; those who were not themselves *socios*, yet who were present on the cooperative sector for long periods at a time, such as ONRA personnel, were included in drinking groups operated by peasant *socios* themselves. And second, the data suggest that all three peasant strata participated in individual groups simultaneously, and that consequently no particular group was the specific domain of one stratum to the exclusion of the others.

TABLE 1 Index for participation in beer drinking groups

Category*	**Participation index§**	
Rich peasant *socios*	34	
Middle peasant *socios*	18	} 66
Poor peasant *socios*	14	
ONRA personnel	13	
Workers	12	
Others	8	
	(100)¶	

Notes:

* For the social composition of each category, see text

§ Weighted index calculated on the basis of the number of participants from each category in relation to total participants

¶ All figures rounded up

SOURCE: COMPILED FROM DATA IN BRASS (1982: APPENDIX F)

When aggregate social composition is adjusted so as to take account of the number of separate occasions on which persons from given categories took part in beer drinking groups, a clear pattern emerges regarding differential levels of participation. As Table 1 indicates, rich peasant *socios* exhibited the highest level of participation, which contrasts with the significantly lower incidence for middle and poor peasants, ONRA personnel, agricultural workers, and the category of 'others'. In general, however, members of the cooperative had a higher overall level of beer drinking group participation when compared with that of the remaining categories.

Table 2 indicates the extent to which different categories participated in the same beer drinking groups. The higher the position of one category in the hierarchy of 'other participants' for another category, the greater the frequency of their appearance together in the same drinking groups. It must be emphasized, however, that participation in the same group did not necessarily result in interaction within the group between the categories involved (although a total absence of interaction would have been extremely unlikely), indicating rather (and only) the extent to which interaction in this particular social arena was made possible. As 'non-free' categories were by their very nature unable to express preference concerning the frequency of beer drinking group

TABLE 2 Indices for social composition of beer drinking groups

*Other participants**	*Level of participation by rich peasant* socios§
Middle peasant *socios*	25
ONRA personnel	22
Poor peasant *socios*	19
Workers	14
Other rich peasant *socios*	11
Others	10
	(100)¶

*Other participants**	*Level of participation by middle peasant* socios§
Rich peasant *socios*	38
ONRA personnel	21
Poor peasant *socios*	11
Others	11
Workers	10
Other middle peasant *socios*	8
	(100)¶

*Other participants**	*Level of participation by poor peasant* socios§
Rich peasant *socios*	41
Other poor peasant *socios*	17
Middle peasant *socios*	15
Workers	12
Others	8
ONRA personnel	7
	(100)¶

*Other participants**	*Level of participation by ONRA personnel§*
Rich peasant *socios*	38
Middle peasant *socios*	25
Other ONRA personnel	19
Others	12
Poor peasant *socios*	6
Workers	0
	(100)¶

TABLE 2 Indices for social composition of beer drinking groups (*cont.*)

*Other participants**	*Level of participation by workers§*
Rich peasant *socios*	40
Other workers	21
Middle peasant *socios*	19
Poor peasant *socios*	15
Others	5
ONRA personnel	0
	(100)¶
*Other participants**	*Level of participation by others§*
Rich peasant *socios*	31
Middle peasant *socios*	23
ONRA personnel	19
Poor peasant *socios*	13
Others	7
Workers	6
	(100)¶

Notes:
* See footnote * to Table 1
§ See footnote § to Table 1
¶ See footnote ¶ to Table 1
SOURCE: SEE SOURCE TO TABLE 1

participation with other categories, they have been eliminated from consideration of data presented in Tables 3 and 4.

Table 3 shows the internal preference of 'free' categories in beer drinking groups; that is, the extent to which persons from one 'free' category participated in groups containing a high incidence of individuals belonging to the same category. It reveals that both ONRA personnel and poor peasant *socios* drank in groups that contained a high level of people from the same category, the opposite being the case as regards rich and middle peasants. Table 4 presents the index for external preference by these 'free' categories, in the form of a hierarchy of categories most sought after by those capable of expressing a choice regarding the social composition of the remaining participants in beer drinking groups. Both rich peasant *socios* and ONRA personnel figured prominently in this respect (in other words, they were the most sought after participants) when compared with middle and poor peasant *socios*.

TABLE 3 Index of internal preference by 'free' categories participating in beer drinking groups*

ONRA personnel	35
Poor peasant *socios*	31
Rich peasant *socios*	20
Middle peasant *socios*	15
	(100)¶

Notes:
* Weighted index of preference by each 'free' category for other participants from the same category
¶ All figures rounded up
SOURCE: SEE SOURCE TO TABLE 1

TABLE 4 Index of external preference by 'free' categories participating in beer drinking groups*

Rich peasant *socios*	37
ONRA personnel	26
Middle peasant *socios*	21
Poor peasant *socios*	16
	(100)¶

Notes:
* Weighted index of preference by each 'free' category for other participants from the different categories
¶ All figures rounded up
SOURCE: SEE SOURCE TO TABLE 1

Crucially. the importance of the cost factor as a determinant of beer drinking group participation emerges most clearly when categories taking part in this form of activity are differentiated in terms of paying/non-paying participants. The index for differential economic participation in beer drinking groups set out in Table 5 demonstrates that, with the exception of rich peasant *socios* who – paradoxically – exhibited high levels of paying and non-paying participation, middle and poor peasant *socios* together with ONRA personnel were the categories with the highest level of paying participation, while agricultural workers, 'others', and poor peasant *socios* exhibited high levels of non-paying

TABLE 5 Index for paying/non-paying participation in beer drinking groups

	Paying participants
Rich peasant *socios*	33
Middle peasant *socios*	26
ONRA personnel	22
Poor peasant *socios*	19
Workers	0
Others	0
	(100)¶
	Non-paying participants
Rich peasant *socios*	34
Workers	30
Others	25
Poor peasant *socios*	19
Middle peasant *socios*	0
ONRA personnel	0
	(100)¶

Note:
¶ All figures rounded up
SOURCE: SEE SOURCE TO TABLE 1

participation.[26] Expressed as an index for relative economic cost to each 'free' category in beer drinking groups, Table 6 suggests that middle and (to a lesser degree) poor peasant *socios* bore the main financial burden of participation as paying individuals.[27]

26 The high level of non-paying participation by poor peasant *socios* was an anomaly, since it was accounted for by their presence at a beer drinking group where all the alcohol consumed was purchased by me. On no other occasion did they participate as non-paying elements.

27 The index for relative economic cost is calculated on the assumption that the larger the number of non-paying participants in relation to those paying, the higher the financial cost to the latter of participation in beer drinking groups. Accordingly, in situations where a large number of paying individuals from a given category were present when this ratio of non-paying participants to paying ones was also high, the former were as a result required to sustain a correspondingly higher level of expenditure. Concretely, the main economic burden of beer drinking group participation fell on middle and poor peasant

TABLE 6 Index for relative economic cost to each 'free' category of participation in beer drinking groups*

Middle peasant *socios*	51
Poor peasant *socios*	24
Rich peasant *socios*	19
ONRA personnel	7
	(100)¶

Notes:
* Relative economic cost derived from ratio of non-paying participants to paying participants in relation to the number of those from the latter from each category taking part in the beer drinking group
¶ All figures rounded up.
SOURCE: SEE SOURCE TO TABLE 1

The significance for each of the categories involved in these different modes of beer drinking group participation can be explained as follows. In the case of peasant *socios*, the pattern of beer drinking was determined principally by its double function as the locus of (informal, pre-emptive) political decision-making on the one hand, and on the other as an arena for the imposition of social control. For these co-owners of cooperative means of production, therefore, beer drinking groups were sites/occasions where/when both a negative form (gossip, social control) and a positive sort (formulation of policies concerning the future direction of the agrarian cooperative) of politico-ideological power was exercised.[28] This dual function of beer drinking groups as loci of politico-ideological power is itself reflected in the hierarchy of preferences expressed by 'free' categories.

Thus, internal preferences are indicative of a tendency towards political consolidation *within* particular 'free' categories, a characteristic of poor peasant

socios, while the least burden fell on rich peasant *socios* and ONRA personnel. It must be stressed, nevertheless, that this was a *relative* economic burden, since in absolute terms rich peasants still engaged in the highest levels of drinking group expenditure.

28 In addition to the expulsion of cooperative members, which was constantly being assessed and reassessed in beer drinking group deliberations, the decision both to occupy and to subdivide cooperative land into private plots was first discussed by peasant *socios* in the course of a beer drinking session. These two issues constitute examples of the beer drinking group as a context in which politically important issues were raised/formulated/circulated. A similar pre-emptive role is ascribed by Szwed (1966: 438) to beer drinking groups in a Newfoundland parish.

socios at this period. External preferences delineate the reproduction of political links *between* particular categories, and reflect the extent to which it was necessary for middle and poor peasant *socios* to maintain political access to ONRA personnel and rich peasant *socios* with the object of being fully involved in this informal decision-making process.[29] Both internal and external preference patterns were themselves connected with the fluctuations in the social composition of the cooperative membership and political executive occurring throughout this period, as political dominance passed from poor peasants to a bloc of rich and middle peasants. Subsequently, poor peasants managed to regain control of the political executive, in the process wresting power from the rich and middle peasant membership. A crucial aspect of these changes was the admission to and/or expulsion from cooperative membership of *socios* belonging to other peasant strata, and the lapse of time during which a deficit in an individual's statutory labour requirement was tolerated before embarking on expulsion proceedings.

The price of this access by middle and poor peasant *socios* to rich peasant *socios* and ONRA personnel was the relatively high economic cost to the former of participating in the same beer drinking groups as the latter. If the first of the ten beer drinking sessions is discounted (since this was financed by me), rich peasant *socios* took part in two of the ten groups as non-paying participants, a portion of the cost being shifted onto the remaining middle and poor peasant participants.[30] In none of these sessions did either middle or poor peasants participate as a non-paying category; consequently, they sustained the cost of the non-paying participants present on each of these occasions. The significance of this economic subvention is that in all instances the participation by agricultural workers in beer drinking groups was conditional on the presence of their employers, and as participation by labourers was always on a non-paying basis its cost was borne by the paying participants.

29 As Table 2 indicates, both rich and middle peasant *socios* enjoyed a relatively privileged access to ONRA personnel through beer drinking groups when compared with poor peasant *socios*.

30 The two occasions when rich peasant *socios* took part in beer drinking groups as non-paying participants were as follows. First, when one rich peasant was on the winning side in a game of football, and as such was not required to contribute towards the purchase of beer. And second, when a rich peasant invited another individual from the same stratum to join in a beer drinking session convened by those privately occupying and cultivating portions of cooperative land. In both these cases, having to pay either for a crate of beer as a result of losing a football game, or for a non-paying individual who had been invited by a rich peasant participant, were risks entailing additional costs that accompanied middle and poor peasant participation in the same drinking groups as rich peasant *socios*.

In such circumstances, middle and poor peasants were compelled to sustain the cost of beer drinking group participation by labourers employed by rich peasants.

III

Drinking Ideology and Politics

How drinking was inscribed in peasant/labourer discourse points to its differentiating function. In addition to separating agricultural labourers from co-owners of the cooperative, the beer drinking group also performed an important role in differentiating both peasant *socios* themselves, and the latter from ONRA personnel. Precisely because it was a situation in which *socios* from all peasant strata met, this was a site where it was possible to articulate either hostility against or solidarity with participants from another peasant stratum. It was in just such a context, for example, that a poor peasant who competed disadvantageously for labour-power expressed publicly his resentment about this towards rich and middle peasants who were present in the same drinking group, because – unlike him – they were able to employ workers. On another occasion, an argument between a middle peasant and an inebriated ONRA *técnico* nearly ended in a fight, when the former questioned the latter's recently acquired qualification as an agronomist. The result was that, in the midst of a drinking session, the ONRA functionary rose to his feet and squared up to the middle peasant, challenging him to 'tell me to my face that you are more of a man than I am'.[31] The use on this occasion of an idiom stressing masculinity, together with its invocation as a mechanism of socio-economic differentiation, is highly significant, a point that will become clearer below.

Equally significant as a differentiating mechanism was the fact that participation in beer drinking groups by peasant *socios* was premised on the concept of multiple reciprocity, whereby each participant was usually required both to purchase one bottle for and accept one bottle from each of the others present.[32] The structure of this intra-group reciprocity was embodied in the term *rachar* (from the Quechua word *rachipay*, indicating the division of something into equal parts), which refers to the dual obligation on the part of every participant not only to purchase a round of drinks but also to consume all the rounds

31 *¿Usted es más hombre que yo? ¡Dimelo en frente!*

32 This was restricted to exchanges between peasant *socios*, and excluded most other drinking group categories, such as agricultural workers and women, who were not expected to adhere to this ritual practice.

purchased for him in return. Failure to comply with this double obligation invited not just strong disapproval but also – and more seriously – possible exclusion from future drinking group sessions, with all that this implied for the individual concerned.[33] This situation was described by one peasant socio thus: 'One is compelled to buy a round, and if one doesn't drink people say "evangelist"...'.[34] Hence either unwillingness or inability to purchase and consume the requisite number of rounds in the beer drinking group identified a person negatively by associating him with a minority and teetotal protestant fundamentalist sect.[35]

In La Convención, this demand to drink and its possible refusal operated at two levels: the first, and most important, was within the beer drinking group itself, while the second occurred between the latter context and those on the outside. As an invitation to take part in a beer drinking group necessarily involved a multiple exchange between an individual and the other participants, it was usually impossible to accept a bottle of beer from just one participant but refuse this when purchased by another. The single exception was an occasion when, in order to demonstrate his power, a rich peasant invited another to join in a beer drinking session, forcing other participants to buy an unreciprocated round for his friend. In private, some beer drinking

33 The inability to refuse an offer of a drink without incurring social sanctions is an aspect of alcohol consumption widely reported in Andean ethnographies (see, for example, Simmons, 1959: 107; Stein, 1961: 101; Doughty, 1968: 122). This is labelled 'demand' drinking by Doughty (1968: 195), who observes that it generally involves just two individuals neither of whom is able to break such a 'contract' to buy-drinks-for/accept-drinks-from the other without incurring the hostility of his partner; Bunker (1987: 338) notes rightly that 'the ability to offer a drink, especially bottled or purchased, suggests wealth and therefore power. Refusal to accept drink from a man who is taking and offering drink as a demonstration of his power is a direct challenge to that power and may provoke anger'. No mention is made, however, why those with power find it necessary to exercise it in this form in such a context.

34 *Le obliga comprar rueda, y si no tome dicen 'evangelista'...*

35 On this point, see also Doughty (1968: 226–227). The negative way of referring to a non-drinker was of some consequence in La Convención, since a number of commentators – including Hobsbawm (1969: 45) and Craig (1969: 286) – have claimed that many of the leaders of the peasant movement which took place there during 1958–1962 were themselves evangelists. A study by Fioravanti (1974: 180–81) has shown this to be inaccurate, since 92 percent of peasant union leaders were in fact Roman Catholics. In view of the fact that it would have also involved challenging both the existence and the extent of beer consumption among rich peasants who played a crucial role in the peasant movement, it is anyway unlikely for this reason alone that evangelists could have had much influence in La Convención. Consequently, it is not possible to agree with Huizer (1970: 191) when he writes that: 'The [peasant] unions in La Convención did a great deal to foster ... anti-drinking habits.'

group participants acknowledged reservations about the quantity of alcohol imbibed in this manner, but added that in the circumstances it was unavoidable. If a drinking session was convened at night, a participant might occasionally knock over a nearly full bottle in order to avoid having to consume it all, but this carried risks if discovered.

A similar opprobrium attached to anyone who refused an invitation to join the beer drinking group itself. Given its importance, however, this kind of invitation was rarely refused. The sole exception during the fieldwork period was the case of a middle peasant *socio* who was the president of the cooperative, and whose unpopularity among the membership was linked to his occasional refusal of invitations to participate in these drinking sessions. Such a response on the part of those who unsuccessfully issued these invitations is unsurprising, but he was also criticized for this refusal by the *socios* with whom he drank. The reason for this was that a refusal on the part of the most important political officeholder in the cooperative was a fundamental non-recognition (and thus undermined the efficacy) of beer drinking groups as a context for political decision-making.

Drinking and Gender

Female drunkenness was ideologically less acceptable than male inebriation, utterances concerning the former corresponding to statements about the presence/absence of 'control' exercised by men over women. Whereas disapproval of excessive and uncontrolled drinking on the part of male peasant *socios* was expressed largely with reference to the competence of the individual in question, as displayed in political and economic arenas, that involving female inebriation took the form of a double attack: against both the woman and her husband, sanctions being directed at the latter on account of an inability to regulate the drinking activity of a wife. When in the course of a drinking session the inebriated spouse of a middle peasant *socio* scratched the face of another middle peasant so badly that the latter was unable to attend the anniversary celebration of the cooperative, both husband and wife were blamed for this behaviour by other *socios*. Similarly, during the celebration itself, a rich peasant ordered his spouse home, saying she had drunk too much and would disgrace him publicly. In both these incidents, a male was either blamed for or feared censure on account of his inability to control the drink-related behaviour of a wife.

The ensemble of symbolic oppositions reproduced in drinking group discourse served also to legitimate the ideological subordination of females to males. An immediate and obvious determinant of this subordination was economic, since with few exceptions women did not own means of production either on the cooperative or on the peasant sector of the ex-estate; many were anyway unable to finance independent participation in beer drinking groups, ever were this ideologically possible.[36] As in the case of agricultural labourers, therefore, female access to beer drinking groups was doubly dependent, characterized both as non-paying and 'non-free'. For women, however, this exclusion was subject to an especially potent form of 'non-freedom', since it included an additional impediment: participation in drinking sessions was in all cases conditional on (and indeed never took place without) the presence in these contexts of a husband.[37] Beer was associated with the authority of males in general, not just that of husbands. When the wife of an absent brother threatened him with legal proceedings for desertion, a rich peasant *socio* purchased two crates of beer in order to mollify her. This was a reminder of the authority of her husband and – in the absence of the latter – her brother-in-law, a symbolic way of dissuading his brother's wife from further action by invoking the double patriarchal obligation which both form and content of the gift itself conveyed.[38]

The ideological dissonance between the concepts 'female' and 'beer' is further illustrated by the fact that women able and willing to purchase beer on the same terms as men were prevented from doing this. Hence the attempt by a spouse of a householder in whose dwelling a drinking group had been convened to purchase a crate of beer as her contribution towards the session was emphatically rejected by all the male participants, saying that 'a woman ought not to have to purchase a crate of beer for us [men]'. This refusal is doubly significant in that not only did such an offer constitute an attempt by a female to penetrate economically a male domain, but it also challenged the very notion of maleness itself. Since masculinity was equated with – and, as has been indicated above, defined in terms of – drinking capacity corresponding to the twelve bottles contained in a crate of beer (= 'a real man'), the attempt by a

36 Just 16 percent of all peasant proprietors in Pintobamba Grande were women, and most of these belonged to the poor peasant stratum. Only three of the 72 cooperative members over the 1972–1975 period were female, and they were amongst those expelled from the membership early on, there being no female peasant *socios* in the cooperative membership after this event.

37 For a similar prohibition on female drinking in a Mexican agrarian reform unit, see DeWalt (1979b: 514)

38 As a single crate contained twelve bottles, two crates signalled the authority of two males – her husband and her brother-in-law.

woman to purchase a ('male') round of beer threatened to transgress gender categories embodied in drinking ideology.[39]

Drinking and Work – I

That social identity was defined with reference to drinking practices – especially the quantity consumed during a single session, the average being six bottles – had implications also for other areas of activity in Pintobamba Grande, not least how an individual was seen as efficient or inefficient when undertaking work. When a poor peasant *socio* who, as an officeholder on the cooperative, failed to appear at a meeting of the political executive, another officeholder commented 'he is only a two-bottle man'. Disapproval relating to work activity, in this case non-appearance amounting to dereliction of office-holding duties, was accordingly expressed in terms of limited beer drinking capacity; inefficiency as worker is coupled with incapacity as drinker, unable to purchase/consume more than two bottles of beer. The upper end of this same spectrum was identified in an analogous utterance by a middle peasant *socio* who observed on another occasion that 'nine bottles of beer is nothing, a *real* man drinks twelve bottles' in the course of a single session. Hence approval was similarly projected with reference to beer drinking capacity.

If low beer drinking capacity was viewed unfavourably by peasant *socios*, then excessive drinking also involved contradictions entailing negative images in discourse. On the one hand, therefore, excessive drinking which resulted in drunkenness was contrasted with drinking that did not, the former condition being associated with personal inadequacy on the part of the drinker and – more importantly – with incompetence and unreliability in the labour process. On the other hand, a possible consequence of excessive drinking which did not lead to drunkenness was suspicions and accusations concerning the source of money used to finance this activity. *Socios* against whom political sanctions were invoked specifically in terms of drinking ideology included two poor peasant officeholders. One was compelled to resign as cooperative Treasurer because of the widely circulated view (reproduced, paradoxically, in

---

39 As significant is the way male drinking invoked images of female sexuality. Thus, the Spanish word for beer (*la cerveza*) is itself female, while the beverage is also defined colloquially in terms of a specifically female (= subordinate) characteristic. Among peasant *socios* beer was referred to as *la rubia*, 'the blonde one', thereby equating beer consumption with the way in which females were regarded as being 'consumed' sexually by males, both in terms of the physical act itself (drinking beer = sex with a woman) and prowess in this regard.

the context of drinking groups themselves) that the holder of such a position 'ought not to drink beer', the inference being that funds had been fraudulently diverted for the purpose of financing this activity. Similarly, a different poor peasant *socio* was subsequently prevented from replacing another officeholder on account of the view that 'he drinks too much'.[40]

The antithesis between controlled drinking (a capacity to hold one's drink) and uncontrolled drinking-to-excess was embodied in the vernacular opposition between *sanito*/sober and *tomado*/drunk. The significance of this discursive couple is that the concept *sano* referred simultaneously to sobriety (as contrasted with inebriation) and health (as contrasted with illness). Licensed thereby was the legitimation of controlled drinking in terms of both its behavioural and economic attributes: competence as drinker is a metaphor for competence as worker, the latter aspect visible both in the efficient discharge of official duties, and in financial probity which precludes accusations of fraud.

Drinking and Work – II

In much of the anthropological literature about rural Latin America, land invasion is usually presented simply as an act of reclamation, the repossession of usurped land in accordance with ancient property titles held by inhabitants of indigenous communities. Most analyses of La Convención contain a passing reference to land invasions which took place in the period 1960–61, a time when this activity took its most dramatic form, described as 'Peruvian peasants invading highland haciendas, blowing horns and carrying flags'.[41] After this date, however, no further reference is made to such activity, since land occupations that correspond to this form had ceased to take place. Instead, the occupation of land took a less dramatic but no less important form of smallscale encroachments occurring on the periphery of post-reform units, amounting in the case of Pintobamba Grande to a process of privatisation of cooperative land. Whereas land invasions in the pre-reform era were an appropriation from resources belonging to the landlord class, during the post-reform period by contrast the same process was a deduction from means of production – and

40 Political officeholders in the cooperative were particularly vulnerable to the second of these two accusations mediated in terms of drinking ideology. Hence the comment made by a middle peasant *socio* of a rich peasant *socio* that the latter 'likes drinking, and neglects his official duties' (excessive drinking = inefficient officeholder).

41 Martinez-Alier (1974: 145).

thus revenues – co-owned by the other peasants who were members of the cooperative.

Dividing a portion of the cooperative land into small plots, to be worked privately by groups of the membership, was raised in an assembly meeting in discussions about the demarcation of land co-owned by the whole membership. The latter agreed to repossess any existing privatised holdings that had encroached since the agrarian reform, and a judicial eviction (*acta de lanzamiento*) was carried out subsequently. However, these plots were not returned to the cooperative membership, and those among them who were occupiers continued to harvest and sell the produce from the privatised land, the judicial eviction notwithstanding. Of the four groups formed by peasants belonging to the cooperative, one was named by its components 'Grupo Hugo Blanco', and what follows refers to the peasants of this group in particular.

Initially cultivation was for subsistence crops only, not involving hired labour, but gradually the emphasis shifted, and occupying groups began to produce cash crops (tomatoes) with their own workers redeployed both from their own peasant enterprise and from the cooperative itself. The plots themselves were favourably located, not just in terms of being situated on the flat, fertile land of the valley floor, but also regarding access to cooperative resources available there (irrigation, transport, machinery, storage). Nearly half of the occupiers were poor peasants, who contributed their own time and personal labour to cultivating such holdings, while the remainder of the occupiers consisted of rich and middle peasants, who for the most part undertook supervisory roles, their manual labour input being undertaken by their wage labourers whom they brought along.

As in other areas of Pintobamba Grande, the work regime on these privatised holdings was categorized by peasants and labourers alike in the following manner: light manual labour, or 'easy tasks' (*trabajos suavecitos*), consisting of furrowing the earth with a sickle, and depositing fertiliser; and heavy manual labour, or 'hard work' (*trabajos duros*), which entailed covering up the rows of earth with a hoe (the furrows having previously been ploughed by a tractor). The main burden of 'hard tasks' – 87 percent of the work – was undertaken by non-occupying wage labourers along with occupying poor peasants, while the 'easy tasks' (13 percent of the work) fell to the occupying rich and middle peasants. In all cases, the labour input of occupiers to their privatised plots was higher than that provided by them to the cooperative sector.[42]

42 Possessing subjects provided 66% more personal labour, 64% more labour of workers accompanying them, and 65% more in total to their privatised plots than they did to the cooperative labour process in the corresponding period.

As well as an increased labour provision to privatised holdings, the working day was significantly longer. On the cooperative, the length of the working day began at 7 am and extended until 4 pm, a total of nine hours; one hour is devoted to the midday meal (*almuerzo*) and the remaining eight to work activity. By contrast, the duration of the working day for labour employed both on the peasant enterprise and on the privatised holdings of the cooperative began at 5 am and lasted until 5 or 6 pm, a total of thirteen hours, of which 1¾ were allocated to rest periods and meal times, and 10¼ to work activity. In terms of the latter aspect, therefore, the working day on privatised land exceeds that on the cooperative by 28%. All possessing groups transferred the extended working day for labourers employed on the privatised land of the cooperative, from where they had been deployed from the rich and middle peasant enterprise.

IV

Drinking and Class

Beer drinking was also a mechanism for distinguishing peasants from labourers, in terms both of general ideology and of the *rite de passage* symbolizing the change from landlessness to property ownership. Signalling the transition from non-owner to owner of means of production, drinking beer was present at the very outset of this transformation. A middle peasant *socio* recounted how in 1952, when he was still a landless labourer, but had nevertheless saved S/.2,500 from a monthly wage of S/.750, the possibility arose of purchasing rights to a sub-tenancy on the adjacent estate. In order to buy the lease to his first smallholding, however, it was necessary for him to borrow a further S/.12,500 from a tenant who was his *compadre*. Although then eighteen years of age, he had never previously consumed beer, and would be compelled to accept and provide drink if invited to do so by his fictive kinsman as part of the loan transaction. Accordingly, he purchased a crate of beer, approached his *compadre*, took part in a drinking session with him, and succeeded in obtaining the loan.[43] The episode confirms the symbolic importance and meaning of drinking in a chain of ideological signification: a crate of beer, composed of twelve bottles, was a metaphor not only for a man but also for a landholder, signalling a shift in his class position.

---

43 When telling this story, it was the peasant *socio* himself who placed the emphasis on the purchase and consumption of beer for the first time as an integral aspect and precondition of the loan transaction.

That agricultural labourers neither owned land nor participated autonomously in beer drinking groups reinforced the perception of them as juniors of subordinate class position (boys-not-men).[44] Perhaps in no other socio-economic arena was the ideological subordination and tangible unease of such workers more evident than in the sense of 'otherness' manifested in relation to – and actually in the context of – beer drinking groups. I myself experienced difficulty on a number of occasions in my attempts to involve workers on the cooperative in beer drinking sessions when peasant *socios* were also present. In one episode I purchased a crate of beer specifically for distribution among the labourers toiling in the courtyard of the ex-estate house, only to see it summarily consumed by peasant *socios* and ONRA personnel overseeing the work in that location.

The concreteness of this exclusion by peasant *socios* of workers from beer drinking groups – unless invited to participate by peasant *socios* themselves – was similarly demonstrated in yet another fieldwork episode. Once again, I purchased a crate of beer as my contribution to an evening drinking session, composed of rich and middle peasant *socios* together with an ONRA functionary, taking place upstairs in the ex-estate house, on the way to which I invited some of the labourers in the courtyard below to join the group. Despite it being after working hours, this suggestion was met with an emphatic refusal, one of the workers pointing out that under no circumstances would it be possible for him (or the other labourers) to accept such an invitation. The fact that the same worker was willing to participate along with other labourers and me in a beer drinking session when no peasant *socios* were present underlines the force of exclusion from this politico-ideological arena.

In a sense, such exclusion should not surprise, given the antagonistic relations between better-off peasants and their workforce in Pintobamba Grande at that conjuncture, a situation reflected in the class-specific and contradictory images about the beer/wealth connection possessed by each category. Thus, the hostility felt by one worker towards his employers on the cooperative was expressed in the following terms, contrasting the hard manual labour undertaken by those like himself with the lack of effort expended by peasant *socios*: 'sweating, we [labourers] work like fools. If they [the peasant *socios*]

44 Drinking sessions were invariably an excuse for *socios* to reminisce about (and to claim a crucial role in) both the peasant movement led by Hugo Blanco and the subsequent *guerrilla* activity in the province, thereby underlining the extent to which these occasions served as opportunities for celebrating the process of becoming proprietors and reaffirming in symbolic terms the achieving of 'manhood' in the most 'male' of social contexts.

have money, they get drunk ...'.[45] From the viewpoint of the worker, therefore, wealth was not only a precondition of excessive drinking but also thereby an indirect cause of their maltreatment at the hands of inebriated peasant *socios* (wealth → excessive drinking → drunkenness → maltreatment of labourers).[46]

This was confirmed by another worker on the cooperative who, when asked if peasant *socios* treated labourers with respect, answered: 'They have no respect [for us], none at all. They drink their beer and come at us cursing. A sober person cannot reason with a drunk. Thus, we are at loggerheads'.[47] On a separate occasion, yet another worker made a similar observation, using the same idiom: 'The cooperative membership is composed of rich bosses, the president comes at us swearing when drunk.'[48]

By contrast, in the discourse about their dealings with workers, peasant *socios* ascribed a different and positive image to the consumption of beer. Since agricultural labourers were unable to purchase beer frequently on their own account, invitations to participate in drinking groups were made by their employers in recognition of effort in the labour process (beer = reward for hard work). Peasant *socio* ideology sought thereby to confer legitimacy/acceptability on beer drinking in general, and to deflect antagonism resulting from the association of wealth and maltreatment of subordinates with beer drinking undertaken by *socios*.[49] Linking beer consumption to hard work in this manner also by inference devalued ideologically the manual labour carried out by the excluded categories of agricultural workers and women. As the latter were the main components of the agrarian workforce on both the peasant and the

---

45 *Sudando nos trabajamos como engañados. Ellos si tienen plata, borrachos así nomás ...*

46 Maltreatment by drunken *socios* was yet another characteristic that agricultural workers shared with females. Alcohol-related physical violence by men against women in the Andes is well documented (see, for example, Harris, 1978: 33–35; Bourque and Warren, 1981: 106–108), and in Pintobamba Grande gave rise to gender solidarity that transcended social boundaries. When an inebriated poor peasant *socio* beat his spouse, she sought refuge with and protection from the wife of a local ONRA *técnico*; on another occasion, the spouse of a rich peasant turned to the same person, who then interceded with the drunken husband in order to prevent him from continuing to beat her.

47 *No tienen respecto, no tienen. Ellos vienen con sus ajos nomasya, metan a ajos. Toman su cerveza y vienen. Un borracho con un sano no puede hablar. Asi es que estamos de a malas.*

48 *Los del comité son patrones, el presidente viene con sus cojudeces cuando borracho.*

49 Another example of the way in which peasants associated drinking with rewards for hard manual labour occurred in in the course of an exchange-labour work party (*mink'a*) on the holding of a middle peasant. The latter, in his capacity as owner/organizer (*chajrayoc*) was engaged in the customary task of distributing two small glasses of liquor (*trago*) to all the peasants and labourers working on his land, when a rich peasant commented: 'I only give one glass of liquor to those who don't work very hard [in exchange-labour working parties on his own land], and two glasses to the rest'.

TABLE 7 Positive/negative identities in peasant socio ideology

Positive	Negative
Beer	*Chicha*
Drinker	Non-Drinker
Peasant	Labourer
Rich	Poor
Hard worker	Idleness
Male	Female
Roman Catholic	Evangelist

SOURCE: AUTHOR

cooperative sector of the ex-estate, an important economic effect was that it justified low (or even, in the case of women, non-payment of) wages.

From the viewpoint of peasant *socios*, therefore, multiple signification – about gender, class, and work – effected with reference to drinking ideology projected the ideological oppositions set out in Table 7. Socio-economic differentiation arising from this same discourse was also reflected in the organisational structure of the beer drinking group itself, where in accordance with the requisite symbolic spacing the central seats were occupied by either *socios* or ONRA personnel. Agricultural labourers and females, by contrast, were positioned differently, and marginalised in physical terms, located on the periphery of the beer drinking group.

The antithesis between drinking and working as part of the class struggle between better-off peasants and the labourers employed by them also emerges clearly from the discourse used in relation to activity undertaken on privatised cooperative land. In the case of 'Grupo Hugo Blanco', class struggle took the form of confrontations and disputes between its possessing components, all of which derived from a single determining cause: the asymmetrical economic position of the different occupiers, and the qualitative/quantitative disparities between the sorts of labour-power (personal, hired) deployed. So acute did this confrontation become that the better-off protagonists suggested sub-dividing the privatised land further, into four separate plots, one for each occupier. A poor peasant in this group argued strongly against this proposal, and it was abandoned. Subsequently, however, a middle peasant divulged that had the land indeed been sub-divided as suggested, he did not discount the possibility that the same poor peasant who opposed this might have poisoned the tomato plants with herbicide.

Poor peasants belonging to 'Grupo Hugo Blanco' that privatised cooperative land were described by their better-off counterparts as unable to contribute economically in the same way, saying 'they do not have a crop-sprayer, they have no capital'.[50] A crucial aspect of this difference involved the inability of one poor peasant to hire labour for work on the privatised holding, an issue that led to conflict with rich and middle peasants in the same group, one of whom he accused of having taken from him a labourer he himself wanted to employ. Although resolved, the antagonism nevertheless remained latent, the accused rich peasant saying: 'It is in my heart, and will never come away. I remain silent because he is my co-parent: were he not, I would tell him his life story, about the shit he really is …'.[51]

Consequences of disputes like this spilled over into the functioning of the cooperative itself. Faced with legal action by ONRA to repossess holdings that had been privatised, a poor peasant occupier who was part of 'Grupo Hugo Blanco' threatened to resign from his officeholding post as cooperative Treasurer, citing as cause 'because I am called a thief, an invader … it is said that I occupy'.[52] He had fallen victim to the contiguity of a familiar discourse where officeholding was concerned: rumour that he stole two kinds of property from the cooperative, both as Treasurer (funds) and as occupier (land). The acuteness of this class struggle was underlined by another cooperative member who observed that two poor peasants who occupied plots of land hated the President of the assembly for having deprived them of this resource, but at the same time 'they hide their hate'.[53]

Conclusion

The element of ambiguity widely associated with the consumption of alcohol in the Andes, and embodied in the simultaneous coexistence and circulation within beer drinking groups of contradictory idioms projecting solidarity and antagonism, may be explained in the case of La Convención by reference not to its ceremonial but to its economic importance, and in particular its operation as a site where the meaning of work, property relations, gender identity, and class position was formulated and reproduced.

---

50 *No tienen mochila, no tienen capital.*

51 *Todo eso es en mi corazon i jamas saldra. Quedo calladito porque es mi compadre: si no fuese mi compadre lo contaria su vida, como es mierda …*

52 *Por que me tratan de ladron, como un invasor … dicen que ocupo.*

53 *Ocultan a su odio.*

On the one hand, therefore, the drinking group was an arena that affected the continuation or dissolution of property rights to the agrarian cooperative itself, insofar as it was a place where political decisions about crucial issues such as the privatisation of cooperative land and the expulsion of *socios* for the non-fulfillment of their statutory labour obligation were raised, discussed, and frequently decided. For this reason, a dislike of consuming large quantities of bottled beer was coupled with the recognition of its necessity, since by this method peasant *socios* either gained or retained access to economic resources available on the cooperative. Hence the 'demand' drinking this entailed had little to do with the individual acquisition of prestige, since within the drinking group all contributed and consumed in equal measure. Instead, it corresponded to a form of capital investment by peasants, and the relatively high level of expenditure involved was a result not of conspicuous consumption as of drinking patterns based on group participation structured by multiple reciprocity.

On the other hand, however, drinking groups were also sites where class struggle took a double form: between between *socios* from different peasant strata, and also between peasant *socios* and agricultural workers. Conflict involving rich, middle, and poor peasants stemmed from unequal access to the means of production, a difference evident in the economics and pattern of drinking. Within these sessions, however, *socios* also proclaimed, affirmed, and reinforced their collective identity, by uniting in the face of the subordinate non-owning categories on the cooperative. Such contexts were by their very nature situations in which politico-ideological domination over agricultural workers and females was projected and reproduced in a particularly forceful manner. A central feature of this discourse was the way drink, drunkenness, and work efficiency/inefficiency, were depicted in opposed ways by those of different class positions, contributing thereby to the struggle between the latter.

Not the least significant aspect of discourse projecting notions of economic difference that featured prominently in beer drinking groups is that its subordinate categories were also components of the post-reform workforce employed on all the sectors – cooperative land, privatised plots, and the holdings forming the peasant enterprise – throughout the ex-estate. As such, drinking group participation challenges the populist view that peasants cannot be differentiated along class lines.

CHAPTER 7

On Anthropological Fieldwork (and Other Things)

> For me the central problem for late twentieth century academic anthropology is not whether we should approach our data as scientists or poets but whether we can fully convince ourselves, as well as our non-anthropological colleagues, that all men and women, past, present and future are of equal standing and that the distinction between savage and civilised upon which the whole edifice of traditional anthropology was constructed deserves to be consigned to the trash can. We may live in a world dominated by scientists but we are no different from the human beings of other times and other places who built their cosmologies around "Mountains of God" rather than "Back Holes in Outer Space". This is hardly a new idea [which] emphasized all the way through that modern anthropology is just as much about "us" as it is about "them". But, whatever they may say, anthropologists have a vested interest in believing otherwise. Their academic qualifications proclaim that they possess specialised knowledge of the life styles of a mythical zoological species called "primitive man". Why should they abandon this most treasured possession? Most of my professional colleagues still talk and write as if observer and observed were beings of quite different kinds who think in quite different ways.
>
> An observation by EDMUND LEACH identifying the interpretation of the divide between fieldworker and the studied 'other' as the central dilemma facing present-day anthropology.[1]

Introduction: Other Times, Other Places

The prominent role of drinking in the research process, and the emphasis it places on a specific (and well-known) form of participation in the range of activity connected to social anthropological practice, highlights in turn the

1 Leach (1989/90: 47), whose view about anthropology has generated acrimonious exchanges (Hallpike, 1992/93a; Kuper, 1992/93a; Hallpike, 1992/93b; Kuper, 1992/93b).

centrality of a personal element. So marked is the overlap in many contexts between having to drink and information gathering that it suggests the two activities – drinking and anthropological fieldwork – may actually be synonymous. Historically, British social anthropology has been the handmaiden of colonialism, and this indeed is undeniably part of its history.[2]

As undeniable is its ingrained empiricism, where fact-finding has for a long time enjoyed the status of a given.[3] For my part, however, I have always valued its methodology, based as it is on long-term going-and-staying. This fieldwork practice, conceivably the most direct form of research engagement outside laboratory work, entails getting as close as possible to what is happening at the rural grassroots, living the existence insofar as an outsider can do this, pursuing issues and following up with further questions, has always seemed to me to be a good way to conduct research.[4]

Of course, this sort of intensive fieldwork, based as it is on participant/observation, is faced with a number of obvious and ever-present dangers. First, of taking everything one is told at its face value – and some anthropologists have done just this – but with luck, persistence, and a critical outlook, it is an approach that can work. Second, the equally marked tendency to slide into empiricism, as embodied in the fallback line of defence used by anthropologists – 'I have been there, and you haven't' – whenever their

2 On this history see, among others, Asad (1973) and Stauder (1974).

3 This all-embracing investigative approach is well described by Malinowski (1967: 290, original emphasis), who in the early part of the twentieth century records that 'I drew up plans ... [w]hat to do, what to work on, etc. Ideas about methods of *field work*. The main principle of my work in the field: avoid artificial simplifications. To this end, collect as concrete materials as possible; note every informant; work with children, *outsiders, and specialists. Take side lights and opinions*.' This privileging of empiricism is acknowledged (Malinowski, 1967: 158): 'Yesterday ... I had some ethnological ideas, but I cannot remember what they were. They had a bearing on the general theoretical "sauce" in which my concrete observations are to be dressed up.'

4 On the importance of participant/observation fieldwork, see Evans-Pritchard (1951: Chapter IV). That it necessarily entails an anthropologist being seen by those studied as one of them is, of course, not the case. On this Barley (1983: 56) observes, rightly, that: 'Much nonsense has been written, by people who should know better, about the anthropologist "being accepted". It is sometimes suggested that an alien people will somehow come to view the visitor of a distinct race and culture as in every way similar to the locals. This is, alas, unlikely.' Currently the idea of conducting this kind of long-term research in far-away places is a practice regarded by some (e.g., Hart, 2022) as questionable, for two reasons in particular. First, due to its strong links with colonial rule; and second, because any attempt to interpret 'otherness' by those who do not themselves share this identity is seen – mainly by exponents of the 'new' populist postmodernism – as a form of cultural appropriation, and thus politically unwarranted.

interpretation of a particular context is challenged.[5] And third, obstacles which take the form of having to negotiate with bureaucracy, research assistants, and informants, or the sort of difficulties which are recorded, if at all, only in diaries kept by an ethnographer when undertaking fieldwork.

This chapter is composed of four sections, the first two of which consider the nature and object of anthropological fieldwork, along with disputes about these aspects, with particular reference to what is recorded in diary form. Sections three and four consist of excerpts from my own fieldwork diaries kept in Peru and India, together with commentaries on them.

I

General Theoretical Sauce

Given the primacy attached to fieldwork, and the resulting emphasis put by ethnography on fact-gathering, it comes as no surprise that such a methodology has been accompanied more often than not by an anti-nomothetic approach to the question of theory, perhaps to a greater extent in anthropology when compared to other branches of the social sciences.[6] In the immediate aftermath of the 1939–45 war, when colonial empires were being dismantled and economic development in decolonized countries moved up the political agenda, social anthropology was in a sense compelled by these circumstances not just to confront but also to accept two interconnected departures from its

5 According to Geertz (1988: 4–5), '[t]he ability of anthropologists to get us to take what they say seriously has less to do with either a factual look or an air of conceptual elegance than it has with their capacity to convince us that what they say is a result of their having … one way or another, truly "been there"'. This line of defence is rightly described by Hart (2022: 47) as the only knowledge rule open to anthropologists. Equally ingrained is empiricism: 'Like most anthropologists in this situation [nothing much happening], I sought refuge in collecting facts', notes Barley (1983: 55, 126–127), who continues 'I often simply fired questions at random in the hope of hitting something to ask further questions about … And so one picks one's way through the morass of data by a process of constant error and revision'.

6 This aspect is emphasized strongly by Evans-Pritchard (1951: 58, 117) in his influential history of the practice and aims of social anthropology: 'I think that the effort to discover natural laws of society is vain and leads only to airy discussions about methods. Anyhow, I am not obliged to prove that there are no such laws; it is for those who say there are, to tell us what they are … I do not think that there is any anthropologist anywhere who would seriously maintain that up to the present time [c. 1950] any sociological laws have been discovered; and if there are no laws known, they cannot be applied.' A different explanation is provided by Lienhardt (1966: 25), who attributes the inadequacy of anthropological theory to a lack of empiricism, whereby 'the fault … was not indeed that [anthropologists] propounded theories, but that the theories were based on very inadequate information …'

usual approach: that henceforth its focus would shift from tribe to peasant, and that consequently the study of the latter component would entail also research into its history. Although commonplace now, the latter departure was regarded at the time as controversial.[7]

For this reason, certain aspects of social anthropological theory were also modified, none more so than in the way ethnographic research was itself constructed: no longer just endogenously determined, in purely empiricist terms, but now also shaped exogenously, as the product of both the assumptions made by and the background of the researcher him/herself. That peasant societies had not merely a history, but one that was documented, both by its own subjects and by state institutions, meant that the anthropologist could either ignore this or delve into the archives.[8] It would not be possible for fieldworkers simply to do what had been done hitherto: record as fact what oral tradition said fact was, now and in the past.[9] Delineating the findings emanating from participant/observation fieldwork in terms of the social context not of those studied but rather of the ethnographer, it was further accepted that 'political views' of the anthropologist would affect the kind of ethnographic account that emerged from fieldwork, and that consequently what was garnered in the course of fieldwork itself could no longer be perceived as self-selecting.[10]

---

7 Writing in 1961, Evans-Pritchard (1969: 46) commented: 'In 1950 I delivered the Marett Lecture at Oxford. In it I said that I regarded social anthropology as being closer to certain kinds of history than to the natural sciences. I will not say that there was a storm of protest, but I had certainly, as the criticisms levelled at me showed, run into a bad patch of anti-historical prejudice. The influence in this country of Malinowski and Radcliffe-Brown, both extremely hostile to history, was still dominant; but elsewhere too there had been hostility, or at least indifference, to historical method.'

8 In the words of Evans-Pritchard (1951: 59): 'This is an issue coming more to the fore today [c. 1950] when social anthropologists are beginning to study societies belonging to historical cultures. So long as they were investigating such peoples as Australian aborigines or South Sea Islanders, who have no recorded history with an easy conscience. Now, however, that they have begun to study peasant communities in India and Europe ... and like communities elsewhere, they can no longer make a virtue of necessity but must choose deliberately to ignore or take into consideration their social past in making studies of their social present.'

9 This issue was central to the debate between Sartre and Lévi-Strauss (1962: Chapter 9) about whether myth or history provided the better account of what happened in the past. See also the contributions to the volume edited by MacClancy (2002).

10 Hence the view (Evans-Pritchard, 1951: 83–84, 87–88) that: 'Within the limits imposed by their discipline and the culture under investigation anthropologists are guided in the choice of themes, in selection and arrangement of facts to illustrate them, and in judgment of what is and what is not significant, by their different interests, reflecting differences of personality, of education, of social status, of political views, of religious convictions, and so forth. ... The essential point to remember is that the anthropologist

In the decades that followed, social anthropologists who conducted fieldwork in Third World countries – me included – benefited from some of these changed approaches.[11] In my case, the most fruitful information gathering during research in rural Peru was done in the context of beer drinking groups, convened by peasants after (and frequently during) the working day.[12] They drank a lot, and could hold their drink, appearing promptly for work the next day, whilst I had to sleep off the effects of the previous night's drinking session. Broadly speaking, it is impossible to overstate the degree to which fieldwork depends on the element of luck. On one occasion, while a rich peasant informant was working elsewhere, I came across a trunk he owned, in which were notebooks containing detailed accounts, including the lending of money to neighbouring poor peasants, all of whom paid off these loans in the form of days they and their kinsfolk worked on the holdings of the rich peasant creditor. While he was absent, all the information contained in his notebooks was rapidly copied into my own fieldwork notes, and these raw data were the source of the subsequent analysis indicating how the debt bondage system (*enganche*) operated in that context.

Locating the issue of debt, its meaning and effects, in peasant society during what had become the 'development decade' and after, underlined the tenacity of residual concepts belonging to earlier anthropological discourse. In these cases, debt relations and their connection to the deployment of labour were usually interpreted merely as a form of pre-capitalist reciprocal exchange, a benign and frequently symbolic intra-kin group transaction to the benefit of all, a way of reproducing and maintaining harmony within the indigenous community.[13] However, this idealised depiction of debt relationships as merely

is working within a body of theoretical knowledge and that he makes his observations to solve problems which derive from it ... in deciding what he is to put into his book and what to leave out of it, he is guided by the relevance of the material for a particular theme designed to bring out significant features of some system of social activities.'

11 Whilst this is generally true, it is nevertheless the case that specific theories – especially Marxism – continued to be viewed disdainfully from within social anthropology: see, for example, the dismissive comments by Evans-Pritchard (1969: 32–33, 36, 44); also, Firth (1972) and Leach (1982).

12 See Chapter 6, this volume.

13 The pervasive nature of this earlier way of interpreting workforce deployment simply as an intra-kin group arrangement is evident also in the ethnographic account by Seligman and Seligman (1932: 435): 'The bridegroom-elect compensates the girl's relatives by working on their cultivations. Not only he, but his father and brothers and other near relatives have to work on the cultivations of the girl's father and uncles, and are obliged to render service when it is required of them by relatives of the future bride.' A similarity exists between this arrangement in Sudan and that encountered in southern Ireland during

one more form of ritualised exchange occurring within the kinship domain, designed to do no more than reproduce family, neighbourhood, or community as such, runs into trouble when these kinds of units are themselves located within the wider capitalist system, and when therefore these same exchanges are driven by a different economic logic.

In order to illustrate the meaning and function of debt as understood by British social anthropology, Evans-Pritchard turns to the way it operated in Ireland during the late 1930s, citing in support of his interpretation the well-known ethnographic case-study by Arensberg and Kimball. Debt is central to the link between townsfolk and country inhabitants, since the countryman – a peasant farmer – 'is always in debt to his shopkeeper kinsman', a tie which Evans-Pritchard regards simply as a *social* relationship, not an economic one.[14] When a countryman 'is angry' with the shopkeeper, he withdraws his custom by paying off his debt, thereby breaking the relationship. For Evans-Pritchard, therefore, debt is 'a measure of status', a social relation that is part of a 'network of social obligations'. Forming as it does a link between kin groups that expresses 'confidence and social obligation', therefore, so desirable is this sort of relationship that debt is inherited, and passed from father to son.

In the opinion of Evans-Pritchard, the Irish case-study indicates that, embedded within kinship affectivity debt has an altogether different meaning from its usual negative one, being simply a positive relation whereby 'a social system is maintained'. He emphasizes that, consequently, a debt must not be seen as an economic arrangement, insisting 'it cannot be understood merely in economic or legal terms but only in relation to kinship and other features of

the same decade (see below), where 'cooring' draws the labour-power of kinsfolk into exchanges between individuals.

14 For this and what follows, see Evans-Pritchard (1951: 107), who in his textbook on social anthropology describes as follows the logic driving the debt relation in late 1930s rural Ireland: 'One of the ways in which the connection between townsmen and their country cousins is maintained and expressed is by debt. The countryman is always in debt to his shopkeeper kinsman, and this chronic debt is part of their social relationship. Indeed, when a countryman is angry with a shopkeeper he pays his debt to withdraw his custom and sever their relationship. The debt … is a measure of status, being a sign of one's ability and willingness to support that network of social obligations which gives oneself and one's family a place in social life. the debt passes down the generations from father to son. It is the bond between the family and kin of the farmer and the family and kin of the shopkeeper by which they express in each other confidence and social obligation. Debt is thus shown in a new light, as one of the mechanisms by which a social system is maintained. It cannot be understood merely in economic or legal terms but only in relation to kinship and other features of the total social structure; and moral judgment about it has to be made in the light of this broader understanding.'

the total social structure.' This idealized interpretation is made explicit in his conclusion 'that in southern Ireland debt serves to uphold *harmonious* relations between countryman and townsman'.[15] Despite the seemingly concrete nature of materials gathered in the course of fieldwork, however, the picture then drawn by the social anthropologist is open to other kinds of explanation.

Thus a later analysis of the same ethnographic case-study materials generates a very different interpretation, pointing out that, far from being a harmonious method of reproducing the town/country link in Ireland at that conjuncture, and operating solely within the affectivity of the kinship domain, debt was much rather the coercive way larger farmers subordinated and then exercised control over less well-off peasants.[16] Known as 'cooring', it involved exchanges between rural inhabitants, whereby the labour-power both of indebted poorer smallholders and of their kin was acquired by better-off producers on a beck-and-call basis.[17] Shopkeepers who 'sprang out of the ranks of the upper echelons of the peasantry ... remained farmers while still engaging in commercial and usurious operations'; owning land themselves, they used such debt relations in order to secure and control labour-power.[18] An effect of this inter-generational debt inheritance, moreover, was that the necessity of meeting payments incurred earlier meant for the children of less well-off

---

15 Evans-Pritchard (1951: 108, emphasis added). Contrast this with Lienhardt (1966: 151), who observes: 'Since the first world war at least, there has been ... a strong current of a kind of liberalism in anthropological thought, which may sometimes have idealized the integration, stability, and equilibrium of many societies ...' Although this refers to contexts 'before European contact', the way Evans-Pritchard misinterprets the Irish case-study indicates such a critique applies to the way some anthropologists explain societies well beyond the so-called 'primitive'.

16 See Gibbon (1973), who – in sharp contrast to the interpretation offered by Evans-Pritchard of the same context – observes (Gibbon, 1973: 491) that 'Arensberg and Kimball's functionalist theoretical position produced an account of [rural Ireland] which had more in common with the visions of obscurantist nativists and revivalists than with concrete reality'.

17 According to Gibbon (1973: 486–87, original emphasis), '"cooring" would involve exchanges between farmers of unequal resources [based on] the incurring of labour-power debts ... there is little question that [the exchange] would have been determined not by mutual convenience ... but univocally by the larger farmer. In this way, the mutual aid system ... must have worked against the small farmer, who would have to wait at the convenience of the larger one for the completion of many important tasks, and who simultaneously might have his family labour-force called away for the day, while it must have worked *for* the larger one. It is clear that the latter participated in it not simply out of cultural obligation'.

18 Noting 'the virtual absence of ruthless entrepreneurs from Arensberg and Kimball's [ethnography]', Gibbon (1973: 490) indicates that the Gombeen man, or 'the entrepreneur engaging in multiple forms of the most primitive and vicious exploitation is one of the most "traditional" figures of all in the post-famine Irish countryside'.

peasants an arrangement that 'represented nothing more than subjection to indefinite and arduous unpaid labour with no foreseeable compensatory reward'.[19]

A similar labour arrangement was found in my Peruvian fieldwork area, where the exchanges consisted of two institutional forms. A dyadic relationship, *ayni*, involving just two smallholders who agree to work on each other's land over a given period; and *mink'a*, which refers to a large work party called for a particular day during which many peasants discharge a day's labour owed to the individual on whose land the *mink'a* takes place.[20] Since both these forms of exchange labour are accompanied by festive drinking and eating, they tend to be regarded as materially reciprocal transactions characteristic of traditional Andean economy. However, much like the Irish 'cooring' arrangement, rich and middle peasants who participated in these reciprocal exchanges contributed not their own personal labour-power to such work parties but rather that of landless agricultural labourers or poor peasants; the latter categories included their own fictive kinsfolk who were also bonded to these better-off creditor-employers by debt, and were thus unfree in relational terms.[21]

Despite the shift in the post-war research agenda of social anthropology, adding to the study of autochthonous tribal populations that of peasants with a history and located in a wider capitalist society, the pervasiveness of earlier, idealised interpretations of debt as essentially a harmonious social relation nevertheless persisted. Hence the view encountered in a later textbook by Leach that '[i]n any context, if a debt is ever fully paid off then the relationship between debtor and creditor ceases to exist', the inference being that since all benefit from the debt relationship, every party is reluctant for it to cease, and thus equally committed to its reproduction.[22] For some later social anthropologists, such as Leach (and others), therefore, debt bondage continued to be seen as nothing more than an egalitarian arrangement operating within the kinship domain.

Reproducing the benign earlier interpretation advanced by Evans-Pritchard of 'cooring', Leach maintains that '[i]n many of the simpler agricultural societies this is also the normal way to organize labour; no wages are paid, but over a period, each household pays back in labour form whatever it has previously

19 Gibbon (1973: 490).
20 On these exchanges, see Brass (1999).
21 In mid-1970s La Convención, rich peasants employing fictive kinsfolk as bonded labour in this manner were small capitalist producers.
22 See Leach (1982: 152).

received in labour form'.[23] Among the social anthropologists who – beyond the development decade – continued to depict debt bondage in the idealized terms of the pre-war era, as a relation involving reciprocal exchanges benefitting each party, was Jan Breman. However, he subsequently changed his mind about the meaning of bonded labour, seen by him no longer as a benign but now as a coercive relation, all of a sudden adopting the very interpretation he had previously deemed wrong.[24]

II

The Feel of Fieldwork

Seen, rightly, as the epitome of a fieldwork diary kept by a social anthropologist, that of Malinowski records the sort of reactions on entering a context to be studied, together with the inner thoughts accompanying this rite of passage, ones that will be familiar to all social anthropologists who have undertaken participant/observation research.[25] Emerging from his field trips to the Trobriand Islands in the period 1914–1918, his account 'does not dwell either on field methodology or anthropological theory [but] does convey most keenly the reactions of a field anthropologist in an alien society'.[26]

23 'In domestic relationships within the household, and in relationships between close neighbours, who see one another very frequently, this is how gift exchange usually operates,' declares Leach (1982: 153–54), adding: 'There is no close accounting of who owes what to whom but there is a tacit understanding by all concerned that there is a moral obligation to balance things out over a period. In many of the simpler agricultural societies this is also the normal way to organize labour; no wages are paid, but over a period, each household pays back in labour form whatever it has previously received in labour form. Wherever I have observed transactions of this kind the balancing of accounts has been very carefully worked out.'

24 On this initial view, together with the reason for the subsequent *volte face*, see Brass (2024a: Chapter 8).

25 See Malinowski (1967), an account which I read only after returning from my Peruvian fieldwork, and one that I wish I had read before embarking on that process. Before Malinowski, the diary as record of fieldwork attracted little attention, featuring if at all in footnoted references; in the words of Geertz (1988: 16, 17) a status akin to other '[e]xplicit representations of authorial presence [which] tend to be relegated, like other embarrassments, to prefaces, notes, or appendixes ... Getting themselves into their text (that is, representationally into the text) may be as difficult for ethnographers as getting themselves into the culture (that is, imaginatively into the culture).'

26 In the words of Raymond Firth, who provides an introduction to the diaries (Malinowski, 1967: xv–xvi): 'But if the diary does not dwell either on field methodology or on the problems of anthropological theory, it does convey most keenly the reactions of a field anthropologist in an alien society. There he must live as a recorder and analyst, but as such he

Although for Malinowski 'the importance of keeping a diary [was] as a means of self-analysis', as a document charting not just the internal physical and mental vicissitudes but also of external difficulties connected with fieldwork it remains unsurpassed.[27] A catalogue of irritations, despondency, and the plain boredom – if not the pointlessness – of research are interspersed with outbursts of rage and racism when things go wrong.[28]

Although these same themes continued to be addressed, from around the 1980s the earlier separation between fieldwork diary and ethnographic account had seemingly ceased to exist. When discussed, the sort of issues previously confined to the diary were encountered now in the ethnography: what used to be the diary moves front and centre of the narrative, it together with its writer becoming as a result the focus of attention. Seen by some as a laudable attempt to demystify fieldwork, a less charitable interpretation is that the methodological approach central to the practice of social anthropology is depicted as a largely unserious endeavour composed for the most part of a random collection of accidents that cannot be avoided. Consequently, no serious kind of fieldwork, or the sort done earlier by Evans-Pritchard, Godfrey Lienhardt, Edmund Leach, or Malinowski, can ever be done again.[29]

---

cannot completely share the customs and values of the people, admire or dislike them as he may. The feeling of confinement, the obsessional longing to be back even if for the briefest while in one's own cultural surroundings, the dejection and doubts about the validity of what one is doing ... the moral compulsion to drag oneself back to the task of field observation – many sensitive fieldworkers have experienced these feelings on occasion, and they have rarely been better expressed than in this diary.'

27 Malinowski (1967: 284).

28 Anger mixed with resignation, frustration, and depression is a constant refrain in the fieldwork diary (Malinowski, 1967: 167, 227, 240, 261, 262, 268, 281, 288), of which the following are symptomatic: 'As for ethnology: I see the life of the natives as utterly devoid of interest or importance, something as remote from me as the life of a dog'; 'There is also the difficulty of doing research under these conditions. The fellows are unpleasant and answer my questions with obvious reluctance'; 'Last day of the month – complete collapse. In the morning I did nothing'; 'Last night and this morning looked in vain for fellows for my boat. This drives me to a state of white rage and hatred ... combined with depression, a desire to "sit down and cry," and a furious longing "to get out of this."'; 'In the morning rain, dampness, wet weather ... Unable to work: uncomfortable situation, irritated by *boys* [= informants], bothered by mosquitoes'; 'Am still subject to petty irritations in my relations with the *boys*, whom I should treat as dogs'; 'Yesterday was completely fouled up'; 'Slept badly ... Awakened by some bastard screaming furiously.'

29 The fieldwork approaches of Evans-Pritchard, Leach, and Malinowski are the target of postmodern critiques by Geertz (1988) and Clifford and Marcus (1990). Similarly, Malinowski is seen negatively by a later anthropologist (Barley, 1983: 28–29, 121) who labels him a 'self-styled inventor of fieldwork' and purveyor of 'fanatical tirades against anthropology'.

This point can be illustrated with reference to the approach of Barley, and in particular his account of research conducted among the Dowayo people in the Cameroons during 1978, 'who were to become "my" people in love and hate from then on'.[30] Well-written, and endeavouring to record what are recognisably still issues of interest to the practice of social anthropology, the analysis not merely features but foregrounds himself and his own agency and responses to fieldwork situations, doing so in a jokey fashion, along the lines of 'look at me, am I not doing silly things, aren't my antics funny to behold'. In his account, the humour becomes a displacement, a way of coping with the negative aspects of fieldwork.[31] Rather than episodes recorded in the diary being an adjunct that shines a light on the ethnographic text, the latter becomes instead an account of the self, what befalls the latter merging with – if not displacing – the ethnography as the main version of what is happening at the fieldwork site.[32] A discourse that might be described as being about anthropology-as-clowning, reinforcing perceptions of its essentially unserious nature.

Privileged in this narrative are not the occasional glimpses of the social anthropologist at work, which have always been referenced in ethnographies, but the role of the fieldworker who now looms large, to the degree that the account is now one where the central position is occupied not so much by the

30 See Barley (1983: 13).

31 In what at times resembles a catalogue of disasters, Barley (1983: 26, 35, 36, 55, 60, 65–66, 73, 93, 98, 113, 137, 139–140) records the many difficulties arising in the course of fieldwork: 'There was an immediate sense of alienation ...'; 'I would probably have accepted my historical role as someone to be robbed ...'; 'I was by now familiar with the disease of optimism ...'; 'the tractors ... fell to pieces, the pumps broke down, the building fell apart'; 'it was pouring with rain, and ... I felt weak and lonely'; 'Faced with the impossibility of eating off the land, I decided to keep my own chickens. This, also, was not a success'; 'I was still subject to huge bouts of depression when trapped in my tiny hut by the rain'; 'a blessed relief from trying to make sense of the Dowayos, from being stared at and pointed at, shouted at and interrogated'; 'while I was in Dowayoland, many people and dogs availed themselves of the opportunity to vomit over me'; 'People were reluctant to talk about rainchiefs and leopards'; 'The next period of my stay was without doubt the most unpleasant I have ever spent anywhere, a time when I wallowed in the sin of despair'; 'This gibberish was just too much for me and I found myself in a great rage ... since this was quite typical of the explanations I was used to from Dowayos ...'; 'As I had feared, the answers I received were evasive and liberally mixed with half-truths'; and 'I had clearly been woken by a large goat that was pensively devouring my field notes ...'. Similarly vexatious are the continuous and ever-present clashes with bureaucracy, and the frustrations occasioned when engaged in the getting of permissions (Barley, 1983: 31ff., 38ff., 72, 111).

32 See Barley (1983: 97), who writes: 'The fieldworker can never hope to maintain a good rate of work for very long ... I estimated that I perhaps spent one per cent of my time doing what I had actually gone for. The rest of the time was spent on logistics, being ill, being sociable, arranging things, getting from place to place, and above all, waiting'.

population studied as by the self and his/her take on what is seen.[33] Clearly, while it is important to know about, for example, the political views of the fieldworker, and how these considerations influence what is studied and how, the problem is that the whole of fieldwork can easily become an inwardly focused exercise, amounting thereby to a reductive approach close to the psychologistic. In keeping with postmodernism, the possibility of conducting participant/observation fieldwork is itself downgraded if not negated, and the diary becomes in effect a subjective account of travel to and residence in another place – much like a travelogue – instead of an attempt to find out, record, and then understand the dynamics and logics driving the way its inhabitants live.[34]

An Unmediated Voice?

It comes as no surprise, therefore, that anthropological fieldwork was not merely caught up in but became a main target of the much touted 'crisis of representation' debate that emerged as part of the 1980s 'cultural turn', when the analytical focus in western academia turned from examining the nature of the 'other' to questioning the role of the 'self'.[35] From this point on, postmodernism

33 As Barley (1983: 10) accepts, his purpose is to 'show students and, it is hoped, non-anthropologists, how the finished monograph relates to the "bleeding chunks" of raw reality on which it is based, and convey something of the feel of fieldwork to those who have not had that experience.'

34 This foregrounding of the role of the researcher, erasing the distinction between diary and ethnographer, is by no means confined to social anthropology. It is also a practice followed by historians who, like anthropologists, have in the past tended to stand outside what is written. This has changed, as is evident from the contrast between MacKendrick (1971) and the history by Fletcher (2024) of the road network covering the Roman imperial domains, interspersed as the latter is with accounts of her own modern-day itinerary and reactions to what is seen en route (unmentioned by the earlier approach). A not untypical example goes as follows (Fletcher, 2024: 32–33): 'The natural salt lagoons in this area were in use well before the Romans got here ... We pass a wind farm, with modern, sleek white windmill blades, and a field of solar panels, silvery black. The Romans might theoretically have had windmills, but there's little evidence they did, favouring watermills instead ... From Seville both road and river lead to Córdoba. I go for the train but almost miss it as I linger over coffee in the station.' An instance of an historian becoming a travel writer, or the reversal of the usual pattern, whereby the travel writer seeks to be like an anthropologist.

35 Hence the view (Clifford and Marcus, 1990: 251) that: 'The metareflections on the crisis of representation in ethnographic writing indicate a shift away from concentrating on relations with other cultures to a (nonthematized) concern with traditions of representation ... in our culture.' An early attempt at introspection, asking the question as to what

is declared to be 'a general condition of multicultural life demanding new forms of inventiveness and subtlety from a fully reflexive ethnography', engaged in 'dislodging canons to make space for alternatives'; the latter, it seems, is 'a new canon, postmodernism'.[36] Among the core practices followed by social anthropological research – indeed constitutive of its very methodological approach – fieldwork (' keeping good field notes') is declared by postmodernists to be an ideology that 'has crumbled'.[37] Because 'many voices clamour for expression', therefore, what is said from-below licenses a polyphony/polyvocality that is not merely privileged, but is elevated to the status of 'real' which in effect puts it beyond the capacity of the ethnographer to interpret. The role of the social anthropologist carrying out fieldwork is now that simply of a conduit, unable any longer to talk about the meaning of what is heard.

These are curious views to hold. To begin with, the research procedure favoured by postmodern theory, in which the ethnographer is nothing more than a conduit with no further role in the intellectual process, is just another form of empiricism, or the approach by British social anthropology that has in the past drawn much criticism. Moreover, postmodernists appear to think that hitherto fieldwork has involved the exclusion of the from-below voice, whereas the object of this anthropological practice has always been exactly the opposite: an endeavour to capture what this voice actually says. It is clear, however, that the objection by postmodern theory is not so much to this as to something else: that between the world and the voice from-below is inserted the ethnographer, someone from another society, culture, nationality, ethnicity.

---

someone doing fieldwork is in fact doing, and how such endeavour impacts on the self, is Mannoni (1956: 7), who observes about Madagascar that 'For years I have been interested in everything I could find out about that country and its inhabitants, but for a long time I deliberately confined myself to ethnological rather than psychological studies ... I found myself taking part either in imagination or in reality in a kind of community life that was quite new to me, and realised with surprise that my own essence was being gradually altered.'

36 Clifford and Marcus (1990: 22–23, 24). Postmodern approaches to anthropology inform not just the latter volume but also those by Geertz (1988) and by Gardner and Lewis (1996). More recently, Clifford (2013) has endorsed as empowering the identity politics of the indigenous 'other'.

37 'No longer a marginal, or occulted, dimension, writing has emerged as central to what anthropologists do both in the field and thereafter,' argue Clifford and Marcus (1990: 2), who continue: 'The fact that it has not until recently been portrayed or seriously discussed reflects the persistence of an ideology claiming transparency of representation and immediacy of experience. Writing reduced to method: keeping good field notes, making accurate maps, "writing up" results.' In the sentence that follows, it is asserted that 'this ideology has crumbled.'

Eliminating the latter, postmodernism implies, allows an 'authentic' voice to emerge and express itself, and as such to deliver an unmediated – and thus ideologically untainted – image of an actually-existing grassroots reality. This, of course, is not the case, since the from-below voice is itself time-bound, and invariably differs from similar grassroots accounts of what is taken as real in the same space earlier. More serious is that in the case of peasant society, this voice from-below is not only internally fragmented along class lines, but also projects external narratives drawn from other, non-peasant – and frequently landlord – voices.[38] In short, a grassroots narrative that cannot be deemed 'authentic', in the sense that it depicts a peasant reality and nothing else. The latter issue is one of those addressed in my own fieldwork diaries, an ancillary record of research undertaken in both Peru and India.

III

Beginnings

Rereading fieldwork diaries kept by me, a half-century before in Peru and three decades ago in India, confirms the trope that what these kind of sources record can throw useful light on aspects unmentioned in the ethnographic accounts published subsequently: namely, the travails that invariably accompany – and sometimes influence – the whole research process. Starting out as a record of money spent, the 1974 Peruvian diary soon became a daily account of conversations, descriptions, and normal routine activity taking place outside the more formal process of information gathering that constitutes anthropological participant/observation fieldwork.

•••

Friday 1st February 1975. Arrive at Quillabamba in early afternoon, a magnificent mountain backdrop, tropical heat similar to Lima, only much more humid. Points of interest: new hospital, out of keeping with the rest of the town – a result of the peasant movement of the early 1960s? Ask where can I find Antonio Ccoscco, the Secretary-General of the *Federación de Campesinos de La Convención y Lares*, and am directed to a lawyer, Ernesto Quispe Ledesma, who is talking to two very deferential campesinos.[39] I wait until 6.30 p.m. when

38 On this, see Brass (2024a: Chapter 9).

39 The *Federación* was the peasant union in the province, and Quispe Ledesma was its lawyer.

they go, and talk to him briefly about my plans. He thinks the main problems of the area are not so much land reform as mechanization and industrialization of the production process.

•••

Saturday 2nd February 1975. In the morning went to *Federación* meeting in a hut on the outskirts of Quillabamba, where delegates from local districts and different agrarian cooperatives were listening to a number of leaders – including a peasant woman – seated round a table, and asking questions about government intentions to eradicate coca and impose land taxes. Crop prices were also heatedly discussed. Approximately fifty persons were in attendance. I had to explain to the meeting my reasons for being there, and the response was generally sympathetic. The general atmosphere appeared anti-government, and the campesinos frequently seemed very indignant about their situation. One of the women present started a long tale of woe, crying halfway through, to the obvious sympathy of those present. I was told that she had a friend who had been killed by anti-union people. Around the mud hut that housed the *Federación* were signs of building, well advanced: was told it would be a two-story headquarters for the *Federación*, paid for from its own funds. Clearly, a rich union. In the afternoon the lawyer Quispe arrived, greeted with much respect by the delegates. His language was distinctly more militant than that used by other delegates. The meeting was still in session when I left at 2.30 p.m. In the evening met an agronomist who worked for the *Reforma Agraria Zona-IX* in Cusco, who said the reform wasn't working because of lack of government inputs: that is, not a question of politics, but of economics only. He seemed anti-military and pro-peasant.

•••

Thursday 7th February 1975. Back in Cusco, where it rained continuously from 1.20 to 3 p.m. In the *Sol* newspaper one of those accidental truths; a photograph of a high-ranking military officer so bad that all one could make out was the shape of a face, the cap and a neck – a typical portrayal of a faceless *gorila*![40] Ripped-off in the market, where I bargain down the price of my purchase from S/.50 to S/40, and hand over a S/.100 note in payment, saying *sencilla no tengo*

40 The reference is to the reputation of the Latin American military as unthinkingly thuggish, a common enough response to proliferation of coups and accounts of torture and 'disappearances' (on which see below).

[I haven't anything smaller].[41] Instead of returning the S/.60 change, he gives me only S/.50, saying he had no change either. In future I must carry small change when shopping in the market.

•••

Wednesday 13th February 1975. It rains all afternoon, as usual. Read some of *Cristianismo y religion Quechua* – its sounds OK for this kind of monograph, but I have yet to be convinced that the linchpin of the hacienda system was – and is – either religion or the fiesta system.

•••

Thursday 14th February 1975. It seems that the rains in the La Convención area are worst during March, the rainy season being January, February March. At about three o'clock a huge downpour takes place, during which I retreat into a café. It rains until about six; floods in the main street, coursing down towards the airport. In the evening supper at a restaurant, then at nine go round to a bar, hoping to meet someone I know: it is shut, so return to lodging and prepare for Quillabamba trip tomorrow.

•••

Friday 15th February 1975. Catch six o'clock morning train to Quillabamba [via Chaullay]. Sit with three Brazilians, two men who are medical students at Rio University, and a woman who speaks English and actually wants to know about anthropology.[42] Talk turns to politics, and they appear to be resigned, good-natured bourgeois who care, but can't do anything. Argentinians and Chileans travelling on the train sing revolutionary songs. From Chaullay to Quillabamba by bus, on the left side of the river, where the view is spectacular, particularly the final approach to Quillabamba itself, with the town nestled in the valley. Instructive is the view the journey provides of the physical agrarian

---

41 The rate of exchange at the time was S/.100 = £1.

42 The presence on the train of these students, together with the fact that it was crowded with passengers when starting out from Cusco, is because half-way along the journey was the station at Aguas Calientes, the stopping off point for anyone travelling to visit the Inca ruins of Macchu Picchu, the main tourist attraction in Peru, if not the whole of Latin America. After that station, where the majority of passengers disembarked, few proceeded on to Chaullay, and even less who then travelled by bus to Quillabamba.

structure on the right bank, with *chacras* stretching up the mountainside.[43] Must enquire about doing fieldwork here, between Quillabamba and Chaullay as against to the north of Quillabamba. Arrive at two o'clock and book into local hotel. It begins raining here at five thirty; have supper at six. Soup is served with a chicken leg sticking up out of the middle – too much!

•••

Saturday 16th February 1975. Morning spent at a meeting of the *Federación*, where the majority of delegates were speaking against two of those present. When asked by me why this was, the response from the person next to me was because they were brothers who were *pequeños proprietarios* [small landowners]. They were better dressed; black leather shoes, new trousers and shirts, and the wife of one was wearing pearl earrings. Of the brothers, one had 11 hectares of land, the other three. Before the agrarian reform, their father owned 900 hectares, and the brothers used *arrendamiento* as a method of working their land.[44] Now they can't get labour, and are hoping to get benefits by joining the *Federación*. Each brother has cafetales, the significance of which they downplayed by saying that the coffee plants were small, *metro y medio*. Both live in Quillabamba, and one has money in the bank. Other features of the meeting: a funeral wake for a dead comrade held inside, while the meeting itself was held outside, in a building without a roof. The lawyer, also present, has been here eight years, and arrived just as Hugo Blanco was being taken away.[45] Among the issues discussed was the role of the big *comerciantes* [traders] in the coca market; the *Federación* lawyer was demanding a free market, at present controlled by the *comerciantes* who possessed government franchises, acting as agents when purchases made from cooperatives.[46] Later in the morning the lawyer heard petitions, including from a woman who was about

43 *Chacra* refers to a peasant smallholding.

44 *Arrendamiento* refers to labour-service tenancy, whereby in exchange for a holding leased on the estate a peasant is required to provide the landlord with a stipulated number of days worked on land belonging to the proprietor.

45 Hugo Blanco (1934–2023) was a leader of the peasant movement and its related *guerrilla* activity in La Convención during the 1958–62 period. He worked as a tenant on the estate of Chaupimayo, adjacent to Pintobamba Grande. Arrested and imprisoned, he was eventually released and went into exile, returning to become a national politician. For more details, see among others, Blanco (1972), Gott (1970); and also Brass (2000b: Chapter 2), which examines the important role in the peasant movement played by agrarian populist discourse.

46 Only smallscale *comerciantes* or petty traders operate in Pintobamba Grande, buying crops directly from peasant smallholders which they in turn then sell on to larger traders

to be evicted. For typing out letters, he charges campesinos S/.10–20. To the *pequeños proprietaries* he charged S/.50.

•••

Sunday 17th February 1975. Set out for the *Comité de Producción* at Pintobamba Grande, four kilometres outside Quillabamba.[47] The *casa hacienda* was empty, only cattle being herded next door; I asked a herdsman with a machete for directions to the school, but that too was empty (holidays until April?).[48] I was greeted with some strange looks by those around, so I walked out, giving the place up for lost, when I met a *peon* who had been asleep.[49] I sat down and we talked; he earned S/.25 a day, whereas prior to the agrarian reform he earned only S/.15. We were joined by a boy who lived in the *viviendas* that I had just visited, who told me that he had just visited his parents who owned a *chacra*, on which they worked all week – no cooperative land.[50] The *peon* had no land and belonged to no union; he didn't seem to care – but this was probably a superficial assessment on my part; the boy didn't like the *técnico* and *ingeniero*, who lived in the *casa hacienda* and looked after the cattle.[51] We walked back down the road to Quillabamba, after which he went home and I continued into town with the peon. Joined in a football game taking place on a nearby field, amidst goats and sheep grazing and vultures wheeling overhead. Have to visit PIP to explain who I am and what I am doing in Quillabamba; then climb quarter of the way up a nearby mountain to look at the *chacras*.[52]

•••

in Quillabamba. It is only towards the latter sort of *comerciante* that peasants are hostile, not the former kind.

47 Unlike the much larger agrarian cooperatives which are able to export directly, smaller units like the *Comité* are unable to do so, and – as I was informed subsequently – are consequently at the mercy of middlemen.

48 The *casa hacienda* was the large house on the rural estate, not unlike the manor of European feudalism, inhabited in pre-reform times by the landlord and his family. In the post-reform era, it served as stores and offices – or habitations – for those holding posts in the agrarian cooperative.

49 *Peon*, like the term *obrero*, generally refers to a labourer who has no land, and obtains a living from the sale of his labour-power.

50 *Viviendas* refers to dwellings located on the ex-estate.

51 Both the *técnico* and the *ingeniero* were employed by the local agrarian reform office, and tasked with supervising the way the livestock herd was managed.

52 PIP refers to the *Policía de Investigaciones del Peru*. It was one of their number who arrested me in the main square of Quillabamba at the end of my fieldwork (see below).

Tuesday 19th February 1975. I ride out to Pintobamba Grande, and come across some *obreros* gathered by the shed; the boss of this group appears to be the *vaquero*, who offers me coca leaves to chew, which makes my gums numb. At about seven fifteen they set out towards the *pasto*; I go with them, and help bring back the bales [of straw], which goes down well.[53] Later in the morning I go out to the tomato field to help there. I explain to two members of the cooperative what I want to do here, and they say I will have to have the approval of the *asamblea*. The two with whom I speak are better dressed than the *obreros*, and appear to be the kingpins around here. After working the tomato field, we all come back about eleven (the *obreros* and me), and they go to the hut of the *vaquero* to have lunch while I sit in the shed and share the lunch of two members of the cooperative: a cup of rice, green pasta and a raw potato – rice and pasta are passed around. Then we go inside the *casa hacienda* where about eight women and girls are knitting – with modern equipment – forming the women's section of the *Comité*. On the wall are small diagrams illustrating *la vida de la mujer campesina*, a very unliberated version, and an equally unliberated version of the *vida del campesino*.[54] They also sell beer – at what price and what kind of franchise I don't know. After a heavy joking session involving male and female peasants, the group settles down to '*chupar chicha*' but end up drinking lots of beer instead, during which I'm asked many questions about England, and everybody gets quite drunk.[55] Am told that peasants of La Convención are communists, and that the *Federación* lawyer had his papers burned by an Aprista.[56] Towards the end an old woman comes in to drink *chicha*, and I am told that she is an old *compañera* who has been fighting against the *gamonales* long before most others.[57] Meanwhile the *obreros* are sitting outside in the central courtyard of the *casa hacienda*, shelling maize.

•••

At this point the diary becomes a fieldwork notebook, but in the two and a half weeks it covers – from the 1st to the 19th February, 1975 – there emerge many of

53 *Pasto* refers to fields on the cooperative land devoted to pasture for livestock grazing.

54 Images depicted in these diagrams are what the Peruvian government thinks the lives of the rural male and female should be like.

55 *Chicha* is a fermented maize alcoholic beverage, much cheaper than bottled beer.

56 *Aprista* is a member of the Peruvian APRA, the *Alianza Popular Revolucionaria Americana*, an anti-imperialist but essentially a bourgeois nationalist political party formed by Victor Raúl Haya de la Torre in Lima during 1930.

57 *Compañera* is the affective political term 'comrade', while *gamonal* is a pejorative word for landlord.

the issues that subsequently became the focus of my fieldwork in Pintobamba Grande. As is invariably the case with social anthropological research, what the diary also reveals are the many common and vexatious aspects of conducting fieldwork: these extend from bureaucratic hurdles; being overcharged for purchases made simply because of being a foreigner; being regarded by inhabitants of the research area with suspicion for the same reason; arranging to meet people who don't turn up; and having difficulties with the rural cuisine. Already two crucial features of conducting research are noticeably present: not just asking questions but also having to answer them (to peasants, to police), and the centrality of drinking as a method of eliciting most kinds of information.[58]

Revealed also are value-judgments, concerning the unliberated depictions of peasant life (albeit as recommended by the Peruvian state) and judgements that turn out to be partially wrong. Although questioning the centrality of the fiesta system to the reproduction of the hacienda system, therefore, I could not have known then that its relative decline in the post-reform era when compared with its role in the pre-reform period was much rather an effect of the rise to power in La Convención of a rich peasantry, who were able to dispense with the landlord capacity to impose on them the economic burden – in terms of cost – of holding religious office.[59] Contrary to the image presented by the *Federación* lawyer as a radical voice, moreover, it later became clear that he was regarded by peasants in the area as somewhat conservative, responsible for holding the union back in terms of policy.

However, not missed in the fieldwork diary were early pointers to issues that emerged as significant, not least the link between the peasant movement and agrarian populism. One of these was signs as to the importance of socioeconomic differentiation occurring within the ranks of the peasantry, and the conflict to which this gave rise. Hence the antagonism expressed by union delegates towards two of their number who were ostensibly not so different from

58 For similar difficulties with the bureaucracy, see Barley (1983: 64–65, 78, 88, 129, 139) who also records the ubiquity of beer drinking, together with its role in fieldwork information gathering.

59 The pre-reform existence – and the post-reform decline – of religious officeholding (*carguyoc*) was because in the earlier period the landlord was able to choose the officeholder, invariably a tenant (*arrendire*) who was a rich peasant. The latter was unable to refuse, since to do so would risk the loss of his tenancy, and had to go into debt in order to meet the expenses, which were considerable. Post-reform expenses were negligible, mainly because officeholding was now spread out among numerous peasants, each of whom was responsible for a single aspect of the fiesta (a puppet show, drinks, fireworks) rather than all its costs, as had been the case previously. On all this see Brass (1986b).

themselves as regards land owned. In the case of the two brothers criticized at the *Federación* meeting, the hostility aimed at them appeared to be the result of a couple of things: as much at what they once had been as what they now were, and how they looked – dressing, so to speak, in a manner so as to distance themselves socially from the rest of the peasant union delegates present.

Signalled as noteworthy in the diary were other instances of resentment stemming from what was seen as actions undermining both peasant solidarity against petty traders and the progress of the cooperative itself. Thus, the display of anger by one peasant against another was caused by the latter not selling his coca crop to the shop set up by the cooperative members in an attempt to cut out the power of the middlemen. The same peasant also pointed out that the *Comité* would never prosper without capital investment, as long as surpluses that ought to be invested were handed back to the cooperative members as dividends. The inference was that public good was being undermined by private advantage, a criticism that applied especially to the better-off peasants who deployed kinsfolk and hired workers onto the cooperative land.[60] Equally, the distinction made by the boy from Pintobamba Grande, between owning a peasant holding but not having anything to do with the cooperative, turned out to be another crucial aspect of my fieldwork research.[61] As significant was the dislike of the agrarian reform *técnico* and the *ingeniero*, a commonly expressed hostility encountered among the peasants who were members of the cooperative.

Endings

Another outcome of the post-war change in the direction followed by social anthropology was that, no longer conducting fieldwork in British colonies, where to a limited extent the researcher was under the protection of the colonial authorities, fieldwork in Third World nations now took place under the

60 As is outlined in Brass (1999: Chapter 2), this dividend stemmed in part from the wage differential between the low daily wage received by workers hired by the peasant enterprise and the higher payment made to those employed on the cooperative sector.

61 This encounter, when I had already given up hope of doing fieldwork in the ex-estate, underlines the significant element of luck in the fieldwork process. A similarly fortuitous encounter is noted by Barley (1983: 93–94) in his search for information about rainchiefs and leopards: 'I only found out by chatting to a boy I bumped into while walking into town on one day of my Friday mail runs … that piece of the picture concerning leopards and rainchiefs had only come my way through sheer luck. If I had not been on that particular road at that particular time I might never had heard it …'

aegis of – and often surveillance by – the local and/or national state apparatus.[62] The latter situation has on occasion generated problems for a social anthropologist engaged in fieldwork.[63] This was especially true of La Convención, the Province in eastern Peru where I carried out my research in 1974–75, an area which some two decades previously had been the site of one of the largest peasant movements in the whole of Latin America.[64] As I learned subsequently, I was watched by the police, who then arrested and transported me to Lima, where I was once again imprisoned and interrogated, a series of events that eventually culminated in my expulsion from the country.[65]

That throughout this episode I was able to retain my final – and in terms of information it recorded – most valuable fieldwork notebook, containing data about the operation of the *enganche* system, was largely due to luck. The notebook was in my possession when in March 1975 I was arrested in the provincial capital Quillabamba, just outside my fieldwork site, but I managed to hide it during police searches, and keep it on me during the whole period of my imprisonment in Peru.[66] Had it been found, and as a result confiscated by the police, this would unquestionably have had a disastrous impact on what

62 Clearly, this is a distinction that did not always apply. The difference alluded to here, it must be emphasized, stemmed from the changed identity of the researcher, and consequently the way s/he was perceived as either an insider or outsider. Hence a social anthropologist carrying out fieldwork in a British colony was not viewed by the authorities as a foreigner, and thus was regarded by them as someone who ostensibly shared the same interests. This was not the case once fieldwork extended into (newly or longstanding) independent nations, where the investigation into politically sensitive issues such as land reform and peasant movements by a foreigner could be seen by local/national authorities as potentially a threat, gathering information that might prove embarrassing or even harmful.

63 Conducting fieldwork in Iraq during 1938, after the end of the British Mandate there, Leach (1940: 60) reports that 'I was the first Englishman for some years to approach the district without some form of military protection, and since it was assumed that I must necessarily be a secret agent of the former mandatory power I was naturally the object of considerable curiosity and suspicion ... though I travelled with an official pass from the Ministry of the Interior, it was generally assumed that in some mysterious way I was plotting against the Government; my curiosity concerning the intimate details of Kurdish life was regarded as a cloak with which to hide my subtler designs.'

64 On the nature of this peasant movement, see Brass (2000b: Chapter 2).

65 Details about this episode can be found in Brass (2017: Chapter 14).

66 Rather than turning out the entire contents of my shoulder bag – a tourist purchase that conveyed a reassuring image of frivolity, as carrying within it nothing of importance – police searches consisted of asking me to hand over a particular item, for example my passport, which I myself then retrieved from the shoulder bag, all other articles inside it remaining unexamined.

I could then have been able to produce as an analysis of my fieldwork site.[67] The element of serendipity that enabled me to avoid such an outcome cannot be underestimated.

A further point which needs emphasis is that had I done my kind of fieldwork a decade later, when Peruvian state agencies were conducting a shoot to kill policy in areas where Sendero Luminoso recruited support among local peasants, I would in all probability not have survived.[68] As it was, in Cusco at the start of my time in Peru I became friends with an Argentinian veterinary student whose politics were very similar to mine. We travelled together to Lima, and then he returned to his own country while I repaired to my fieldwork site in La Convención. He was to become, sadly, one of the 'disappeared' in the dirty war that the armed forces waged against the people of Argentina over the period 1976–83. Years later, once I was back in Cambridge, looking through the University Library copy of the President's Special Commission, *Nunca Mas* (Never Again), I came across his name in the Appendix: he was one of those listed as having been 'disappeared' by the military dictatorship.[69] A reminder, were it needed, that there but for the grace of God, etc.

IV

In certain important respects, subsequent research conducted in India, at various points throughout the 1980s, was different from that undertaken by me in mid-1970s Peru.[70] To begin with, unlike the latter fieldwork, that in India was of shorter duration and involved research assistants.[71] Furthermore, by this

---

67 Loss of fieldwork notes is not always catastrophic, as the case of Srinivas (1976) underlines. When all his processed notes garnered from Indian fieldwork conducted during 1948 in a Karnataka village were burned in a fire started by arsonists in April 1970, he simply reconstructed his account from memory, the resulting published monograph being acclaimed as the classic it has now become.

68 A guerrilla organization inspired by Maoist theory, Sendero Luminoso emerged in Peru during the 1980s and conducted operations well into the new millennium; it was subjected to violent repression by state military and police agencies in the 1990s. For accounts of its objectives, activities, and support, see among others Stern (1998) and Gorriti (1999).

69 His is one of the recorded 8,960 disappearances, registered in the long appendix to the main report (Comisión Nacional sobre la Desaparición de Personas, 1984).

70 Fieldwork trips to India took place in Punjab during 1983, Bihar in 1985, Haryana and Bihar in 1987, and Bihar in 1989. On the first of these, in 1983, I was assisted by Amanda, my wife, who also joined me in the course of the 1987 field trip.

71 To some degree, this adheres to the model described by Evans-Pritchard (1951: 61–62), who differentiated a first and more intensive fieldwork process from subsequent ones, a trajectory whereby '[h]aving isolated these structural patterns in one society, the social

time other personal issues supervened, and consequently had to be considered. I had developed a medical condition which – although it did not rule out fieldwork – nevertheless placed restraints on what I was able to do in terms of long-term research.[72] Being married and having, towards the end of my fieldwork trips to India, the first of three children meant an additional source of anxiety when far away from home. Research itself had also become more focussed, this time on the incidence and effects of unfree labour, as distinct from a more open-ended study of rural society as a whole.[73]

The single entry from my 1983 fieldwork diary is included to underline the fact that the kind of research I was pursuing now – into the structure and dynamics of unfree labour – was difficult not merely in terms of fieldwork itself (as proved to be the case), but also as regards obtaining the necessary institutional support in order to be able to enter a fieldwork site in the first place. Fortunately, my assistant K. Gopal Iyer, then a Reader at Panjab University in Chandigarh, indicated we could proceed without such official institutional backup, and that his own academic status and research experience was sufficient to ensure access to fieldwork areas (as proved to be the case). Difficulties within such contexts remained, however, and stemmed largely from obtaining access not to fieldwork areas *per se* as to labourers in situations where employers were not present.

The following entries from my fieldwork diaries illustrate what were the most relevant issues surfacing during the course of research in India over the 1983–89 period.

• • •

Wednesday, 16th March 1983 – New Delhi. Discussion with M.S.A. Rao, Professor of Sociology, Delhi University. Saw Rao briefly at 3 pm. Had tried to get him by phone previously, but phone lines out of order. On the 14th had gone originally

anthropologist … compares them with patterns in other societies [since] the study of each new society … enables him to construct a typology of forms, and to determine their essential features and the reasons for their variations.'

72 Two years after returning from my Peruvian fieldwork, I fell ill and was diagnosed with type 1 Diabetes, since when I have been on an insulin-dependent medical regime entailing daily injections. The latter were taken in rural India in somewhat public and trying circumstances; having on one occasion disposed of my used syringes in Bihar, I later found that they had been dug up and reused by someone else.

73 It must be emphasized that, the focus notwithstanding, as what was happening in the context studied was obviously important to an understanding of the dynamics structuring unfree labour, it too was analysed as before, but not in the same long-term fashion.

to Delhi Uni in order to chase up contacts suggested by Scarlett Epstein.[74] Saw Arvind Shah & B.S. Baviskar. Shah indicated that affiliation would be OK, but that this would have to be settled by Rao, the head of the Dept. He also said that either Rao could take a decision on this himself, or else he would have to process it. On the issue of bonded labour, he [Shah] said there were problems of identification; he did not agree that this form of labour existed in the Punjab, only migrant labour. Baviskar was friendlier, but not in a position to do anything except make introductions. When I at last got to see Rao, who spends most of his time administering & working on committees, he asked about the project and for whom I was working. He said he would have to process the affiliation request through academic committees & then send it to the Ministry of Education. I said that this would take time, & he replied that this was the way of all bureaucracy. He then indicated that the subject of debt bondage was extremely sensitive politically, & that all research projects from abroad to do with either bonded labour or tribals were refused (had a red mark against them). For this reason he could not affiliate me, but was quite willing to give me informal affiliation – use of the library, to consult staff, giving seminars, etc. I got the impression that I was being given the brush-off; it also left me in no doubt as to where the university stood vis-à-vis the government. Subsequently Manjari said this is what would in fact happen; but she thought I should find out for myself, rather than be told, in case I thought that she was trying to pre-dispose me against them.[75]

•••

Friday, 8th May 1987 – Haryana. Conduct interviews in a village near Panipat, in conjunction with a student of Gopal Iyer, who for personal reasons cannot himself act as a research assistant on this occasion.[76] At six we start out to interview farmers in this village, beginning with a sharecropper. After this, it having got dark, we go to the house of a capitalist farmer who was listening to the earlier interview, and interview him; he is important, owns 40 acres, and is on the panchayat. When asked about attached permanent labour (*naukar*), he

74 Based at the Institute of Development Studies at Sussex University, the social anthropologist Scarlett Epstein had herself conducted fieldwork in India, and provided much valuable advice together with useful contacts.

75 A dynamic and radical scholar/activist, Manjari Dingwaney was not just knowledgeable about the conditions generating bonded labour (Patnaik and Dingwaney, 1985) but also helpful in establishing non-academic contacts in rural India.

76 Gopal suffered a family bereavement shortly before fieldwork was scheduled to start, and was thus unable to participate in fieldwork until the later trip to Bihar.

makes out he is at their mercy, that they are not bonded. Also says he makes no surplus, which it transpires is untrue. The branch of the State Bank of India at the edge of the village is where the rich farmers put their Green Revolution profits. On the way back we encounter labourers sorting & storing wheat grains by lantern light, the farmers looking on. We ask to interview two of these, which we arrange to do nearby [away from the farmers]. Only one labourer, a free worker, turns up, & tells us lots of interesting things in the course of a long interview, by candlelight.

•••

Saturday, 9th May 1987 – Haryana. From 9.30 to 11.30 am we go around the village interviewing agricultural labourers from the Scheduled Castes. First, Ziwars, who express a strong disinclination for work as attached labour ('It is better to ask for alms [i.e., beg] than being an attached labourer'). Much the same is told us during our second interview with Chamars & Balmiki caste members, who also indicate a strong resentment against farmers in the village, & a dislike of attachment. At about midday we return to the house, where I rest for a couple of hours. At two we have the midday meal, and then set out for further interviewing sessions. The first is the village sarpanch, a rich farmer owning about 60 acres of land, who gives us a lot of info about production. Then his brother brings along his attached labourer, who is my age but looks about 80, and we interview him in front of his employer (a situation to the liking neither of me nor of the labourer). Finally, we interview the employer himself, who surprisingly tells us much about peasant/labourer conflicts in the village, & how these escalate to the point of physical confrontation. We return to the house, have tea, & then I take my camera & go around the village taking photos, followed by the inevitable group of children who stop everywhere I stop & unselfconsciously start when I do. At seven go out for a final round of interviews, hoping to find an attached labourer, but they will all be working. Go instead to the Gujjar section of the village & interview a marginal farmer & his son. The latter asks a lot of questions about me, wondering whether I worked collecting information about India as a foreign agent. His mother places her hand on my head & blesses me.

•••

Sunday, 10th May 1987 – Haryana. Together with a JNU student and his friend, I go to Baniyani village, some 10 kms away from Rohtak town. In the village have a frustrating first interview with the *sarpanch* & other peasant farmers.

When I ask what special linkages farmers in this village have with workers to stop them going off to work on the nearby brick kilns & construction sites, he guesses I'm talking about bondage & says we have nothing of that here. Lies, as I find out later, as is his claim to own only 45 acres (he owns 90) and to pay his workers Rs.25–30 daily (Rs.10–15 is the rate). Interestingly, as in the village yesterday, it is the so-called 'free' workers who are the ones to give clues about their bondage through debt. Arrive back at 7.30 pm, having enjoyed my field visit more than I thought I would.

•••

Saturday, 23rd May 1987 – New Delhi. Had terrible [hypoglycemic] attack at about 8.30 pm, just as we were about to begin our evening meal in the IIC [Indian International Centre] dining room.[77] I had my [insulin] at 6.45, & let too much time elapse – very stupid. Unlike other attacks, where the onset is signalled by acute hunger, this one was marked by a strong nausea: I suddenly felt very, *very* ill, a feeling compounded by not knowing what was happening – I didn't think it was an attack, the symptoms were *so* unfamiliar. Very quickly I felt faint: dizziness, accompanied by a blocking out of sound & a wavering of sight. I came near to passing out. Gradually I recovered, but didn't feel like eating. A warning that I should take more care – lucky it happened here rather than in rural Bihar.

•••

Saturday, 30th May 1987 – Motihari, Bihar. The first day in the field was bad, but the morning session in the S.C. *toli* did produce some good information re. the link between free & unfree labour, & the enforcement of bondage via kinship links & obligation. I managed to restrain Gopal from proceeding ever onwards at midday for some hours of welcome rest; he seems to regard fieldwork as a manic race, the victory going to the person who carries out most interviews (regardless of their banality) in the course of a day. I prefer quality to quantity, & here lies one major point of difference. The evening interview with the frightening landlord in village Sisua Patwa was also very useful. He provided us with the crucial info I was after in the last 5 minutes of a very long session, when, in response to my question about how he recruited local

77 Amanda had arrived in India shortly before, and we were both staying at the Indian International Centre prior to departing for fieldwork in Bihar. Not for the first time – nor, indeed, the last – she was instrumental in ensuring that I survived a hypoglycemic attack.

casual 'free' labour, he indicated that this was done through the giving of loans in hard times, which 'obliged' the recipients to work for him. Earlier, he had complained about labour shortages, with locals going to other parts (Assam) as migrants, so clearly this was significant. Also, his treatment of one of his annual servants (*salana naukar*) who did not have one moment's rest throughout the period there, his tasks varying from giving us food & drinks, fetching food, doing agricultural tasks in the yard, to fanning us towards the end. The latter task was taken up in response to a barked order from the landlord. Later we had tea in front of another crowd, watched toddy tappers at work on palm trees. A clash with Gopal occurred on our way to the harijan toli, when I said that I hoped the two peasants (high caste) from the village where we were staying would not be present while we interviewed the S.C. workers. Gopal replied that they would, & thought that we had to work within these limits. I continued to point out the futility of such an interview situation, but he didn't appear moved. Finally, the two 'guardians' went, leaving us to carry out the interviews unpoliced.

•••

Sunday, 31st May 1987 – Motihari, Bihar. We went with Gopal's CPM contact to the village of Bhopatpur, an initially unpromising location where a landlord/labourer conflict was in progress. On the way into the village we passed the landlord's house, & looking into the veranda I saw an armed policemen sitting on a chair. The interviews were useful, particularly the one with the wife of a S.C. bonded labourer falsely imprisoned for trying to leave his landlord in search of higher wages. We gave Rs.500 to the CPM activist to help in the struggle against the landlord, & another Rs.200 for the wife of the bonded labourer, so that she wouldn't have to take a loan to subsist. Gopal created a sense of danger (see fieldwork notes), so we left the village abruptly at about 2 pm. As we all cycled out past the landlord's house, I saw the same policemen move his hand onto his gun – so perhaps there was danger after all. Later, Gopal took down details of the 7 killings of CPM activists by landlords in that village. We were also told of the existence of 18 villages in the neighbourhood where labour was bonded, & – significantly – that there was a scarcity of labour in 4 blocks of the district, workers migrating because of low agricultural wages.[78]

78 My fieldwork notes record that a hundred local workers migrated to Assam, a pattern arranged by contractors who come in October to recruit. Each migrant is provided by the contractor with a cash advance of Rs. 100, a debt that is deducted from future earnings, and works in Assam until the end of May, in brick kilns there. The debt itself has to be

In the village itself, Gopal held court, & had some migrants summoned. Two of these were worse than useless (a petty landowning businessman & a frontier policemen), but the third was potentially very interesting. He combined migration to Assam (because of low agricultural wages, he said, bravely, surrounded by peasants) with local agricultural and non-agricultural work. I managed to establish the fact that he also had periods of unemployment & that to cover these he took loans (from local landowners). When I wanted to ask the conditions governing these loans – they carried a 60% interest rate – Gopal refused to put this question saying it was irrelevant, & slammed his book shut, indicating the interview was at an end. Before I could explode – as I surely would have done – a young boy beside me had a fit & fainted, causing a diversion. I was furious, & refused to speak to Gopal for the rest of the evening. His response was not only unwarranted but, more seriously, bad social science: *no* interviewer should ever make assumptions about an issue & refuse as a result to put questions. Gopal's policing of my questions in this manner is unforgivable; it is not the first time he has done this (see my 1985 fieldwork diary). His authoritarian attitude (which [another Indian academic] warned me against) contrasts with that of his students, who were models of fieldworking co-researchers.

•••

Tuesday, 9th June 1987 – Singbhum District, Bihar. On the way back to Chakradhapur from a fieldwork trip, Gopal, a colleague of his, and I are caught in the monsoon break. Rain comes down in stair rods, while the whole landscape is lit up with pink flashes of sheet lightning. I, together with Gopal, am riding on the back of a motorbike driven by his colleague, nearly falling off as it goes along. Get soaked, and we finally arrive safely at Chakradhapur, where I learn that our hair-raising ride took us through dacoit-infested forests, travelling across what was dangerous bandit-infested terrain. Amanda was convinced she would never see me alive again, and was already thinking how she would have to arrange for the return of my body to England.

•••

Friday, 26th June 1987 – New Delhi. Discussion with K.B. Saxena, who tells us he had great difficulty with government IAS [Indian Administrative Service] officers identifying bonded labour in Singhbhum District, Bihar, since these

cleared before the migrant is permitted to seek alternative employment. This is now an established pattern of outmigration that began only 5–6 years ago.

had their own ideas about debt bondage & therefore said it didn't exist.[79] Their ideas were essentially *visual* (= physical oppression). KBS said well-disposed District Magistrates were important; without them, nothing would happen. Gopal mentioned that the District Magistrate at Nellore, Andhra Pradesh, had got hold of surplus lands, government money, and united these in an integrated programme with freed bonded labourers. The latter were *not* given land titles: these remained the property of the government, so that bonded labourer land could *not* be sold. KBS confirmed that attached labour was bonded, & that the contrary argument – that attachment did not constitute bondage – was developed by the Bihar government to frustrate the bonded labour abolition programme. His view was that academics who had developed this notion – AL ≠ BL – were very unhelpful politically, because they gave this separation an intellectual respectability.[80] His opinion was that labour was – and could only ever be – *either* free *or* bonded.

•••

Tuesday, 26th December 1989 – Purnia District, Bihar. I, along with Gopal and M.C. Sarkar, go to the Circuit House, and am introduced to the Additional Collector (Land Ceilings), spending most of the morning talking with the latter.[81] He gives us a very rosy view of landlordism in the District, saying that *adivasis* now have landlords at their mercy & that all *adivasis* have to do is to step on a landlord's land & it is theirs. The landlords do dare commit atrocities against them, he maintains, because the gov't will come down hard on them. Also, there is no bondage or semi-slavery, since workers who stay with one or two landlords do so because they have faith in them. Interestingly, I managed to establish that in Bihar, unlike other states, a landlord exercises very strong resumption rights over land held under land ceiling laws. If, e.g., a landlord has 15 acres under the ceiling, & leases this all out under sharecropping arrangements, then he retains the legal right to take back this land,

79 Known for his probity and pro-poor stance, K.B. Saxena has been a member of the Indian Administrative Service who has held important government roles, including Secretary for Land Reforms, Chief Secretary of the Government of Bihar, Principal Adviser to the Planning Commission, and various Ministerial Secretaries for the Government of India. Background to our discussion was his role in ensuring that the 1976 Bonded Labour Abolition legislation was implemented throughout Bihar.

80 He named these academics, many of them senior and still research active, so for obvious reasons it is better that they remain anonymous.

81 M.C. Sarkar, of the A.N. Sinha Institute of Social Studies at Patna, assisted with the fieldwork in Purnia District.

a right which overrides that of sharecroppers to land which they work (i.e. landlord rights supersede tenancy laws favouring the sharecropper). The sole exception is the occupancy rights sharecroppers have as a result of spending 12 years on the same piece of land, but landlords manage to avoid this by rotating sharecroppers.

•••

Wednesday, 27th December 1989 – Purnia District, Bihar. Visit two villages in Kritynand block, and there are no bonded labourers in either, although I get some interesting reactions to the possibilities of this. In the second village, Gopal & accompanying bureaucrat interview one section about land, while Sarkar & I interview Santals in the Adivasi tola, where women state that under no circumstances would they enter bondage even for the sake of obtaining full employment.

•••

Thursday, 28th December 1989 – Purnia District, Bihar. I want to get away before the gov't official arrives, and we start out for Forbesganj, some 80-odd kms to the north [on the frontier with Nepal]. There we find out about the incidence of attached labour, the effect of outmigration to Punjab, & the labour shortages in the area. In one village we find classic instances of unfreedom effected through withholding wages, both from attached labour & casual workers. Attached labour is of two kinds: the ploughman (*harwaha*) and the permanent servant (*naukar*), the latter being more arduous than the former. Towards the end of our interviews we hear a commotion in some adjacent dwellings: a woman labourer has just been beaten up by a farmer for daring to ask for back wages. A public commotion ensues, in which a Congress (I) representative from the scheduled caste community of Musahars claims to be acting on behalf of the latter, & is told by Gopal that he is a stooge of the landholders. We move on rapidly ...

•••

Friday, 29th December 1989 – Purnia District, Bihar. We decide to concentrate the research in the bottom SW of the district. En route we see lots of females harvesting & threshing in the fields, and stop by the side of the road to conduct interviews with them. They are day labourers, Oraon tribals, working for a male Yadav labour contractor supervising them on behalf of a large Yadav landholder. The women take small cash advances and are not allowed to work for anyone else as long as he [the landholder] wants their labour-power. During the interview the women turn on the labour contractor and accuse him of forcing them back to the fields when they go to work for another employer. At about 3 pm we reach Rupauli block, where there are large landlords owning 11,000 and 50,000 acres apiece, untouched by land reforms because their owners are VIPs in the Congress (I) party. We start back to Purnia, agreeing that this is a risky area in which to do fieldwork.

•••

Saturday, 30th December 1989 – Purnia District, Bihar. Today we spend gathering secondary data from the bureaucracy in town, at the office of the District Collector. Confirmed is the changed pattern of economic development, as evidenced by tractorization & the commercialization of crops, very different from what was happening in the recent past. Gopal informs the District Collector about the eviction of registered tenants & the withholding of wages. The DC is remarkably frank about this, & agrees that the problem of eviction, land surplus evasion, & withholding wages is widespread in Purnia. He also thinks that a study of outmigration from Purnia to Punjab & the Green Revolution areas of UP (Meerut) would be a good idea, and provides us with a letter instructing full cooperation from all concerned.

•••

Sunday, 31st December 1989 – Purnia District, Bihar. Decide to forget about going to Raniganj Block, our original destination, & to return instead to Rupauli Block in the SW of the District. At Mataili village we conduct interviews in the Harijan tola. Instead of starting with – or even mentioning – debt, I approach the issue through the work history of the subject, & this proves successful. I interview a ploughman, an attached labourer, although he does not identify himself as such, & then a daily agricultural labourer. Both are unfree workers, one over a 3-year period & the other for briefer periods. Find that debts are inherited, the witness system operates (as in Haryana), social pressure is exercised against children to honour fathers' debts, and that employers prevent children & young adults who inherit debts of parents from themselves migrating to Punjab.[82] All very interesting, & a fruitful visit.

82 This involves passing any outstanding debt onto remaining kinsfolk, in most cases females in the household who – if a male who originally inherits parental debt himself migrates

...

Monday, 1st January 1990 – Purnia District, Bihar. We depart for the field at 10 am, and drive to Kisanganj, about 90 kms to the NE of the District. The area is one of immigration from Bangladesh, & all the landholders are Muslims who are good cultivators, having purchased their property after East Pakistan became Bangladesh. We find an Adivasi tola inhabited by Santals who have migrated from elsewhere in Bihar. Both AL & casuals are in debt to Muslim landholders from whom they borrow, & for whom they work. In this village also there is withholding of wages, inheritance of debt, & landlord force against AL in general and their offspring who do not work off their father's debts when old or dead. I am happy with the interview materials, & we go to a harijan tola nearby to collect supplementary material. The 2 main informants who owned land, were suspicious of me as a foreigner, and tended to evade questions or give dubious answers. As we are leaving, the other inhabitants of the tola warn us that the 2 are not to be trusted, & sure enough one of them rushes past us on a bike. We all agree he is on the way to the landholders to report our visit, & I begin to worry. Immediately we travel back to Purnia ...

...

An emerging theme recorded in these Indian fieldwork diaries, one that eventually became central, was that unfree production relations – widely regarded within the development community as indicating the presence of an economically backward, pre-capitalist, agrarian sector, a sign of at best the existence of semi-feudalism or at worst a still embedded feudalism – were much rather not merely compatible with the accumulation process but in many instances for commercial producers the employment arrangement of choice. Production relations such as the *enganche* in Peru and attached labour in India enabled small agrarian capitalists – consisting of rich peasants and/or better-off ones in these contexts – to operate a labour regime that combined lower costs with better control over their workforce.

Not the least important aspect of this was when outmigration, from Bihar to Punjab, led to a decline in the numbers of agricultural labourers available for employment locally. So as to retain their workers, commercial farmers in Purnia ensured that debts incurred were met by remaining kinsfolk, usually females, who were required to work for a creditor-employer in lieu of a male

(= 'absconds') – then have themselves to work in the fields of the creditor-employer in order to pay off with their own labour-power what is owed.

family member who migrated. State officials in India were not uniform in their reaction to our presence and research agenda, some being helpful, others not. The same was true of academics: Gopal Iyer and M.C. Sarkar facilitated and participated in fieldwork, in contrast to those at Delhi University.

Although an energetic and knowledgeable assistant in the field, coupled with periodic and welcome humorous asides uttered in the course of its longueurs, Gopal was nevertheless used to following his own research agenda. He tended not to want to focus on production relations and unfree labour, initially at least, to the extent of on one occasion discontinuing an interview following this line of questioning. Because of this, our fieldwork collaboration oscillated in terms of mood, between an initial frustration, to a more usual amicable disposition subsequently, leading overall to fruitful cooperation. This, as others have pointed out, is a recognisable fieldwork pattern, albeit one not often acknowledged by social anthropologists.[83]

Conclusion

From theory to fact-finding, both the practice and the paradigm of social anthropology have been the object of criticism spanning two conjunctures: first, after the 1939–45 war, when decolonization was accompanied by a questioning of fieldwork and the notion of the 'other' as backward and 'primitive'; and second, following the 1980s rise to academic prominence of the cultural turn recuperated criticisms of fieldwork but reinstated 'otherness', now as empowering. One crucial mutation, important in the sort of risks faced by the ethnographer, was that in contrast to pre-war research (in colonial settings) was that the fieldworker no longer occupied the position vis-à-vis local and national political authorities of a relatively privileged 'insider' (as part of the overarching colonial apparatus, however unlikely this may actually be).

During the first stage, leading into what became the 1960s development decade, fieldwork was confronted with the need to address the wider context

83 Hence the observation by Barley (1983: 44, 66): 'The anthropologist's assistant is a figure who seems suspiciously absent from ethnographic accounts ... The position of a fieldworker's assistant is a difficult one. He is expected by the locals to take their part in any clash of loyalties with his employer ... At the same time, his employer expects him to act as his agent in dealing with the local people and tipping him off on strategies and contacts.' He continues (Barley, 1983: 68): 'An important feature of "collecting the mail" [from the local town] was that it provided me with a break from my assistant. I have never in my life spent so much time in the uninterrupted company of one person and had begun to feel like one married against his will to a most unsuitable partner.'

in which its subject, hitherto perceived as autochthonous, now had to be situated. Hence the change in post-war social anthropology signalled a transition not just from one period to another, but also from one kind of research, the focus of which was on subsistence economy of tribal populations in colonial settings, to another sort of fieldwork, among peasant smallholders operating in the wider capitalist market. This shift exposed the theoretical shortcomings of the discipline, as illustrated by the idealised meaning ascribed to unfree labour: not as an harmonious effect of kinship affectivity, but rather as a coercive relation in which better-off farmers acquired and controlled the labour-power of poor peasants.

Over the latter stage, from the 1980s onwards, postmodern theory not only doubled down on the earlier critique, equating fieldwork once again with a colonial gaze, but also maintained that its continuation was acceptable solely in a distinct form. Henceforth social anthropological practice would be converted into a way of expressing what was seen by postmodernism as an 'authentic' and unheard grassroots voice, in the process relegating the ethnographer merely to a conduit who made available this unmediated from-below discourse. Challenged by postmodernism, fieldwork seemingly would be able to survive only by a double transformation in the authorial voice: initially as unserious (anthropology-as-clowning), and then as a channel for what postmodernism thought – wrongly – was an ideologically untainted, and thus pristine, voice-from-below.

The search by postmodernism for an unmediated grassroots voice, in effect reducing the ethnographer to a conduit, is destined to fail. This is because in pre-capitalist situations peasant society is itself mediated by non-peasant ideology, and once agrarian sector is penetrated by capitalism, the notion of an unmediated voice – a pristine 'from below' discourse – vanishes. Moreover, the approach licensed by postmodernism amounts to replacing one kind of subjectivity, that of the ethnographer, which is interrogated for its inherent biases, with another, that of the informant, which often remains unexamined in quite the same way.

Evidence for all the usual vexations and satisfactions linked to anthropological practice are generally found, if at all, not in the ethnography but the fieldwork diary. Excerpts from my own fieldwork diaries covering a period from the mid-1970s to the end of the 1980s underlines the veracity of a trope central to social anthropological practice: fieldwork combines good days with bad ones, episodes that frustrate together with those yielding significant information. This is as true of fieldwork conducted in the Trobriands by Malinowski and by Barley in Cameroon as it is of mine in the rural locations of Peru and India.

In the latter context, diary entries pointed not just to the existence of unfree production relations, but also to their being a response by commercial farmers to outmigration, making it necessary for such producers to exercise more effective control over their workers, by – among other things – withholding wages and enforcing debt repayment on remaining kinsfolk and/or family members. Hence the presence in the labour process of workers who were female: an effect of male outmigration was that women left behind become bonded labour in their place.

More generally, and unsurprisingly, the fieldwork diary reveals the kinds of difficulties facing research conducted by an 'outsider', not the least significant being suspicions – by bureaucrats and those studied alike – as to what really is the object of investigation carried out in their own society by someone necessarily regarded in such contexts as 'other'. Inevitably, perhaps, fieldwork carries the ideological taint of (and thus also the potential threat from) 'foreignness': in my case, police surveillance led to arrest, imprisonment, interrogation, and expulsion. Insofar as the diary highlights the personal component of research, it licenses a follow-up question as to what kind of background does the anthropologist have; this is explored in the next chapter.

CHAPTER 8

Fragments of a Life, or Drawing a Line

> The historian A.J.P. Taylor, applying for a fellowship at Oxford, was asked an anxious question by one of the dons interviewing him. He had heard that Mr. Taylor regrettably suffered from a dubious condition known as Strong Opinions: was this the case? Yes, Taylor confirmed, he did indeed have Strong Opinions, but it was all right, because they were Weakly Held. (And he got the job.)
>
> An observation on the perils in academia (and in life generally) of holding Strong Opinions that are not Weakly Held.[1]

•••

> The world, however wide, has folds and wrinkles that bring distant places together in strange ways. An adage says: "All politics is local". This is a special case of the truism that all experience is personal. A corollary is that in some sense there is no exotica. Everything gets compared to your own experience. Paradoxically, what is closest to home can seem exotic.
>
> An observation by ETHAN COEN in the Introduction to the script of the film *Fargo*.[2]

∴

Introduction: Till All Our Strivings Cease

As one rushes each towards his or her own personal abyss, seemingly accompanied on this final stage of a journey by humanity itself, there surfaces – inevitably – a desire to reconsider prefiguring aspects of the point now arrived at. Rather than an all-conquering forward march, the trajectory recorded here is composed more often than not of institutional exclusion or defeat. Assembled, therefore, is a random selection of personal episodes, things that have happened to the self (and those close to one), a collection that seems at times to illustrate the old trope of 'a chapter of accidents', which, of course, it is not (or

1 Barnes (2025: 31).

2 See Coen and Coen (1996: ix).

not quite). Inescapable, however, is its non-triumphant character, approximating to the much-reviled sociological epithet, amounting nearly to an insult, of 'ordinary', which is probably the only accurate description of the life most of us get to lead.[3]

By contrast, some academic memoirs reveal the influence on them of celebrity culture, thereby fostering the construction of a personality cult. The object of the latter process is to depict its subject as a world-changing individual, someone who – because s/he is not ordinary but extraordinary – is the centre of attention by colleagues, and even perhaps the global media.[4] Academics in this particular category either depict themselves, or are portrayed by others as all-conquering intellects, whose interventions are said to transform existing thought and knowledge for ever. Even when not in this category, however, university lecturers with a public profile feel the need constantly to provide the world with their opinions about everything and anything.[5] This mimicking of celebrity culture is in turn an effect of competition for attention within a university system experiencing funding cutbacks, where having a public impact not only attracts research grants but also to some degree ensures success – or at least survival – in an increasingly competitive jobs market. One reason for setting out here what amounts to a personal history is that, because unrecorded,

---

3 Being seen to be nothing more than 'ordinary' is categorized by Sennett and Cobb (1977) as one of 'the hidden injuries of class'. A variant of the same interpretation is found in Thompson (1963: 12) when taking issue with historiographical approaches in which 'Only the successful ... are remembered. The blind alleys, the lost causes, and the losers themselves are forgotten.'

4 In contrast to me-me-me accounts criticized elsewhere, the personal one here is separated off and presented as what it is, whereas the former kind tend to be inserted into whatever is written, regardless of its relevance. Furthermore, here the emphasis is on the individual as bystander ('this happened to me') rather than as hero ('I made this happen').

5 See, for example, Beard (2009), who – among other things – inadvertently reveals the gap between on the one hand special pleading that academic life is not the cushy number many believe it to be ('hard work ... all too often misrepresented ... [b]ecause we have very few fixed hours of work, university teachers are often assumed to have loads of free time ... [f]eel some sympathy for Oxford and Cambridge, please', 'dispel a few of the myths about our long holidays', 'the hard-working fellows of Newnham ...', 'there are a few misapprehensions about our leisurely life that need to be put right', etc., etc.) and on the other the many descriptions by her of numerous foreign 'gigs' ('I am at Pompeii, getting some work in for the next book ...', 'If you venture deep inside the pyramids, as I did on my Egyptian "holiday"', 'I went to Mexico on a quick holiday from the Getty Research Institute in LA', 'Just back from the fleshpots of Los Angeles (the hard-working fleshpots, I should say) ...', 'My trip to Mexico ... A few months in the USA', 'I am now in Naples for seven days ...'. etc., etc.) involving frequent travel to and stays in 'exotic' foreign locations. Commenting on the role of myths, Beard (2009: 275) is not above subscribing to one of the most common ('Cambridge is a place where academic freedom still means something').

other sorts of lives are invariably regarded as devoid of wider significance and perhaps even of meaning.[6] Hence the description attached to them: the demeaning label 'ordinary'.[7]

What follows is neither a lament nor a memoir, but the presentation of a number of personal episodes arranged chronologically, depicting in unheroic mode a world passing by, teaching lessons, some learnt, others not. If there is a common theme, it is the impact of politics, and how one is shaped by this, a cliché but true: not only on me but also on both my parents. In the latter instance, directly, in the form of the Spanish Civil war and the 1939–45 global conflict; in mine, indirectly, a consequence of radicalization by the 1968 student movement. For me, political difficulties linked initially to cartooning persisted long after the latter activity ceased, and were generated subsequently by what was written. In my case, therefore, cartoons are images from a discontinued past.

This chapter consists of four sections, the first of which recounts – briefly – the political (and other) experiences of my parents in wartime, while the second covers mine at boarding school and university. Outlined in the third are incidents connected to work (and other things) before conducting research abroad, and the politics of academic employment as this affected me is considered in the fourth.

I

Sleep and Forget

As is well known, the historical era stretching from the 1930s, through the 1939–45 global conflict, and then the Cold War, was marked by, among other things, the actions of the 'Cambridge Five' who over this period delivered secret information to the Soviet Union. The group consisted of Guy Burgess,

6 Moving beyond the 'ordinary' involves a number of distinct processes. As well as a life composed of episodes regarded as being 'out of the ordinary' (= 'extraordinary'), therefore, it also depends on the acquisition of what Bourdieu (1984) terms 'cultural capital', a process requiring knowledge and adoption of a battery of social codes and practices. Here it is not so much the latter route as the former identity that is of interest, insofar as it raises questions regarding to whom the concept might apply, and why. Since it could be argued that the element of 'cultural capital' is itself on display in the correspondence between John Cairncross and my mother, this can be said to be a process which resonates in the personal domain.

7 This sort of negative characterization informs the film comedy *The Rebel* (1961), directed by Robert Day and starring Tony Hancock. His risible earnestness (or pretentiousness) notwithstanding, Hancock is depicted as a mediocre artist *because* he is ordinary, and punished for a failure to rise above this condition: to be 'extraordinary', in other words.

Donald Maclean, Kim Philby, and Anthony Blunt, along with the 'fifth man', John Cairncross.[8] Conducting intelligence-gathering operations at the Foreign Office and code-breaking at Bletchley Park, Cairncross was recruited as a spy by James Klugmann in 1937, and his girlfriend at the time was my mother, Gloria.[9] At that point, when he was aged 24, she was 21 and had recently arrived in England, having left Spain in the company of her parents after the start of the Civil War the previous year. In 1937 both were still unmarried; she wed my father just short of a decade later, and Cairncross married his first wife in 1951. Evidence of their earlier relationship is contained in a series of letters sent by him to her subsequently, throughout the 1940s.[10]

These letters from Cairncross to Gloria, together with a couple of photos, one of which depicts him doing the washing up, were inserted into her copy of his book.[11] I came across them when going through her effects after she died in 2012.[12] No copies of letters written by her to him were found, the only record to what she wrote being the references contained in his correspondence with

---

8 The reason given by Cairncross for spying for Russia is similar to that expressed by the character Bill Haydon (played by Ian Richardson) in the 1979 television series *Tinker Tailor Soldier Spy*. Having at last been unmasked as a mole, Haydon is asked by George Smiley (played by Alec Guinness) why and when he spied for Russia, and replies: 'Why? You ask that? Because it was necessary, that's why! Someone had to! Do you know what's killing Western Democracy, George? Greed ... moral, political aesthetic ... Britain ... oh dear ... no viability whatever in world affairs ... I suppose that's when it began, turning my eyes to the east, when I saw how trivial we'd become as a nation, say the forties. At the time I was scrupulous not to give Moscow anything harmful to ourselves, our own agents in the field'.

9 In 1937, when he was recruited by Klugmann (on which see Andrews, 2023a, 2023b), Cairncross was at the Foreign Office. By 1942 he was undertaking cryptoanalysis at Bletchley Park, and in 1943 he moved to MI6. 'With Russia as an ally,' writes his brother Alec in the Preface (Cairncross, 1997: ix), 'he ... came to a deliberate decision while at Bletchley Park to become an agent for the duration of the war ... What he transmitted in 1943 is now known to have included intercepts of German radio messages that were of critical importance to the USSR in what proved to be the decisive battle at Kursk on the Eastern Front.' It was only in 1964 that Cairncross was revealed to have been providing the Soviet Union with secret information, when he was given immunity from prosecution.

10 Whilst not certain, it is likely that they met when in February 1937 Cairncross was transferred to the Western Department of the Foreign Office, which included Spain (Cairncross, 1997: 55, 61–62); he was still with the Spanish section when, in May 1937, Cairncross was recruited by the KGB.

11 Cairncross (1997). The letters themselves contain occasional references to his 'abominable handwriting', observing that 'I'm sure *you* can't decipher *my* familiar handwriting straight away'. Some words are indeed difficult if not impossible to decipher.

12 This discovery emphasizes the accuracy of the old trope about leaving it too late to ask questions about the lives of parents. Although vaguely aware of the Cairncross link, not realising its significance for her I failed to ask my mother about this until it was no longer possible to do so. One of life's many regrets.

her. The Cairncross letters to Gloria (see Appendix 1) span the decade from December 1941 to January 1950, a period in which she met and married my father in late 1945. Unsurprisingly, none of them contain any reference to secret activity undertaken by him at the time: he did not divulge his link to the USSR, even to his brother, the economist Alec Cairncross.[13]

The sole mention in the correspondence of what Cairncross was doing is to his being called up in 1942 'to become a soldier', adding that he 'will be doing special work' and was 'not at all unhappy at the prospect'.[14] Later, in 1944, he writes that '[t]he only thing I've done during these years has been to learn Russian', but this, he adds, is necessary only to read literature. References to events focus on day-to-day wartime travails, along the following lines: 'These last four years have been hard, exhausting, often depressing but they've been a magnificent experience and most of us have come out of them tired but tougher, more rigorous and more humble than we went in'; 'Unfortunately life has not been easy these last few months, with flying bombs etc.'; and 'you will not find [London] much changed. Even now the lights are going up again, the scars are healing over and most of the old places remain.'; and, latterly, 'Life here is more normal'.

Observing in April 1944 that 'I feel much less subhuman than I've done since 1937', Cairncross then adds: '1937 – it seems a long way off, doesn't it. Heaven, by comparison with the events of the past seven years, and alas a heaven that we, like most people, didn't fully appreciate at the time.' He continues: 'Would we have broken off, I wondered[,] if we had known what was coming, it was a very great loss to me ... I've still got your letters.' Five months later that same year, he writes that 'our relationship must have struck deep roots. It is interesting to speculate what would have happened had I met you after you had had a taste of life on your own and I had developed a rather more understanding attitude to various aspects of life. It is probable that we might have understood each other much better instead of colliding as we did.' This expression of regret, however, is then qualified by a pessimistic note: 'But again

---

13 In the Preface his brother Alec (Cairncross, 1997: vii) writes that 'During his lifetime [John] maintained a rigorous silence about those contacts and at no time confided in me. Even when I wrote to him in 1964 after hearing officially, to my utter astonishment, that he had been a Soviet agent, I received no reply or comment. Nor did he indicate to me at any time in later years the part that he had played.'

14 About this 'special work', Cairncross (1997: 95) writes much later: 'My fate, I soon learned, was that my service in the armed forces would not be as a humble infantryman ... my next assignment took me into the heart of the war effort. I was posted to the secret and vital operation of deciphering signals of foreign military forces carried out at the Government Code & Cypher School (GC&CS) ... at Bletchley' – breaking the ENIGMA cipher machine.

it is possible that your views, which I deeply respect, would have precluded closer relations.' One can only guess as to the source of this regret, and at what caused the disagreement that terminated their relationship: possibly religious, national, cultural incompatibility, since the Cairncross background was Scottish Presbyterian, whereas that of Gloria was Spanish Roman Catholic.[15] Or simply being and growing apart during wartime, 'a taste of life on your own'.

During the early 1940s, letters from Cairncross display a fondness that hinted at the possibility of marriage, from 'toasting my toes in front of the fire ... [t]oo bad you weren't there to see them', via enthusiasm ('writing to you seems to have some magical effect on me', 'a fresh voice from an exquisite past'), regret at her absence together with remedies for this ('I'm terribly sorry you're not coming back. I see that the only thing for me is to come out to Spain to visit you', 'When you come back to London, if you ever do ...'), combined with oblique enquiries as to her current marital state ('that you are still alive and an autonomous unit', 'are you now an independent young lady', 'I am still unmarried and rapidly developing into a crusty but bibulous old bachelor'). Towards the end of that decade, when Gloria was already married and had children, the tone alters somewhat, and by 1950 in the last of the letters he informs her that 'I have a really enchanting girlfriend', signing off 'your humble constant and distant ... admirer, John.'[16]

Like my mother, my father Denis Brass lived the sort of life that might be described as 'ordinary'. Whilst a student he travelled in Germany during the mid-1930s, and witnessed there the rise and consolidation of Fascism.[17] In the early 1940s, when British Council Music Officer based in Portugal, he escorted Leslie Howard during the actor's visit, and put him on the plane home from Lisbon that was then shot down over the Bay of Biscay.[18] Later that same dec-

---

15 However, cultural incompatibility can only with difficulty be regarded as a cause for disagreement, since it is clear from the letters that cultural issues were a frequent topic of discussion between them.

16 The 'enchanting girlfriend' was Gabriella Oppenheimer, who became his wife in 1951 (Andrews, 2023b: 158).

17 In his papers was found the following note: 'Suffocating complacency about [the] risk of Hitler [who] tended to be regarded as a kind of Charlie Chaplin – few politicians read *Mein Kampf*. As a student in Germany during 1935, I became rapidly aware of the danger.' Interestingly, a year earlier, John Cairncross was also in Germany, and had come to exactly the same conclusion (Cairncross, 1997: 32): '[I] saw for myself, with alarm, Hitler's rise to power and the impact of his totalitarian imprint on the country.'

18 Since wartime Portugal was neutral, Lisbon was a place where spying was rife, as agents from the opposed combatants sought information from those fleeing European nations invaded by the Nazis. No individual or institution based there at the time can be said to have been uninvolved in this process.

ade he gave the first concert performance in Franco's Spain of Piano Concerto No. 1 by Alan Rawsthorne, which ended with a musical quotation from the Italian song *Bandiera Rossa*, closely associated with the defeated Spanish Republican cause. Throughout this period, Denis championed and translated into English the work of the Portuguese writer Miguel Torga, whose leftist publications were banned in his own country until the 1974 revolution.[19] All in all, a far from 'extraordinary' life.

II

Part of the Crowd

Just as the life of my parents might be described as 'ordinary', so too the same notion applies to me. At boarding school, I played cricket and rugby, drew cartoons, read books and (occasionally) wrote essays, in many respects no different from others there at the time. Whilst in the sixth form I indicated a wish to study ancient history at S (or scholarship) level, but the classics master – a priest – refused to teach me and another boy who also wanted to do this, giving as a reason that as neither of us had been in his class hitherto, we would undoubtedly fail the exam and thus bring down his success rate. Both of us continued to study on our own, my special subject being the Emperors Trajan and Hadrian, while his was the campaigns of Julius Caesar.[20] Not only did we pass the exam, but each did so with high marks, much better than those awarded to students taught ancient history by the classics master.

A year later, when on a visit to the school, I looked him up in order to pay my respects, and on entering his room noticed the honours board prominently displayed on his wall, listing all the names of students that he had taught who had done well in examinations. The most recent additions consisted of the

19 After a posting to Vienna during the late 1940s and early 1950s, my father left the British Council and taught in the Department of Spanish and Portuguese at Bristol University. For her part, my mother joined the Labour Party and became a local councillor in Bristol.

20 Although I studied ancient history on my own, reading books in local libraries, my father not only copied out sections from Mommsen but also took me to see a friend of his, Colin Hardie – who taught classics at Oxford and had been Director of the British School at Rome during the early 1930s when Mussolini was in power – for advice as to what I should read. Hardie recommended the *Social and Economic History of the Roman Empire* by Rostovtzeff, and when I asked (somewhat brashly) if I might borrow his copy, he reluctantly agreed, immediately and rather pointedly writing his own name on the front endpaper in order to emphasize that the book was his and he wanted it returned (which of course it was, after the exam).

names of the two S level candidates he had refused to teach, myself and the other student. The *sole* point of telling this story is that in a very real sense it presaged the kind of experiences I was to encounter later on in academic life, where those who were quick to dismiss concepts advanced by me about labour regime change and other things, soon afterwards incorporated these very same views into their own published work, invariably accompanied by claims either to have argued thus all along or to have 'discovered' them in the first place. A lesson taught and learned at school early on, indeed, but an important one about the sort of unmentioned dynamics often found in academia.

Like many others, I was politicized whilst an undergraduate at Essex University, a development evident in the cartoons drawn there, becoming part of what might be termed the generation of '68.[21] It is perhaps no accident that a number of those associated with the Angry Brigade in the early 1970s had been students at this particular institution, one of the 'new' universities.[22] At this period, in this place, two examples show the kind of political problems arising from what I drew, both of which attracted unwelcome attention from state agencies. The first concerns what was perhaps the cartoon that generated the most controversy whilst at Essex, one featuring the monarchy, entitled 'Not Standing Up for the Queen', and published in the *Manifesto of Rationalism* distributed during a revolutionary festival that took place on the university campus during the spring of 1969.[23] It was the subject of a front-page article in the *News of the World* condemning it as 'an objectionable cartoon of Prince Philip'.[24] Shortly after I was interviewed by two police officers, one an Inspector from Scotland Yard, who warned me that if I drew a similar cartoon in the future 'the whole system will be moving against you'.

The second example concerns what nearly happened to one of the Essex students (and me) in Spain that same year, where a group of us was attending

21 One of my cartoons, depicting a number of students and staff then at the university ('Some people who matter, and some who think they do'), has been reproduced in Pellew and Taylor (2020: 244, Figure 8).

22 On the direct action undertaken by the Angry Brigade against conservative, commercial, and corporate targets, see Anonymous (n.d.), and Christie (1980).

23 For obvious political reasons these days it is not possible to republish this particular cartoon, now considered too 'scurrilous' to be put on public display.

24 See 'A cartoon of Philip starts probe', *News of the World*, 16th February 1969. Among the expressions of moral outrage on the part of the journalist who wrote it were the following: '[The publication] was handed to me by a group of businessmen from the University town ... I saw the cartoon, which was in a distinctive style [and] passed my copy ... to one of Britain's top detectives, who ordered an immediate investigation ... [w]hen I tried to speak to ... the Vice-Chancellor of the University about the magazine though, I was told by a secretary that he did not want to discuss it'.

a language course at the University of Granada. When we attempted to engage Spanish students in a discussion about politics, the University rector summoned the police, and one of the group was arrested and held for questioning.[25] He featured in a cartoon I had made of him as a matador fighting a bull in the shape of Franco, the Spanish dictator. The rolled-up drawing of what was 'a highly scurrilous piece' was sticking out of his rucksack he had with him whilst in police custody awaiting deportation, and although never searched, would most probably have resulted in his imprisonment and my arrest had it been examined.[26]

III

A Life Not Led

The year 1971–72, between Essex undergraduate and Sussex postgraduate, was spent working as a cleaner at the Mermaid Theatre in London, a period during which I drew many cartoons, both of productions it put on and of persons employed there. Located in the city, by the side of the Thames, the Mermaid was the project of Bernard Miles and Josephine Wilson, both of whom had long careers in theatre and cinema, each having appeared in a Hitchcock film.[27] Although at the time I had considered – briefly – the possibility of drawing political cartoons as a career, it was clear to me that I was not good enough

25 Because he was putting up a wall poster containing the agenda for the political discussion, Chris Allen was the one who was arrested by the police. Also, part of the group was the poet Tom Raworth, who includes a (very) brief mention of this period in his autobiography (Raworth, 1969: 93–94).

26 In a message to the *Essex May 1968–30 Years On* reunion held in 1998, Chris Allen writes: 'Now Tom Brass – who was one of the Essex mob in Spain at the time – had done a poster-sized cartoon of Franco and me [and] Tom's loathing of the former was manifest in his [drawing that] was a highly scurrilous piece. The sort of work that would deeply upset the old dictator and his cronies. As I was led off, I could see the offending document still poking out of the top of the rucksack. I spent an anxious few hours … But it was OK. [The police] never did search my rucksack and, rather gratefully I boarded the plane.' As is outlined in Chapter 7 of this volume, overlooking items deemed by the authorities to be politically incriminating also happened to me in Peru during 1975.

27 Wilson was in *The Lady Vanishes* (1938), and Miles in *The Man Who Knew Too Much* (1956), both directed by Hitchcock. About the former Strachan (2023: 37) observes that 'Josephine found some work too [including] a small part she played [as] the enigmatic nun with the high heels under her habit in Hitchcock's *The Lady Vanishes*.' This is quite simply wrong: the part that Wilson had in the film was not the nun-in-high-heels (played by Catherine Lacey) but rather that of Madame Kummer, who is substituted for abducted Miss Froy (the lady who 'vanishes').

to do this, particularly given the quality produced by others then making a living from drawing cartoons professionally.[28] For this reason I continued on an academic path, applying to Sussex in order to do anthropological research on peasant economy and society, and from this point on I ceased to produce cartoons.

Among the drawings made at this time was one of Bernard Miles himself (see Appendix II/7), while the productions featured in cartoons included *Othello* and *Dick Turpin*. A propensity to want to be at the centre of any play at the Mermaid, regardless of the role he was playing or indeed the play itself, was a widely recognized characteristic of Miles, as of other actor/managers.[29] I saw evidence of this when he played Iago in the 1971 production of *Othello*, not least because in connection with the latter performance I drew a cartoon in which he featured as the central figure, a depiction which he liked so much – since it reflected his own importance to the play as he saw it – that he insisted on its being displayed in the Mermaid foyer (see Appendix II/5).

In order to boost ticket sales, Strachan reports that 'Bernard's keen sense of publicity' introduced a novel aspect into this production: that 'for the death-bed scene towards the close when Othello kills Desdemona the actress should be naked'.[30] Unsurprisingly, this generated moral outrage among the press, a response satirized by me in another cartoon which depicted the theatre logo as a mermaid of easy virtue (see Appendix II/6). Another cartoon was of the cast of *Dick Turpin* (see Appendix II/4): it, too, was put on display in the theatre, and part of that drawing accompanied a review of the production which appeared in the *Financial Times*.[31] In order to produce images of the players, I sat at the back of the auditorium during rehearsals, filling sketchpad pages with likenesses.[32]

It was clear, even then, from the frequency of meetings taking place in and around the theatre the focus of which was simply on raising money – at

---

28 It was clearly impossible for me to approach – let alone match – the brilliantly accomplished draughtsmanship of cartoonists like Gerald Scarfe, Steve Bell, Gary Trudeau, and Posy Simmonds.

29 On this see Strachan (2023: 64, 138), who refers to the fact that Bernard Miles always privileged – most often wrongly – his own ability to perform a role as 'misguided self-castings'.

30 Strachan (2023: 157–58).

31 See *Financial Times*, 15th December, 1971.

32 Actors depicted included Gary Raymond and Neil McCarthy, both of whom had appeared earlier in big budget film epics: Raymond in *El Cid* (1961), directed by Anthony Mann, and McCarthy in *Zulu* (1964), directed by Cy Endfield, and *Where Eagles Dare* (1968), directed by Brian G. Hutton.

the conclusion of which Bernard Miles would exit muttering furiously – that financial difficulties were on the horizon, and indeed in the following decade the site on which the Mermaid stood was sold off and repurposed, no longer functioning as the kind of theatre he wanted it to be.[33] Ironically, it was some of those on its own governing board – appointed by Miles – who thought the site better suited to commercial activity, an object in keeping with the rise and consolidation of Thatcherism, which underlines yet again what is a familiar problem: the folly of extending friendship to those who subsequently betray its trust. It is possible, as has been argued, to regard Bernard Miles as somewhat naïve for misrecognizing the attraction to capital of developing for alternative use a theatre site by the Thames.[34] Indeed, in his many radio and television monologues he adopted the persona and language of a rural ingénue, lacking the sophistication necessary for city life.[35]

The Ground Moves

At Sussex, the period late 1972 to early 1974 was spent following anthropological coursework, preparing for fieldwork in Peru; the latter would involve a participant/observation study of an agrarian cooperative in the lowland

33 There is contrast between the optimism expressed by most contributors to early publications addressing future prospects (Fay, *c.*1953; also contributions to The Mermaid Theatre Review), and the few pessimistic voices counselling wariness in dealings with the City. For the most part, optimists saw the main threat to its survival as coming not from the City but rather from television, an alternative form of popular culture that might undermine theatre-going. A more cautionary note was sounded by the film director Lindsay Anderson (1959: 107), who observed that '[t]he Welfare State has developed its decently-paid working class, who can afford and who deserve good theatre; but it has abandoned them to the potent mediocrity of television', and then warned that because '[g]overnments of Right and Left ... leave [culture] in the hands of profit-makers who [are] content to see theatres torn down', argued for the need 'to resist the pressure of commercialism and conformism alike'.

34 'In some ways', writes Strachan (2023: 182, 186–87), 'Bernard was something of an innocent. He believed that by and large people behaved well to each other. Always busy looking to the future at the theatre, he [failed to notice] that the City was now [in the 1980s] ruled by a breed utterly removed from [earlier] values ... It was a much more venal world, tougher and less sympathetic ... His belief was that the City ... had played an adroit but shady hand in the later years of the Mermaid.'

35 In keeping with pastoral images linked to the agrarian myth, Miles emphasized his connection to and love of the rural, observing (Strachan, 2023: 13, 45) that 'the country and all that belongs to it has run like a steel cord through everything I have done', as embodied in his 'countryman persona'. As noted elsewhere (Brass, 2021: 18–19, 23), this identity is evident also in the film he directed, *Tawny Pipit* (1944).

Amazonian area of the Department of Cuzco.[36] In order to conduct research in that country, it was necessary periodically to renew visa and other forms of documentation, which entailed returning from the field and visiting the British Embassy in the Miraflores area of Lima. The Embassy itself was located on the sixth floor of a skyscraper, and on top the building was a huge neon sign for Philips electronics. To one side was a two-lane highway linking the city centre with the southern suburbs, down the centre of which ran a pedestrian causeway planted with tall palm trees that were home to a sizeable population of parakeets, the constant screeching of which almost drowned out the noise of the heavy traffic. At nine in the morning on the 3rd October, 1974, having completed my visit to the Embassy, I crossed onto the central reservation between the two-lane highway where it immediately became evident that all the birds in the trees there had fallen silent.

Within seconds a subterranean rumble was followed by the ground shaking, an earthquake that registered 8.1 in terms of magnitude.[37] Managing with difficulty to keep my balance, I saw the Embassy building swaying from side to side, as was the neon sign on its top. Paving stones on the pavement opposite were hurled up in the air by continuous seismic waves travelling the length of the road network. Screams could be heard in the distance. The earthquake lasted for about six seconds, and was over almost as soon as it had begun. I began to walk back towards the centre of Lima, since no traffic appeared to be moving anywhere. Further along the highway, there was a large crater right down the centre of the road. Far away, screaming could still be heard. Once in the city centre, I joined a large queue of people telephoning family or friends to confirm that they had survived.

Earlier that morning the bus on which I was travelling had passed through the village which – four hours later – became the epicentre of the earthquake. Some two hundred persons – mostly in the shanty towns round the outskirts of Lima – lost their lives. The military government made light of the earthquake, and the newspapers next day carried headlines proclaiming that even the earth shook before the revolutionary government (the military had seized

---

36 It was originally intended to conduct fieldwork in rural Chile, examining the agrarian reform programme of President Allende and its impact on the peasantry, but the 1973 coup put an end to that.

37 As reported by the US Geological Survey Earthquakes Hazards Programme, and published in 'Historic Earthquakes: Peru 1974, October 03', *Earthquake Information Bulletin*, Volume 7, Number 2 (March–April 1975).

power some years before, claiming to be a revolutionary new regime).[38] The birds went quiet, I was told later, because – unlike humans – they sensed what was coming. Of all the destabilizing occurrences that might befall one, therefore, the least expected is that underfoot the earth itself will move.

IV

Perhaps It's Some Political Thing[39]

As for episodes drawn from my time spent in academia, these have frequently been referenced in what I have already published, mostly as asides located in the footnotes. For the rest, it is sufficient to record that this time has been devoted to consolidating and building on views formulated in the 1980s about the agrarian question – broadly speaking, what happens to the peasantry in a developing economy, how and why. From that point on, my focus extended to include not just the pattern of accumulation in rural sector of Third World countries (Latin America, India), the differentiation of the peasantry, the formation/consciousness/struggle based on class, plus the emergence of new social movements, but also the link between capitalism and unfree production relations, the globalization of the industrial reserve, the populist/nationalist response to this in Europe and the US, the political and ideological effect of leftist entry into academic posts, the displacement of Marxist theory by the identity politics of the cultural turn, together with what connected them all.[40]

This has involved following the trajectory begun by Marx, via Lenin and Trotsky (among others), through the modernization approach and culminating in the 'cultural turn', formulating both a theory about the way peasants do (or do not) change, and what this implies for the way capitalism itself develops. It entails drawing a contrast between Marxism, which has in the main argued that peasants must be differentiated into their separate class elements – that is, into rich, middle and poor components – each of which in economic

38 Other events connected with fieldwork in Peru, but not examined here, include my arrest, imprisonment, and ultimately expulsion from the country in April 1975, an episode the details of which are recounted elsewhere (Brass, 2017: Chapter 14).

39 Said by Gilbert, one of the two main protagonists in Hitchcock's film *The Lady Vanishes* (1938), just as the MacGuffin is about to be revealed.

40 On peasants in Latin America and India, see the volumes edited by Brass (1995, 2003). Of additional significance is the way agrarian myth discourse has in the past structured and continues still to inform both film and travel writing, on which see Brass (2014: Parts 2 and 3; 2023b: Part II).

and political terms possesses not merely distinct but antagonistic identities and interests, and current variants of non-Marxist (and even anti-Marxist) approaches. The latter, in the shape mainly of the 'new' populist postmodernism (underpinned epistemologically by the agrarian myth), tends to view rural petty commodity producers as an undifferentiated economic category wanting only cultural empowerment.

Of my two main arguments, the first concerned the acceptability to capitalism of labour-power that was not free.[41] Evidence from Latin America and India suggested agribusiness enterprises, commercial farmers and rich peasants reproduced, introduced or reintroduced unfree relations. Such workforce restructuring involved replacing free labour with unfree equivalents, a procedure frequently resorted to by employers. This labour process decomposition/recomposition was labelled by me deproletarianization, a concept based on Marxist theory about class struggle. Its object was to discipline and cheapen labour-power, an undeniable economic advantage in a global context where capitalist producers had to become increasingly cost-conscious in order to remain competitive. Following on from the adoption of the Green Revolution in the Third World, coupled with labour market deregulation in metropolitan capitalist nations, workforce restructuring benefitted from the capacity of producers to draw on a burgeoning industrial reserve army.

To some degree, the second argument concerned the political and ideological effects of these same economic developments. Among them has been the rise in Western capitalist nations of populism/nationalism, a change accompanied – not to say abetted – by the academic shift away from Marxist theory and towards postmodernism.[42] The latter approach privileged the non-economic identity of the subject, recasting peasant economy as a form of cultural empowerment, ignoring the fact that large numbers of rural cultivators separated by capital from their means of labour were on an increasing scale joining the ranks of the global industrial reserve army. By not addressing the wider systemic logic – that of continued accumulation – advocates of non-class identity as empowering overlooked the implications of this process. Among

41 Empirical and theoretical details of the case about the acceptability to capitalists of labour-power that is unfree, a process of restructuring conceptualized as deproletarianisation, has been presented in numerous articles, and is summarized in two monographs (Brass, 1999; 2011) and my contributions to two edited volumes (Brass and van der Linden, 1997; Brass, 2010b).

42 The rise of nationalism and populism, together with their links to the emergence/consolidation within academia of postmodernism, is covered in Brass (2000b, 2014, 2017: Ch. 18, 2018, 2021) and my contributions to the volume edited by Fasenfest (2022: Chapters 7 and 13).

the developments such non-Marxist approaches failed to anticipate, therefore, were the political effects of the impact on advanced capitalist economies of a burgeoning industrial reserve army, fuelling the rise there of populist and far right ideology.

Strong Opinions, Strongly Held

Political engagement and in my case its accompanying institutional difficulties, stemmed from challenging two of the main orthodoxies – semi-feudalism, the cultural turn – in the development community. These orthodoxies, held by many on the academic left, consisted of dual claims, each of which dominated theory about emerging patterns of agrarian change in Third World countries. Of these orthodoxies, the first insisted that, as it penetrated the rural sector in such contexts, capital would replace labour that was unfree with free equivalents. Unfree production relations, said to belong to the pre-capitalist past, were consigned by many leftist academics to history, and for the most part forgotten. However, the class struggle argument based on deproletarianisation effectively wrong-footed analyses that agrarian capitalists replaced – not retained, let alone actively sought out – production relations that were unfree. The irony of unfree labour-power increases accompanying the global expansion both of *laissez-faire* policies and of the industrial reserve will not be lost on any Marxist.

Whereas historically an ability to conduct struggle 'from above' – one favouring capital over labour – has been restricted to particular national contexts, with the onset of globalization, and a concomitant decrease in skill levels required of workers coupled with an increase in the source and quantity of the industrial reserve in a context where capitalism itself is deregulated, employers are now able to access labour world-wide. In such circumstances, racism can and does arise where capital draws on this enhanced reserve army, generating acute competition for jobs between workers of different ethnic/national identity. This sort of rivalry is itself fostered by employers for two reasons: to maintain or enhance profitability when competing with other producers in the market; and in order to pre-empt or prevent the emergence or consolidation of consciousness based on class, a solidarity which might threaten the ownership/control of the means of production/distribution/exchange currently enjoyed by capital.

When unfree production relations were discovered to be alive and well in the midst of capitalism itself, therefore, the implausible response was either to redefine them as free labour, or to claim that such 'anomalies' would quickly be sought out and then abolished by the state. Having been decoupled from capitalism, and then recoupled to the latter by the Marxist class struggle argument (= deproletarianization), the issue of unfree labour was then recaptured by revisionists who again linked its eradication to capital, maintaining that a benign state apparatus could be relied on to eliminate such production relations. This view was itself linked to the second orthodoxy, which maintained that the most effective struggle against capitalism was not (as Marxists argued) based on class and revolutionary agency designed to bring about socialism, but rather (as postmodernists maintained) based on non-class identities – including ethnicity and nationality. For those in the latter categories, emancipatory agency (by what were claimed to be 'new' social movements) involved nothing more than quotidian resistance, the object being either a return to a non-capitalist social order or the realization of a benign (= 'kinder'/'nicer') form of accumulation.

Even if we on the political left have learned nothing else, therefore, one unavoidably clear issue nowadays is that there is no reality that capital does not – and will not – attempt to turn to its own advantage, and thus adjust to, in order to generate profit. It is perhaps no more than a sign of the times that it is still necessary to point out that it is not the task of socialists (and progressives more generally) to assist in this endeavour, by making it easier for capitalism as a system to survive and prosper. Yet it is precisely this that academic opponents of *laissez-faire* seek to do when calling not for a transcendence of capitalism but rather only for a return to a 'nicer', more 'caring' sort of accumulation. Coming to terms with capitalism in this fashion is evident throughout development studies. Among the more implausible arguments made by its exponents are: that the solution to *laissez-faire* is a return to a more benign pattern of accumulation; that capital can and will eradicate unfree labour; that immigration is simply an issue of human rights and citizenship, unconnected with either the industrial reserve, labour market competition, or accumulation; and that where populism is concerned, as well as a 'nasty' version there is also a 'nicer' variant, which ought to be supported politically.

To challenge any or all these revisionist orthodoxies in the name of revolutionary Marxism has been accompanied by difficulties. Advocating a more radical interpretation of economic development, and no longer confining it simply to what occurred in Third World nations, was at the time not a popular view to hold, not least because it did not fit the prevailing narrative. Hence the alarm of some in the development community when not just unfree production relations, but also the industrial reserve, the agrarian myth, and populism itself – phenomena that in intellectual terms had been overlooked or downplayed where the study of capitalism was concerned – resurfaced in the midst of capitalism. Unsurprisingly, perhaps, Marxists who challenged such orthodoxies and their exponents were subject to many complaints on the part of those criticized, hostility that contributed in my own case to an enforced departure both from Cambridge and from editing *The Journal of Peasant Studies*.[43]

Conclusion

Outlined in this chapter are personal trajectories as part of a crowd, located within particular historical collectivities, either during wartime in the case of my parents or in education and employment in my case. Just as both the former were affected politically by the Civil War in Spain and the 1939–45 World War, so I was a product of the late 1960s student movement. For the most part these trajectories are composed of non-triumphant episodes designated 'ordinary', lives situated within – and more often than not on the fringes of – a wider agency exercised by different kinds of crowd. Common to each of these trajectories is that the focus moves from the self to the context, and how this has shaped the life of its subject: my mother whose encounter with John Cairncross took place whilst he was providing the Soviet Union with information that had an impact on the outcome of the war against fascism; similarly, in the course of postings abroad my father saw at first hand the rise of fascism in Germany and Iberian peninsula, leading to his championing the work of a Portuguese leftist.

Where my personal trajectory is concerned, what is an ordinary life has entailed a twofold shift in focus: from cartooning to academia, and a corresponding transfer of political difficulties encountered as a result from what is drawn to what is written. The latter involved examining the way the capitalist labour regime changed, together with the kinds of contradictions arising from this: the connection between on the one hand employer preference not for free but for unfree production relations when restructuring of their labour process; and on the other the rise of populism as the political and ideological effect of a globally expanding industrial reserve army. Accordingly, along with others, the

43 Details about these enforced departures are set out in Brass (2015; 2017: Ch. 6). As suggested by the epigraph, the political obstacle to university employment consists in what for institutional authority and senior academics is an unacceptable combination: strong opinions strongly held. A situation in which strong opinions are weakly held, however, do not pose the same danger (strong + strong = x), since this combination (strong + weak = ✓) offers for them the acceptable prospect of such opinions either not being defended strongly or else abandoned. The latter position was expressed more succinctly by Groucho Marx: 'Those are my principles, and if you don't like them ... well, I have others.'

rationale for what I publish has been akin to conducting a rearguard action in academia, defending Marxism from varieties of revisionism; it is a task, moreover, which at the present conjuncture has not been an easy one.

Appendix 1: Correspondence with John Cairncross, 1940s[44]

31st December 1941 from 409 Keyes House, Dolphin Square, SW1, addressed to Miss Gloria Barraclough, HM Embassy, Madrid, by diplomatic bag.[45]

I hope nothing has happened to prevent your light and joyous pen turning out the amusing letters which are the only solace of my aged days – and nights.

I have gone on toasting my toes in front of the fire until they were done to exactly the right colour. Too bad you weren't there to see them! In fact as a certain poetisa mejicana says:[46]

Mas¿cuando (¡ay gloria mia!)
Mereceré gozar tu luz serena?
¿cuándo llegará el día
Que pongas dulce fin a tanta pena?
¿cuando veré tus ojos, dulce encanto,
y de los mios quitarás el llanto?

Life is quite agreeable here, but deadly dull. What's wanted is something, or more accurately, some one with feeling[,] perversity humour temper, temperament [,] sweetness, ferocity, and a whole host of other plants that don't seem to thrive in our norther climate.

I am shortly to have my peaceful existence changed. In April [1942] I am to be called up and then I will be whisked away into the country to become

44 Text not included is signalled thus: ..., while text that is indecipherable is indicated thus: [...]

45 In his book Cairncross (1997: 90) explains that he 'decided, for safety from bombing and air-raids, to move to a modern flat in Dolphin Square, overlooking the Thames.'

46 The quotation is an extract from the poem by Sor Juana Inés de la Cruz (1651–1695), composer, philosopher, and nun, the English translation of which reads as follows:
But, when (o glory mine!)
Will I deserve to enjoy your serene light?
When comes the day
That you put an end sweetly to such pain?
When will I see the sweet enchantment of your eyes,
That take away the tears from mine?

a soldier ... and will be doing special work. I am not at all unhappy at the prospect.

Well what about a short note reestablishing diplomatic relations, and incidentally informing me that you are still alive and an autonomous unit ... All my love, write soon, John.

•••

17th April 1944, from 16 Lansdowne Court, Lansdowne Crescent, W11, addressed to Miss Gloria Barraclough, Instituto Britanico, Calle de Méndez Nuñez 17, Madrid.

Dearest Gloria,

I was more than delighted to receive your exquisite telegram, and if I haven't replied earlier it is partly because I felt that it would be easier for you to decipher my abominable writing in sunny spring weather and partly because I thought I'd better wait till I got the long letter you promised me. I'm sure that you're still writing it and that it is now very long indeed, so that I look forward all the more to receiving it.

In the meantime this is just to tell you that I'm still in existence and that partly because it's spring, partly because the world situation is so much more favourable, but most of all because writing to you seems to have some magical effect on me, I feel much less subhuman than I've done since 1937. 1937 – it seems a long way off, doesn't it. Heaven, by comparison with the events of the past seven years, and, alas a heaven that we, like most people, didn't fully appreciate at the time. Would we have broken off, I wondered if we had known what was coming, it was a very great loss to me, even though I still kept in touch with your sunny personality through the medium of correspondence – such charming correspondence. I've still got your letters. They have a lightness, a vivacity and a joie de vivre (with its complementary – a rather pensive melancholy) which recent history has just blotted out completely.

I'm terribly sorry you're not coming back. I see that the only thing for me is to come out to Spain to visit you and that I hope to do within about a year's time since I'm quite confident the war in Europe will be over by then, and I'm thirsting to get a sight of the old continent again.

These last four years have been hard, exhausting, often depressing but they've been a magnificent experience and most of us have come out of them tired but tougher, more rigorous and more humble than we went in.

How have your own affairs (*not* as you used to spell it affaires) been going? Still at the same job? Still with the same relatives? Or are you now an independent young lady? I should so like to know.

It won't be long till your birthday comes around again. Heartiest congratulations in advance. Perhaps it would be as well to wish you a merry Xmas too. One can never be too careful these days when postage is 2½, and Xmas cards are lousy anyway.

Do write to me soon, dearest Gloria. It is such a pleasure to hear from you – a fresh voice from an exquisite past although the recipient is a bit musty and senile.

I enclose a little poem inspired by the reminiscences of years ago. It's practically impersonal. So don't judge it too severely. *Do* write soon. All my love, John.

To Gloria

Nocturne
The dusk has not yet come
Nor the sun set.
The time for rest and sleep
Is not there yet.
The warm all seeing light
Flows through the air
Crowds stirring, sounds of life
Are everywhere

But night drops noiselessly
– more exquisite
Than song or woman's touch
The peace of it.
Then the hard outlines fade
Bright sorrows set
When the time comes for sleeping
Sleep and forget.

John C.

•••

19th September 1944, from 16 Lansdowne Court, Lansdowne Crescent, W11, addressed to Miss Gloria Barraclough, Paseo de Gracia 35, Barcelona.

Dearest Gloria,

I am horrified to see from the date of your last letter how slow I have been in replying to it. I should have liked to reply at once for, if you like receiving letters from me, I am even more delighted to hear from you, especially as one letter is more enchanting than the previous one.

Unfortunately life has not been easy these last few months, with flying bombs etc and there has not been much time for quiet correspondence. Things are better now and the arrears of letters are declining at least the priority arrears such as letters to you.

I envy you your holiday in the Basque country.[47] From such knowledge as I have of them, the Basques (both French and Spanish) seem to be a remarkable people. They must have had tremendous tenacity to retain their language. You know that apart from Etruscan (the language spoken in Florence before the Romans conquered the country) Basque is the only pre Indo European language known in Europe. ...

When you come back to London, if you ever do, you will not find it much changed. Even now the lights are going up again, the scars are healing over and most of the old places remain – and by then the USA and other allied soldiers which are at present such a frequent sight, will have removed to other theatres of war.

I expect you relish your independence more in Spain than you would here since, especially since the outbreak of war, young persons have had to look after and to look out for themselves much more than before.

As you say our friendship must have struck deep roots. It is interesting to speculate what would have happened had I met you after you had had a taste of life on your own and I had developed a rather more understanding attitude to various aspects of life. It is probable that we might have understood each other much better instead of colliding as we did. But again it is possible that your views, which I deeply respect, would have precluded closer relations.

Whatever that may be I am very moved at being still remembered and can only assure you that the feeling is reciprocal. ...

I am sure that Rilke is much the greatest German poet. I dislike his metaphysical stuff but his other poems are magnificent – and unfortunately quite untranslateable. The only other poet in German who is comparable (apart from Goethe) is Holderlin. I doubt though if he would appeal to you.

Hopkins I am not so fond of. He was unquestionably a poet of the very highest gifts but he is too rugged and terse for me. He has none of Rilke's liquidity even in his (R's) most involved passages.

47 Gloria used to visit the Basque country where her godfather, Julio Caro Baroja (1914–1995), whose family home, Itzea, was in the village of Vera de Bidasoa, in Navarra. An anthropologist, he was the nephew of the novelist Pio Caro Baroja (1872–1956), a member of the generation of '98.

Yeats is naturally much closer to me. He is a fellow Celt, and I like his Celtic twilight poems (in the earlier period) 'I will arise and go now' etc and his more sinewy vigorous stark poems of the later period ('For it's much more fun in going naked') his luscious trappings.[48]

I'm ashamed to say I haven't read any poetry for months but I'm determined to do so now that I've at last (after 3 years of this useless life) to get down to it.

The only thing I've done during these years has been to learn Russian. I can now struggle through some of the Russian lyricists which are quite outstanding. There is a poem by Lermontov for example about the white sail [:]

> But he, the restless one,
> Seeks the storms
> As if in the storms it were
> To find peace.

There too I am hoping to extend my reading and really plunge into the better known authors.

I must end now as it is getting late. Tomorrow I must get my day's work done in the morning as I am taking half of my weekly free day off to see The Marriage of Figaro.

Do write soon. The well known writing never fails to gladden my heart. Love, John.

•••

27th October 1947, from Lansdowne Court, Lansdowne Crescent W11, addressed to Mrs D Brass, Mount Alvernia Nursing Home, Guilford, Surrey. [original emphases]

Dear Gloria,

This is just a very brief note to offer you my congratulations on the arrival of son no 2. There was no need for me to look for your name inside – I recognized the familiar handwriting at once. I'm sure *you* can't decipher *my* familiar handwriting straight away! ... I am still unmarried and rapidly developing into a crusty but bibulous old bachelor! Love John.

•••

---

48 The references are to W.B. Yeats, 1889, 'The Lake Isle of Innisfree', *The Wanderings of Oisin and Other Poems*, London: Kegan, Paul, Trench & Co., and 'A Coat', 1914, *Poetry*, where the line reads 'For there's more enterprise / in walking naked.'

31st January 1950, from 16 Lansdowne Court, Landsdowne Crescent, W11, no envelope.

Dear Gloria,

It's a bit late in the year to answer your simpatico Xmas card but I took a good New Year's resolution to improve my handwriting and it took at least a month for it to wear off. ... it wouldn't have been fair, either to your intuitive powers of decipherment or to old times to write to you in any other than my normal hand.

So you're in Wien,... I'm sure you really like Vienna as much as you liked all the other places. At least it isn't middle class and people's sense of colour (especially as regards [...]) is pretty good.

Life here is (a) more normal (that's to say one no longer meets dirt and is [...] a lot of the little annoyances of the poorly structured security austerity economy of 1947–48) and (b) more exciting (I have [...] but exacting job on Western Union military coordination, and have more energy and time to go out and about and enjoy life). And I have a really enchanting girl friend who, however, is probably going off to America for a time at least.

Well, well, *im seben gecht alles variber*, but not I think for you (after all, Brass is a durable material) and though you may love change, I'm sure you enjoy stability, too.[49] Upon which high or low philosophical ending I sign myself, dear lady, your humble constant and distant if illegible admirer, John.

Appendix II: Cartoons

Presented here is a selection of cartoons drawn by me over the four-year period from 1967 when at Essex University to 1971 whilst employed as a cleaner at the Mermaid Theatre, after which I ceased altogether to draw. Those produced at university were published in a variety of student magazines (Wyvern, Ginger), whereas the Mermaid ones have not been published before. Of the eight cartoons reproduced here, three were drawn at Essex (Figures 1–3), and five at the Mermaid (Figures 4–8).

One of the Essex drawings portrays the Duke of Edinburgh (Figure 3), who had complained that the monarchy was poorer than thought, giving a message to impoverished inhabitants of Africa. Two of the others feature David Triesman, a prominent student leader at the university in the late 1960s, depicting him as a sheep in wolf's clothing (Figure 1) and subsequently heading a

49 Translates into English as 'in fact everything changes'.

Parliamentary Commission into student unrest in 1984 (Figure 2). The latter was drawn in May 1969 and to some degree anticipated what was to happen some three and a half decades later, as Triesman followed a familiar rightwards political trajectory. Subsequently a businessman and member of the House of Lords, Baron Triesman held political office in the 'New Labour' government of Tony Blair, and then resigned from the Labour Party radicalised under the Corbyn leadership.

Cartoons done at the Mermaid Theatre were all drawn during 1971, and feature the casts of *Dick Turpin* (Figure 4) and *Othello* (Figure 5), both of which were playing there at that time. Another drawing shows Desdemona pictured as a wanton mermaid (Figure 6), an image that incorporates the theatre logo, and refers to the scandalised press coverage over the appearance in *Othello* of a naked Desdemona. Also portrayed in separate drawings are the actors Bernard Miles (Figure 7) and his wife Josephine Wilson (Figure 8).

FIGURE 1 Mirror, mirror on the wall, who is the fiercest of them all? (Wyvern, 16th February 1968)

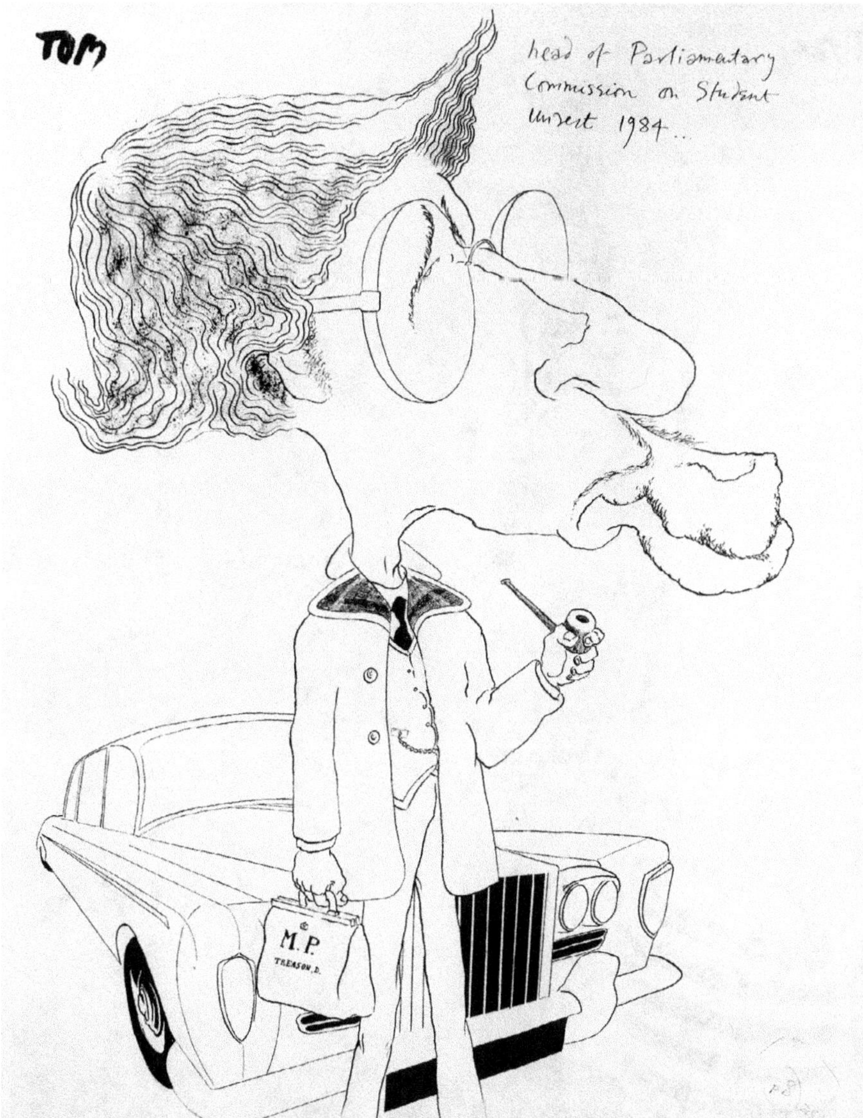

FIGURE 2 Head of Parliamentary Commission on Student Unrest 1984 (Wyvern, 9th May 1969)

FIGURE 3 Message from the new poor to the old poor
(Wyvern, 28th November 1969)
© TOM BRASS

FIGURE 4 Cast of *Dick Turpin* at the Mermaid Theatre, Christmas 1971
© TOM BRASS

FIGURE 5 *Othello* at the Mermaid Theatre, 1971
© TOM BRASS

FIGURE 6 Desdemona, or the Scarlet Lady of Puddle Dock as seen by Fleet Street, September 1971

FIGURE 7 Bernard Miles at Saint Olave, Hart Street, London, 14th October 1971
© TOM BRASS

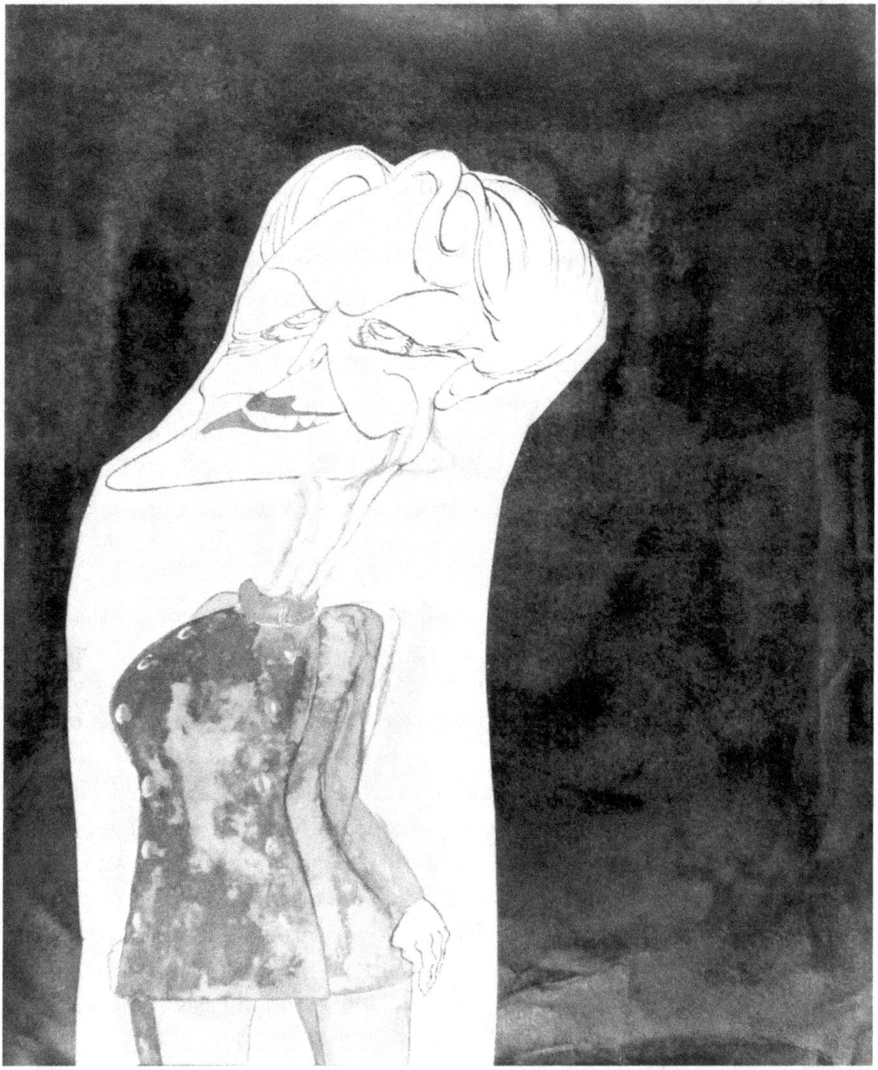

FIGURE 8 Josephine Wilson, Mermaid Theatre 1971
© TOM BRASS

Conclusion

Recent history reveals a congruence between what Marx and Marxism long ago said could not be avoided, and what indeed has occurred. It is possible, therefore, to trace a pattern behind the unfolding capitalist crisis, one that emerged from the 1980s deregulation of labour and capital markets. A result of accumulation combined with depeasantisation was an upsurge in the global industrial reserve, as an effect of competition between producers was the search for cheaper labour, in the form either of outsourced employment abroad or insourced migrants to metropolitan capitalism. In the latter contexts, grassroots reaction against enhanced labour market competition empowered populism electorally, leading to the imposition of tariffs in order to 'bring back jobs' in the name of protecting working class livelihoods. Not the least of the many ironies structuring this trajectory is that the connection between its different components has remained unrecognized by many in academia, including by self-proclaimed Marxists.

Leftist opposition to open-door borders as a way capitalism accessed the industrial reserve was not merely absent but, in some instances, supportive of this policy in the name of empowering the migrant 'other'. Lacking support from this end of the political spectrum, workers increasingly backed a nationalist discourse framed by populist calls to halt immigration so as to safeguard employment, in effect splitting what might otherwise take the form of class solidarity uniting local and migrant components of the workforce. However, the populist claim to represent national interests by combining labour and capital in the same political movement, taking the side of 'the people', is destined to fail. Where profitability and even survival are concerned, a contradiction arises between the interests of business which depend on continued access to ever cheaper sources of labour-power, and those of the working class, who want less not more labour market competition.

This in turn highlights the significance for Marxism of the potential divide between the individual and the crowd, and the distinction between the self as outside the crowd and as part of this collectivity. Accordingly, where personal histories are concerned, there is a difference in the kind of narrative examined in the early chapters of this volume, and that encountered in the later ones. The historical pursuit by the self of an identity that is 'extraordinary' constitutes an individual quest encouraged by and to the advantage of capitalism, embodied conceptually in paradigms such as rational choice theory and economic man. Linked to the myth of upward mobility, an escape from class, it eschews the broader collective designation and its forms of political consciousness and solidarity. In the world of capitalism, therefore, one is drawn into the discourse of difference, a shedding of an ordinariness shared with those possessing a similar identity and its replacement with a selfhood that transcends the ordinary, one which confers a distinctiveness that proclaims a not-belonging to a previous category. 'I am not as others', this narrative asserts, or alternatively 'I am not what I was', claims it is inferred that stem from – and are an effect of – individual achievement.

Valorized thereby is not just the latter but also labour market competition and its form of material rewards. A case, perhaps, of 'because I'm worth it'. A discourse mobilized especially by bourgeois politicians wishing to project a commonality of origin with the masses, yet at the same time a transcendence of this, it reproduces and privileges the notion that a benign accumulation does not exclude the possibility of plebeian empowerment, by ceasing to be plebeian. It is an ideological trope that misleadingly proclaims, 'I am still as ordinary as – and thus no different from – all the rest of you', an ill-disguised but politically effective form of special pleading the object of which is to gain public support. This ideologically seductive narrative holds out the prospect of ceasing to be ordinary, conditional on striving and individual achievement, all objectives supportive of capitalism. However, such a declaration of difference, of no longer being part of a crowd, is itself conditional on not challenging the logic of the accumulation system itself.

Emphasis on the redeeming and innate features of individual achievement and status helps indict those who are perceived as not conforming to these empowering drives. Hence the characterization of anyone who does adhere to them as 'ordinary', and consequently in some sense as lacking, deserving labels such as 'feckless', 'lazy', and generally being without motivation. The same kind of narrative structures the proclamation of ethnic or national difference within a wider population, the basis of an identity politics now deemed progressive and empowering. Recuperation of what are claimed to be historically innate and enduring forms of 'otherness', is part of this same process, a rising above – and thus dissolution of – the crowd, in order to form another one, based on non-class identity that is exclusionary and invariably opposed to socialism.

Rather than separation from the crowd of the 'extraordinary' individual, therefore, Marxism instead embraces the 'ordinary' as located within and represented by the crowd. This, it could be argued, is not negated but expressed by a consciousness of class. In this form, and for this reason, the agency of the crowd becomes the sort of political action feared by the bourgeois as that of the revolutionary mob-in-the-streets. Conceptualized here is an 'ordinariness' that does not entail reproducing a subordinate position based on class: insofar as its form of agency prefigures a socialist transition, being and remaining 'ordinary' cannot be an endorsement of apolitical stasis. Nor is it the kind of celebration advocated by exponents of the 'new' populist postmodernism: that of 'otherness', or the identity politics that divides the crowd once formed, and sends its different components off along distinct paths, in what are ultimately incompatible directions. Many of those going down the identity politics route want not to overturn the capitalist system, but only a better deal within it: consequently, disassembling the crowd on these lines opens the door to claims that class has to wait until non-class identities have been fully empowered, at best postponing class empowerment, at worst cancelling it.

It is not without significance, therefore, that non-Marxist responses to the onward march of laissez-faire capitalism tend to take one of two forms. On the one hand, an inclusionary variant, which advocates political mobilisation based on the idea of everyone-against-neoliberalism. On the other, by contrast, is an exclusionary variant, which supports the notion of opting out based on identity politics: that is, the individual ceases to be part of the larger crowd. Since a concept of struggle founded on class is absent from both responses, neither version backs a progressive transcendence of capitalism as a system, in the form of a socialist transition. Marxism opposes abandoning – as so many do these days – class as no longer a basis either for politics or for mobilization.

Without class, the position becomes unity and agency by all those opposed to some vague notion of an out-there capitalism, which in effect advocates a unity between categories with political and economic interests that are not just different but antagonistic. So many attempts at mobilization which start from this premise quickly fragment along class lines, as – for example – rich peasants who as tenants originally fought alongside labourers against landlords quickly turn against their erstwhile allies once they have secured property rights to their holdings. Such instances have been recorded in India and Peru, and despite attention being drawn to this difficulty many of those who claim to be on the left simply ignore the problem, expressing bafflement about the breakup of anti-landlord alliances.

Much the same is true of current attempts similarly to mobilize under a single umbrella of 'all-against-neoliberalism', which likewise overlooks that such movements have been historically and continue to be the anti-capitalism of the political right. They include not just workers (for whom socialism is the objective) but also better-off farmers, rich peasants, and even small capitalists, all of whom are opposed to worker empowerment and (of course) socialism, and want nothing more than to do away with rival producers who out-compete them in the world market. Hence the rise and consolidation of populism, an ideology which encourages and caters for just such a mobilisation: namely, employers and workers who share a particular nationality or ethnicity opposing capital that is 'foreign'. Progressives have been here so many times before, and it seems are fated to do so again and again, until they – including the 'left' – realize finally the folly of going down this path.

In the case of the exclusionary variant, an identity as projected by the diasporic subject becomes a portable identity, one that informs the ideological, political, and economic framework of postmodern theory, and as such is taken from the past and studiously applied not only to all as-yet unknown futures but also to every historical conjuncture and geographical place. Among the unresolved difficulties confronting this non-ethnographic form of renunciation advocated is what 'authenticity', from what specific epoch of the past, and not wanting to be part of 'the Empire' yet cherishing a current position within it as a writer. Insofar as 'integration' is seen as a step on the path to modernity, therefore, both are elements in the same rejected process. History beyond the confines of 'otherness', of the barbarian, has no place in this discourse, since the process of becoming is seen as a loss of barbarian identity, and thus a negative development to be resisted. Consequently, history which is not barbarian has neither relevance nor much that is positive to teach, from which the 'other' can benefit, can learn.

Political mobilisation as the 'other', which excludes those plebeian components who do not share this identity, departs fundamentally from Marxism ('the white saviour') which advocates grassroots agency based on *class*, and makes no distinction between those of different ethnicities or nationalities as long as they hold the same economic position in the labour process. In effect, therefore, the innateness of difference, together with its non-transcendent nature, suggests the impossibility of a dialectical synthesis (white + non-white unite and fight against capitalism and its *class* structure) in the struggle against 'the Empire'. Not the least of the many difficulties with this exclusionary approach is the inference that the barbarian 'other' is an homogenous category, undifferentiated in terms of division of labour and class position, as such all regarded and treated in the same oppressive manner, whereas this is not so. Unlike 'others' who are simply wealthy, or occupy a privileged location in the class hierarchy (writers, film makers, etc.), those of the same identity in lower socio-economic positions are indeed viewed as 'acting out the desires of the primitive', a pejorative description applied to a category that includes whites as well as non-whites.

Another version of this argument criticizes the rise of identitarian discourse, but this is attributed solely to the political right, omitting from the critique those purportedly leftists endorsing the same identity politics. Here the problem is that the left appears to mean simply 'groups below', which are not necessarily leftist. Avoided thereby is an indication of where the left that ought to be indicted for this identitarianism is actually located: in academia, where discourse about the nature of victimhood and desired empowerment has indeed shifted, from class to race. There is where the main problem is located, in the rise and rise of the 'new' populist postmodernism and the consequent abandonment – with very few exceptions – by the left of a class-based political narrative. Because this is not addressed, its significance is missed.

Where leftist politics are concerned, therefore, it is an argument that has done this cause no good by telling us only part of the story – that the right attacks the working class, which we already know, and missing out an analysis, and thus also a critique, of what these days passes for leftist politics. The latter requires examining both why academic debate shifted from class to race, together with its impact on the wider debate (in the media, politics), and why that shift occurred in the first place: that is, the post-1960s entry by leftists into academic jobs, where continued adherence to Marxist theory and politics was an obstacle to advancement. From this stemmed the subsequent embrace of postmodernism, which was a safe way of presenting an oppositional discourse, and its privileging of non-class identity, ethnic/national 'otherness' especially. That is where the main problem can be found – the age-old role of intellectuals in society, and how they frame debate that has an impact on politics and policy. Of no social science discipline is this more true than in the case of social anthropology, and its form of practice: fieldwork.

Far from being a triumphal onward march, fieldwork – much like life itself – is a messy process, frequently daunting in terms of the political difficulties it entails. The move away from empiricism or the colonial origin of the ethnographer as problem, the focus of critique turned to the ethnic/national/cultural identity of the voice speaking or the gaze looking. This change, starting in the post-war era, gathering momentum in the 1960s development decade, became more pronounced still with the onset of the 1980s 'cultural turn'. Where fieldwork is concerned, therefore, nothing is so predictable as that an attack on its logic at this last conjuncture emanated from postmodern exponents; given their privileging of 'otherness', any description of the latter obtained as a result of a gaze by a social anthropologist who did not share this identity was viewed as illegitimate and dismissed as inauthentic.

The first step in this process was usually to declare the very notion fieldwork itself as invalid, quickly followed by the argument that if anyone had the right to be able to do this then it is only someone belonging to the context to be scrutinized in this fashion. The sole licence extended to a social anthropologist not of this category appeared to be when s/he folded what was once confined to the fieldwork diary into the main ethnography, a transition whereby a narrative about 'they' became one principally about 'me'. Once again, the individual ceases to be part of the crowd, in this instance those studied.

Much present-day writing about populism decontextualises it politically, adopting as a result a mistaken view as to its progressiveness. Overlooked as a result is that, where the left has discarded its critique of the accumulation process, abandoning core political elements such as class and socialism, a discourse supportive of non-class identity quickly cedes ground in the struggle to conservatism and the far right. Capitalism is seen by popular culture in two distinct ways, split between on the one hand a discourse of despair (nothing can be done) and on the other an advocacy of non-integration (opting out). The latter takes the form of promoting 'barbarian otherness' as the only feasible objective, a retreat into an endorsement of pre- or non-capitalist social forms that mimics the historical attempts by agrarian populism to resuscitate peasant economy as innate, eternal, and thus non-transcendent.

Contrary to the programmatic objective of agrarian populists, which is to establish and maintain smallholding agricultural units functioning as such in any existing mode of production (feudalism, capitalism, socialism), most family farms consisting of those belonging to its middle and poor strata are unable to reproduce themselves economically simply from the process of cultivation. Where capitalism is concerned, repeasantisation in the sense of a steady-state petty commodity producing economy involving self-sufficient units operating with and by family labour-power is a chimera, since in this kind of context smallholders are either depeasantised, and their land is acquired by and consolidated within a larger enterprise, or else they continue in form only, because they are a local source of cheap labour-power required by commercial producers. When applied retroactively, as in the case of ancient Rome, however, such a model encounters serious problems.

Because wage labour – albeit 'disguised' – is equated with capitalism, each is regarded as ubiquitous, present historically in all epochs and places. The corollary is that the Roman empire is perceived as not having declined, an interpretation dismissed by those who hold this view as 'catastrophism'; much rather, it is regarded as having flourished. Just as spectacle-driven CGI film images of ancient Rome increasingly resemble superhero epics set in the future, so historiography of the Roman empire these days tends to depict it as an economy little different from modern capitalism. This kind of interpretation is an attempt to dismantle two sorts of historiography: that dealing with ancient Rome, and that informed by Marxist theory. It fails in each case, not least because of its confusion: about not only modes of production, but also definitions of production relations, what these consist of, and where/when they were found. Epistemologically, the reason for this is clear: the receipt of a wage is conflated with labour-power that is free, the presence of the latter being misinterpreted as an effect of the former, a combination that in turn serves as evidence for the existence in such contexts and epochs of capitalism.

More broadly, this non- or anti-Marxist interpretation of ancient Rome, based as it is on claims about the historical ubiquity of capital and free labour, in effect doing away with not only the idea of modes of production and the transition from one to another, but also with their connection to a shift from unfree to free labour-power as a necessary pre-condition to the move from capitalism to socialism, possesses implications for Marxist theory generally. If the Roman empire did not decline but much rather thrived, if production relations were not unfree but free, and if a benign form of capitalism was consequently reproduced everywhere, the connection that is central to Marxist historiography – between economic crisis and struggle leading to systemic transition – no longer holds. Among the counter-narratives overlooked by claims about the absence of crisis, struggle, and systemic transcendence is the retardation thesis, which shows how the cheap labour-power of slaves prevented investment in labour-displacing technology, as such checking the development of the productive forces, constituting thereby an obstacle to economic growth.

This in turn foregrounds what for leftists should be a question of central importance, but one than is currently rarely posed: can there be a Marxism without a transition to socialism, without that as being the sought-after object of any political agency designed to bring about fundamental transformation undertaken by its historical subject, the working class; or is it much rather the case that the only end towards which such mobilisation is – and ever can be – aimed is nothing more than a 'nicer' form of capitalism? If the latter, then what is termed Marxism (or 'Marxism') is little different from other non- or even anti-Marxist theory, such as that of liberalism or conservatism, which seek only to reproduce democracy + accumulation based on private property ownership. That is to say, with the very processes that prefigure and culminate historically in a global *laissez-faire* system, driven by deregulation, outsourcing, downsizing, and an intensification in labour market competition leading to yet further inequality, oppression, and poverty.

Bibliography

Akram-Lodhi, Haroon, *et al.* (eds.), 2021, *Handbook of Critical Agrarian Studies*, Cheltenham: Edward Elgar Publishing.

Albo, Greg, and Stephen Maher, 2025, 'Preface', in Greg Albo and Stephen Maher (eds.), *Socialist Register 2025: Openings and Closures – Socialist Strategy at a Crossroads*, London: The Merlin Press.

Anderson, Lindsay, 1959, 'No War', *The Mermaid Theatre Review*, Westerham, Kent: The Westerham Press Ltd.

Andrews, Geoff, 2023a, *The Shadow Man: At the Heart of the Cambridge Spy Circle*, London: Bloomsbury Academic.

Andrews, Geoff, 2023b, *Agent Molière: The Life of John Cairncross, the Fifth Man of the Cambridge Spy Circle*, London: Bloomsbury Academic.

Anonymous, n.d. [c. 1975], *The Angry Brigade*, Port Glasgow: Bratach Dubh Publications.

Asad, Talal (ed.), 1973, *Anthropology and the Colonial Encounter*, London: Ithaca Press.

Assies, Willem, 2005, 'The Challenge of Diversity in Rural Latin America: A Rejoinder to Jean-Pierre Reed (and Others)', *The Journal of Peasant Studies*, Vol. 32, No. 2.

Badian, E., 1968, *Roman Imperialism in the Late Republic*, Ithaca, NY: Cornell University Press.

Banaji, Jairus, 1978, 'Capitalist Domination of the Small Peasantry: Deccan Districts in the Late Nineteenth Century', in Rudra A., *et al.*, *Studies in the Development of Capitalism in India*, Lahore: Vanguard Books.

Banaji, Jairus, 2000, 'India: Workers' Rights in a New Economic Order', Oxford: QEH Working Paper 55.

Banaji, Jairus, 2001, *Agrarian Change in Late Antiquity: Gold, Labour, and Aristocratic Dominance*, Oxford: Oxford University Press.

Banaji, Jairus, 2003, 'The Fictions of Free Labour, Contract, Coercion, and So-Called Unfree Labour', *Historical Materialism*, Vol. 11, No. 3.

Banaji, Jairus, 2010, Theory as History: Essays on Modes of Production and Exploitation, Leiden: Brill.

Banaji, Jairus, 2018, *Exploring the Economy of Late Antiquity*, Cambridge: Cambridge University Press.

Banaji, Jairus, 2023, *Wanting Something Completely Different: 111 Vignettes of Left-Wing Figures, Themes, Films, and Writers*. Helsinki: Rab-Rab Press.

Banaji, Jairus, 2024, *A Marxist Mosaic: Selected Writings 1968–2022*, Brill: Leiden.

Bang, Peter Fibiger, 2011, 'Predation', pp. 197–217 in Walter Scheidel (ed.).

Barker, Ernest, George Clark, and Paul Vaucher (eds.), 1954, *The European Inheritance – Volume 1*, Oxford: At the Clarendon Press.

Barley, Nigel, 1983, *The Innocent Anthropologist: Notes from a Mud Hut*, London: British Museum Publications Ltd.

Barnes, Julian, 2025, *Changing my Mind*, Kendal: Notting Hill Editions.

Beard, Mary, 2007, *The Roman Triumph*, Cambridge, MA: The Belknap Press, Harvard University Press.

Beard, Mary, 2008, *Pompeii: The Life of a Roman Town*, London: Profile Books Ltd.

Beard, Mary, 2009, *It's a Don's Life*, London: Profile Books Ltd.

Beard, Mary, 2013, *Confronting the Classics: Traditions, Adventures and Innovations*, London: Profile Books.

Beard, Mary, 2016, *SPQR: A History of Ancient Rome*, London: Profile Books Ltd.

Beard, Mary, 2017, *Women and Power: A Manifesto*, London: Profile Books Ltd.

Beard, Mary, 2018, *How Do We Look? The Eye of Faith*, London: Profile Books Ltd.

Beard, Mary, 2021, *Twelve Caesars: Images of Power from the Ancient World to the Modern*, Princeton, NJ: Princeton University Press.

Beard, Mary, 2023, *Emperor of Rome: Ruling the Ancient World*, London: Profile Books Ltd.

Beaumont, Charles, 2023, *A Spy Alone*, London: Canelo.

Berger, John, 1972, *Ways of Seeing*, London: The British Broadcasting Corporation & Penguin Books.

Bernstein, Henry, 2018, 'The "Peasant Problem" in the Russian Revolution(s), 1905–1929,' *The Journal of Peasant Studies*, Vol. 45, No. 5–6.

Bernstein, Henry, 2024, 'Retour sur les études agraires critiques: Henry Bernstein – entretien réalisé par Paul Guillibert et Edouard Morena', *Actuel Marx*, No. 75.

Beveridge, W.H., 1931, *Unemployment: A Problem of Industry (1909 and 1930)*, London: Longmans, Green and Co.

Beverley, John, 2004, 'Subaltern Resistance in Latin America: A Reply to Tom Brass', *The Journal of Peasant Studies*, Vol. 31, No. 2.

Blanco, Hugo, 1972, *Land or Death*, New York: Pathfinder Press.

Bourdieu, Pierre, 1984, *Distinction: A Social Critique of the Judgement of Taste* (Translated by Richard Nice), Cambridge, MA: Harvard University Press.

Bourque, Susan C., and Kay Barbara Warren, 1981, *Women of the Andes: Patriarchy and Social Change in Two Peruvian Towns*, Ann Arbor, MI: University of Michigan Press.

Bowman, Isaiah, 1920, *The Andes of Southern Peru: Geographical Reconnaissance along the Seventy-third Meridian*, New York, NY: American Geographical Society.

Brass, Tom, 1980, 'Class Formation and Class Struggle in La Convención, Peru', *The Journal of Peasant Studies*, Vol. 7, No. 4.

Brass, Tom, 1982, *Class formation and class struggle in La Convención, Peru*, D.Phil. Thesis, University of Sussex.

Brass, Tom, 1983, 'Agrarian Reform and the Struggle for Labour-Power: A Peruvian Case-Study', *The Journal of Development Studies*, Vol. 19, No. 3.

Brass, Tom, 1986a, 'The elementary strictures of kinship: unfree relations and the production of commodities', in Alison M. Scott (ed.), *Rethinking Petty Commodity Production*, a Special Issue of *Social Analysis*, 30.

Brass, Tom, 1986b, '*Cargos* and Conflict: The Fiesta System and Capitalist Development in Eastern Peru', *The Journal of Peasant Studies*, Vol. 13, No. 3.

Brass, Tom, 1989, 'Trotskyism, Hugo Blanco and the Ideology of a Peruvian peasant movement', *The Journal of Peasant Studies*, Vol. 16, No. 2.

Brass, Tom, 1991, 'Moral Economists, Subalterns, New Social Movements and the (Re-) Emergence of a (Post-) Modernized (Middle) Peasant', *The Journal of Peasant Studies*, Vol. 18, No. 2.

Brass, Tom, 1999, *Towards a Comparative Political Economy of Unfree Labour: Case Studies and Debates*, London: Frank Cass Publishers.

Brass, Tom, 2000a, 'Unmasking the Subaltern, or Salamis without Themistocles', *The Journal of Peasant Studies*, Vol. 28, No. 1.

Brass, Tom, 2000b, *Peasants, Populism, and Postmodernism: The Return of the Agrarian Myth*, London: Frank Cass Publishers.

Brass, Tom, 2001, 'Reel Images of the Land (Beyond the Forest): Film and the Agrarian Myth', *The Journal of Peasant Studies*, Vol. 28, No. 4.

Brass, Tom, 2005, 'Late Antiquity as Early Capitalism?', *The Journal of Peasant Studies*, Vol. 32, No. 1.

Brass, Tom, 2006, 'Subaltern Resistance and the ("Bad") Politics of Culture: A Response to John Beverley', *The Journal of Peasant Studies*, Vol. 33, No. 2.

Brass, Tom, 2010a, 'Fiends, Friends and Fools: Screen images and/as rural struggle', *Dialectical Anthropology*, Vol. 34, No. 1.

Brass, Tom, 2010b, 'Capitalism, Primitive Accumulation and Unfree Labour', in H. Veltmeyer (ed.), *Imperialism, Crisis and Class Struggle: The Enduring Verities of Capitalism – Essays Presented to James Petras*, Leiden: Brill.

Brass, Tom, 2011, *Labour Regime Change in the Twenty-First Century: Unfreedom, Capitalism and Primitive Accumulation*, Leiden: Brill.

Brass, Tom, 2012, 'Jairus Banaji's Mode of Production: Eviscerating Marxism, Essentialising Capitalism', *Journal of Contemporary Asia*, Vol. 42, No. 4.

Brass, Tom, 2014, *Class, Culture, and the Agrarian Myth*, Leiden: Brill.

Brass, Tom, 2015, 'Peasants, Academics, Populists: Forward to the Past?', *Critique of Anthropology*, Vol. 35, No. 2.

Brass, Tom, 2017, *Labour Markets, Identities, Controversies: Reviews and Essays, 1982–2016*, Leiden: Brill.

Brass, Tom, 2018, *Revolution and Its Alternatives: Other Marxisms, Other Empowerments, Other Priorities*, Leiden: Brill.

Brass, Tom, 2021, *Marxism Missing, Missing Marxism: From Marxism to Identity Politics and Beyond*, Leiden: Brill.

Brass, Tom, 2022a, *Transitions: Methods, Theory, Politics*, Leiden: Brill.

Brass, Tom, 2022b, 'Marxism, Peasants, and the Cultural Turn: The Myth of a 'Nice' Populism', in David Fasenfest (ed.), *Marx Matters*, Leiden: Brill.

Brass, Tom, 2022c, 'Neo-populist Fables: The Other World of A.V. Chayanov', *Critical Sociology*, Vol. 48, Nos. 7–8.

Brass, Tom, 2023a, 'Critical Agrarian Studies as Populist Land-Grab', *Critical Sociology*, Vol. 49, No. 3.

Brass, Tom, 2023b, *Transitions: Methods, Theory, Politics*, Leiden: Brill.

Brass, Tom, 2024a, *Critiques: In Defence of Development*, Leiden: Brill.

Brass, Tom, 2024b, 'Did Someone Mention Socialism?', *Science & Society*, Vol. 88, No. 3.

Brass, Tom, 2024c, 'A Vanishing Army? Redefining the Industrial Reserve', in Tom Brass and Raju J. Das (eds.), *Interrogating the Future: Essays in Honour of David Fasenfest*, Leiden: Brill.

Brass, Tom, 2024d, 'Recovering the Subject(s)? Self and Others on Parade', *Class, Race and Corporate Power*, Vol. 12, No. 2.

Brass, Tom, 2025a, 'Marxist Mosaic or Non-Marxist Kaleidoscope?', *Critical Sociology*, Vol. 51, No. 2.

Brass, Tom, 2025b, 'Ranajit Guha and *The Journal of Peasant Studies*: An Enduring Legacy', in Sourav Chattopadhyay (ed.), *Ranajit Guha (1923–2023): A Centenary Collection by Bhabuk Sabha*, Kolkata: Alochana Chakra.

Brass, Tom (ed.), 1995, *New Farmers' Movements in India*, London and Portland, OR: Frank Cass Publishers.

Brass, Tom (ed.), 2003, *Latin American Peasants*, London and Portland, OR: Frank Cass Publishers.

Brass, Tom, and Marcel van der Linden (eds.), 1997, *Free and Unfree Labour: The Debate Continues*, Bern: Peter Lang AG.

Breman, Jan, 2023, *Fighting Free to Become Unfree Again: The Social History of Bondage and Neo-Bondage of Labour in India*, New Delhi: Tulika Books.

Brisseau, Janine, 1981, *La Cuzco dans sa région: Étude de l'aire d'influence d'une ville andine*, Bordeaux: Centre D'Études de Géographie Tropicale.

Brown, Adrienne Maree, 2021, *We Will Not Cancel Us*, Chico: AK Press.

Brown, Peter, 1971, *The World of Late Antiquity AD 150–750*, London: Thames and Hudson.

Brown, Peter, 1978, *The Making of Late Antiquity*, Cambridge, MA: Harvard University Press.

Brown, Peter, 2012, *Through the Eye of a Needle: Wealth, the Fall of Rome, and the Making of Christianity in the West, 350–550 AD*, Princeton, NJ: Princeton University Press.

Brown, Peter, 2023, *Journeys of the Mind: A Life in History*, Princeton, NJ: Princeton University Press.

Brunt, P.A., 1988, *The Fall of the Roman Republic and Related Essays*, Oxford: At the Clarendon Press.

Brush, Stephen B., 1977, *Mountain, Field and Family: The Economy and Human Ecology of an Andean Valley*, Philadelphia, PA: University of Pennsylvania Press.

Buck, Solon J., 1920, *The Agrarian Crusade: A Chronicle of the Farmer in Politics*, New Haven, CT: Yale University Press.

Bulwer-Lytton, Edward, 1834, *The Last Days of Pompeii* (in three volumes), London: Richard Bentley, New Burlington Street.

Bunker, Stephen G., 1987, 'Ritual, respect and refusal: drinking behaviour in an Andean Village', *Human Organization*, Vol. 46, No. 4.

Cairncross, John, 1997, *The Enigma Spy: The Story of the Man Who Changed the Course of World War Two*, London: Century.

Camilleri, Andrea, 2020, *The Sicilian Method* (Translated by Stephen Sartarelli), London: Penguin Books.

Camus, Renaud, 2018, *You Will Not Replace Us!* Plieux: Chez l'auteur.

Camus, Renaud, 2023, *Enemy of the Disaster: Selected Political Writings* (Edited with an Introduction by Louis Betty), Blowing Rock, NC: Vauban Books.

Camus, Renaud, 2024a, *The Deep Murmur*, Blowing Rock, NC: Vauban Books.

Camus, Renaud, 2024b, *Ørop* (Translated by Ethan Rundell), Blowing Rock, NC: Vauban Books.

Camus, Renaud, 2024c, *The Great Replacement: Introduction to Global Replacism*, Plieux: Éditions du Château.

Caute, David, 2013, *Isaac and Isaiah: The Covert Punishment of a Cold War Heretic*, New Haven, CT: Yale University Press.

Cawkwell, Tim, 2004, *The Filmgoer's Guide to God*, London: Darton, Longman and Todd, Ltd.

Chayanov, A.V., 1966 [1923], *The Theory of Peasant Economy* (edited by Daniel Thorner, Basile Kerblay, and R.E.F. Smith), Homewood, Illinois: Published for the American Economic Association by Richard D. Irwin, Inc.

Chilver, G.E.F., 1941, *Cisalpine Gaul: Social and Economic History from 49 B.C. to the Death of Trajan*, Oxford: At the Clarendon Press.

Christie, Stuart, 1980, *The Christie File*, Sanday, Orkney Islands: Cienfuegos Press.

Clifford, James, 2013, *Returns: Becoming Indigenous in the Twenty-First Century*, Cambridge, MA: Harvard University Press.

Clifford, James, and George E. Marcus (eds.), 1990, *Writing Culture: The Poetics and Politics of Ethnography*, Delhi: Oxford University Press.

Coen, Ethan, and Joel Coen, 1996, *Fargo*, London: Faber and Faber.

Comisión Nacional sobre la Desaparición de Personas (CONADEP), 1984, *Anexo del informe de la Comisión Nacional sobre la Desaparición de Personas*, Buenos Aires: EUDEBA.

Conlin, Sean, 1974, 'Igualdad y vergüenza en la fiesta', *Allpanchis Phuturinqa*, Vol. 7.

Conticello, Baldassare (ed.), 1992, *Rediscovering Pompeii*, Rome: Marchesi Grafiche Editoriali.

Cooper, Paul, 2024, *Fall of Civilizations: Stories of Greatness and Decline*, London: Duckworth.

Craig, Wesley W., Jr., 1969, 'Peru: the peasant movement of La Convención', in Henry Landsberger (ed.), *Latin American Peasant Movements*, Ithaca, NY: Cornell University Press.

Creighton, John, 2000, *Coins and Power in Late Iron Age Britain*, Cambridge: Cambridge University Press.

Croce, Benedetto, 1927, *An Autobiography* (Translated from the Italian by R.G. Collingwood, with a Preface by J.A. Smith), Oxford: At the Clarendon Press.

Cuadros, Carlos Ferdinand, 1949, 'El "arriendo" y la reforma agrarian en la Provincia de La Convención', *Revista Universitaria del Cusco*, Vol. 38, No. 96.

Dabiri, Emma, 2021, *What White People Can Do Next*, London: Penguin Books.

de Ste Croix, G.E.M., 1981, *The Class Struggle in the Ancient Greek World, from the Archaic Age to the Arab Conquests*, London: Duckworth.

Desmarais, Annette-Aurélie, 2002, 'The Vía Campesina: Consolidating an International Peasant and Farm Movement', *The Journal of Peasant Studies*, Vol. 29, No. 2.

DeWalt, Billie R., 1979a, *Modernization in a Mexican Ejido*, Cambridge: Cambridge University Press.

DeWalt, Billie R., 1979b, 'Drinking behaviour, economic status, and adaptive strategies of modernization in a highland Mexican community', *American Ethnologist*, Vol. 6, No. 3.

Diamond, Jared, 2003, *Collapse: How Societies Choose to Fail or Succeed*, London: Penguin Books.

Dobb, Maurice, 1955, *On Economic Policy and Socialism: Collected Papers*, London: Routledge and Kegan Paul.

Doughty, Paul L., 1968, *Huaylas: an Andean District in Search of Progress*, Ithaca, NY: Cornell University Press.

Doughty, Paul L., 1971, 'The social uses of alcoholic beverages in a Peruvian community', *Human Organization*, Vol. 30, No. 2.

Duff, A.M., 1928, *Freedmen in the Early Roman Empire*, Oxford: At the Clarendon Press.

Duyker, Edward, 1987, *Tribal Guerrillas: The Santals of West Bengal and the Naxalite Movement*, Delhi: Oxford University Press.

Dyer, Thomas H., 1867, *Pompeii: Its History, Buildings, and Antiquities*, London: Bell & Daldy, 6 York Street, Covent Garden.

Eisenstadt, S.N., 1963, *The Political Systems of Empires*, New York: The Free Press.

Elley, Derek, 1984, *The Epic Film: Myth and History*, London: Routledge & Kegan Paul plc.

Erdkamp, Paul, Koenraad Verboven, and Arjan Zuiderhoek (eds.), 2020, *Capital, Investment, and Innovation in the Roman World*, Oxford: Oxford University Press.

Evans-Pritchard, Edward E., 1951, *Social Anthropology*, London: Cohen & West, Ltd.

Evans-Pritchard, Edward E., 1969, 'Anthropology and History [1961]', in *Essays in Social Anthropology*, London: Faber & Faber.

Fasenfest, David (ed.), 2022, *Marx Matters*, Leiden: Brill.

Fasting, Mathilde (ed.), 2021, *After the End of History: Conversations with Francis Fukuyama*, Washington, DC: Georgetown University Press.

Fay, Gerard, c. 1953, *The Mermaid: A record of performances and prospects*, London: The Mermaid Theatre.

Fioravanti, Eduardo, 1974, *Latifundio y Sindicalismo en el Perú: el caso de los valles de La Convención y Lares (1958–1964)*, Lima: Instituto de Estudios Peruanos.

Firth, Raymond, 1972, *The Sceptical Anthropologist? Social Anthropology and Marxist Views on Society* (Inaugural Radcliffe-Brown Lecture in Social Anthropology), London: Published for the British Academy by the Oxford University Press.

Fletcher, Catherine, 2024, *The Roads to Rome: A History*, London: The Bodley Head.

Fogel, Robert William, and Stanley W. Engerman, 1974, *Time on the Cross: Volume I – The Economics of American Negro Slavery*, London: Wildwood House.

Fowler, Don Paul, 2000, *Roman Constructions: Readings in Postmodern Latin*, Oxford: Oxford University Press.

Frank, Tenney, 1920, *An Economic History of Rome*, Baltimore, MA: The Johns Hopkins Press.

Freu, Christel, 2013, 'Les salaries de la terre dans l'antiquité tardive', *Antiquité Tardive: Revue international d'histoire et d'archéologie*, No. 21.

Furedi, Frank, 2024, *The War Against the Past: Why the West Must Fight for Its History*, Cambridge: Polity.

Gardner, Katy, and David Lewis, 1996, *Anthropology, Development and the Post-Modern Challenge*, London: Pluto Press.

Garnsey, Peter, and Richard Saller, 2014, *The Roman Empire: Economy, Society and Culture*, London: Bloomsbury Academic.

Geertz, Clifford, 1988, *Works and Lives: The Anthropologist as Author*, Stanford, CA: Stanford University Press.

Geiser, Urs, 2023, 'Reflections on Critical Agrarian Studies in Sri Lanka', *Polity*, Vol. 11, No. 2.

Giardina, Andrea, 2007, 'Marxism and Historiography: Perspectives on Roman History', in Chris Wickham (ed.), *Marxist History-writing for the Twenty-first Century*, Oxford: Published for the British Academy by Oxford University Press.

Gibbon, Edward, 1995 [1776], *The History of the Decline and Fall of the Roman Empire* (Edited by David Womersley), Volumes 1–3, London: Penguin Books.

Gibbon, Peter, 1973, 'Arensberg and Kimball revisited', *Economy and Society*, Vol. 2, No. 4.

Gibbon, Peter, and Michael Neocosmos, 1985, 'Some Problems in the Political Economy of "African Socialism"', in Henry Bernstein and Bonnie K. Campbell (eds.), *Contradictions of Accumulation in Africa: Studies in Economy and State*, London and Beverley Hills, CA: Sage Publications.

Gibson, Charles, 1964, *The Aztecs Under Spanish Rule: A History of the Indians of the Valley of Mexico, 1519–1810*, Stanford, CA: Stanford University Press.

Gifford, Douglas, and Pauline Hoggarth, 1976, *Carnival and Coca Leaf: some traditions of the Peruvian Quechua Ayllu*, Edinburgh: Scottish Academic Press.

Glyn, Andrew, 2006, *Capitalism Unleashed*, Oxford: Oxford University Press.

Goad, Jim, 1998, *The Redneck Manifesto*, New York, NY: Touchstone/Simon & Schuster.

Goodwyn, Lawrence, 1976, *Democratic Promise: The Populist Moment in America*, New York, NY: Oxford University Press.

Gorriti, Gustavo, 1999, *The Shining Path: A History of the Millenarian War in Peru*, Chapel Hill, NC: University of North Carolina Press.

Gott, Richard, 1970, *Guerrilla Movements in Latin America*, London: Nelson.

Grant, Michael, 1997, *The Roman Emperors*, London: Orion Books.

Grantham, George, 2004, 'A Review of Agrarian Change in Late Antiquity: Gold, Labor and Aristocratic Dominance', *EH.NET* (May).

Guillet, David, 1979, *Agrarian Reform and Peasant Economy in Southern Peru*, Colombia, MO: University of Missouri Press.

Hall, Edith, and Henry Stead, 2020, *A People's History of Classics: Class and Greco-Roman Antiquity in Britain and Ireland 1689 to 1939*, London: Routledge.

Hallpike, C.R., 1992/93a, 'Is There A Primitive Society?', *Cambridge Anthropology*, Vol. 16, No. 1.

Hallpike, C.R., 1992/93b, 'On Primitive Society and Social Evolution: A Reply to Kuper', *Cambridge Anthropology*, Vol. 16, No. 3.

Hanson, Victor Davis, 2001, *Why the West Has Won: Carnage and Culture from Salamis to Vietnam*, London: Faber & Faber.

Harris, Olivia, 1978, 'Complementarity and Conflict: an Andean view of women and men', in Jean La Fontaine (ed.), *Sex and Age as Principles of Social Differentiation*, London: Academic Press.

Hart, Keith, 2022, *Self in the World: Connecting Life's Extremes*, Oxford: Berghan Books.

Heath, Dwight B., 1971, 'Peasants, revolution, and drinking: interethnic drinking patterns in two Bolivian communities', *Human Organization*, Vol. 30, No. 2.

Heath, Dwight B., 1987a, 'Anthropology and alcohol studies: current issues', in B.J. Siegel, A.R. Beals, and S.A. Tyler (eds.), *Annual Review of Anthropology*, Vol. 16, Palo Alto, CA: Annual Reviews, Inc.

Heath, Dwight B., 1987b, 'A decade of development in the anthropological study of alcohol use: 1970–1980', in Mary Douglas (ed.), *Constructive Drinking*, Cambridge: Cambridge University Press.

Heather, Peter, 2000, 'Introduction' to Thomas Hodgkin (2000).

Heather, Peter, 2006, *The Fall of the Roman Empire: A New History*, London: Pan Books.

Heather, Peter, and John Rapley, 2023, *Why Empires Fall: Rome, America and the Future of the West*, London: Allen Lane.

Hecker, Julius F., 1934, *Russian Sociology: A Contribution to the History of Sociological Thought and Theory*, London: Chapman & Hall Ltd.

Hicks, John D., 1931, *The Populist Revolt: A History of the Farmers' Alliance and the People's Party*, Minneapolis, MN: The University of Minnesota Press.

Hitchens, Christopher, 2000, *Unacknowledged Legislation*, London: Verso.

Hobsbawm, Eric J., 1969, 'A case of neo-feudalism: La Convención, Peru', *Journal of Latin American Studies*, Vol. 1, No. 1.

Hodgkin, Thomas, 2000 [1892], *The Barbarian Invasions of the Roman Empire* (Volume I: The Visigothic Invasion), London: The Folio Society.

Holmberg, Allan R., 1971, 'The rhythms of drinking in a Peruvian coastal community', *Human Organization*, Vol. 30, No. 2.

Houellebecq, Michel, 2022, *Interventions 2020*, Cambridge: Polity Press.

Houellebecq, Michel, 2024, *Annihilation*, London: Picador.

Huizer, Gerrit, 1970, *Peasant unrest in Latin America: its origins, forms of expression, and potential*, Doctoral thesis, University of Amsterdam.

Huntington, Samuel P., 1996, *The Clash of Civilizations and the Remaking of World Order*, New York, NY: Simon & Schuster.

Ignatieff, Michael, 1998, *Isaiah Berlin: A Life*, London: Chatto & Windus.

Ionescu, Ghiţa, and Ernest Gellner (eds.), 1969, *Populism: Its Meaning and National Characteristics*, New York, NY: The Macmillan Company.

Isbell, Billie Jean, 1978, *To Defend Ourselves: Ecology and Ritual in an Andean Village*, Austin, TX: University of Texas Press.

Jasny, Naum, 1972, *Soviet Economists of the Twenties: Names to be Remembered*, London: Cambridge University Press.

Jones, H. Stuart, 1928, 'The Sources for the Tradition of Early Roman History', in S.A. Cook, F.E. Adcock, M.P. Charlesworth (eds.), *The Cambridge Ancient History*, Volume VII, Cambridge: At the University Press.

Joyce, Patrick, 2024, *Remembering Peasants: A Personal History of a Vanished World*, London: Allen Lane.

Judt, Tony, 2010, *Ill Fares the Land: A Treatise on Our Present Discontents*, London: Allen Lane.

Kaerger, Karl, 1979, *Condiciones Agrarias de la Sierra Sur Peruana (1899)*, Lima: Instituto de Estudios Peruanos.

Kalecki, Michał, 1943, 'Political Aspects of Full Employment', *The Political Quarterly*, Vol. 14, No. 4.

Kapuściński, Ryszard, 2007, *The Soccer War* (Translated from the Polish by William Brand, Afterword by Bill Buford), London: Granta Books.

Kapuściński, Ryszard, 2008, *The Other* (translated by Antonia Lloyd-Jones, with an introduction by Neal Ascherson), London: Verso.

Kennedy, Paul, 2017, *The Rise and Fall of the Great Powers*, London: William Collins.

Kornbluh, Peter, 2003, *The Pinochet File: A Declassified Dossier on Atrocity and Accountability*, New York, NY: The New York Press.

Kuper, Adam, 1992/93a, 'Against Primitive Society: A Rejoinder to Hallpike', *Cambridge Anthropology*, Vol. 16, No. 1.

Kuper, Adam, 1992/93b, 'Primitive Anthropology', *Cambridge Anthropology*, Vol. 16, No. 3.

Lampert, Evgenii, 1965, *Sons against Fathers: Studies in Russian Radicalism and Revolution*, Oxford: Clarendon Press.

Leach, Edmund R., 1940, *Social and Economic Organization of the Rowanduz Kurds* (Monographs on Social Anthropology No. 3), London: Published for The London School of Economics and Political Science by Percy Lund, Humphries & Co., Ltd.

Leach, Edmund R., 1982, *Social Anthropology*, London: Fontana.

Leach, Edmund R., 1989/90 [1986], 'Masquerade: The Presentation of the Self in Holi-day Life', *Cambridge Anthropology*, Vol. 13, No. 3.

Lendon, J.E., 2009, 'Historians without History: Against Roman Historiography', in A. Feldherr (ed.), *Cambridge Companion to Roman Historians*, Cambridge: Cambridge University Press.

Lenin, V.I., 1960, 'The Characterization of Economic Romanticism [1897]', *Collected Works*, Vol. 2, Moscow: Foreign Languages Press.

Leonard, Spencer A., and Sunit Singh, 2010, 'The Maoist Insurgency in India: An Interview with Jairus Banaji', *The Platypus Review*, Issue 26, August 6th.

Lévi-Strauss, Claude, 1962, *The Savage Mind*, London: Weidenfeld & Nicolson.

Lienhardt, Godfrey, 1966, *Social Anthropology*, London: Oxford University Press.

London, Leslie, 1999, 'The "dop" system, alcohol abuse and social control among farm workers in South Africa', *Social Science and Medicine*, Vol. 48, No. 10.

Long, Norman, and Bryan Roberts (eds.), 1978, *Peasant Cooperation and Capitalist Expansion in Central Peru*, Austin, TX: University of Texas Press.

MacClancy, Jeremy (ed.), 2002, *Exotic No More: Anthropology on the Front Line*, Chicago, IL: University of Chicago Press.

MacKendrick, Paul, 1971, *Roman France*, London: G. Bell & Sons.

Maher, George, 2021, *Pugnare: Economic Success and Failure*, London: Kilnamanagh.

Malinowski, Bronislaw, 1967, *A Diary in the Strict Sense of the Term* (Preface by Valetta Malinowska, Introduction by Raymond Firth, Translated by Norbert Guterman, Index of Native terms by Mario Bick), London: Routledge & Kegan Paul.

Mann, Abby, 1961, *Judgment at Nuremburg: The Script of the Film*, London: Cassell.

Mannoni, Octave, 1956, *Prospero and Caliban: The Psychology of Colonization* (Translated by Pamela Powesland, with a Foreword by Philip Mason), London: Methuen & Co. Ltd.

Marshall, Herbert, 1965, *Mayakovsky* (Translated and edited by Herbert Marshall), New York: Hill and Wang Inc.

Martinez-Alier, Juan, 1974, 'Peasants and Labourers in Southern Spain, Cuba and Highland Peru', *The Journal of Peasant Studies*, Vol. 1, No. 2.

Marx, Karl, 1972, *Theories of Surplus Value – Part III*, London: Lawrence and Wishart.

Marx, Karl, 1976, *Capital – Volume 1*, Harmondsworth: Penguin Books.

Marx, Karl, 1979, 'The Eighteenth Brumaire of Louis Bonaparte [1852]', *Karl Marx Frederick Engels Collected Works*, Volume 11, London: Lawrence & Wishart.

Marx, Karl, 1981, *Capital – Volume 3*, Harmondsworth: Penguin Books.

Marx, Karl, and Frederick Engels, 1934, *Correspondence 1846–1895*, London: Martin Lawrence Ltd.

Marzal, Manuel, 1971, *El Mundo Religioso de Urcos*, Cusco: Instituto de Pastoral Andina.

Mayer, Philip (ed.), 1980, *Black Villagers in an Industrial Society: Anthropological perspectives on labour migration in South Africa*, Cape Town: Oxford University Press.

McBride, George M., 1936, *Chile: Land and Society*, New York: American Geographical Society.

McClintock, Cynthia, 1981, *Peasant Cooperatives and Political Change in Peru*, Princeton, NJ: Princeton University Press.

Medwid, Linda M., 2000, *The Makers of Classical Archaeology*, Amherst, NY: Humanity Books.

Miers, Suzanne, and Igor Kopytoff (eds.), 1977, *Slavery in Africa: Historical and Anthropological Perspectives*, Madison, WI: University of Wisconsin Press.

Miles, Richard, 2014, 'Declinism', in Kurt Almqvist and Alexander Linklater (eds.), *Civilisation*, Stockholm: Axel and Margaret Ax:son Johnson Foundation.

Mitrany, David, 1951, *Marx Against the Peasant*, Chapel Hill, NC: The University of North Carolina Press.

Mitrany, David, 1968 [1930], *The Land and the Peasant in Rumania*, New York, NY: Greenwood Press, Publishers.

Mörner, Magnus, 1979, *Notas sobre el Comercio y los Comerciantes del Cusco desde fines de la colonia hasta 1930*, Lima: Instituto de Estudios Peruanos.

Mouritsen, Henrik, 2005, 'Freedmen and Decurions: Epitaphs and Social History in Imperial Italy', *The Journal of Roman Studies*, Volume XCV.

Mouritsen, Henrik, 2011, *The Freedman in the Roman World*, Cambridge: Cambridge University Press.

Murray, Oswyn, 2024, *The Muse of History: The Ancient Greeks from the Enlightenment to the Present*, London: Allen Lane.

Narr, Wolf-Dieter, 1980, 'The Selling of Narcissism', *Dialectical Anthropology*, Vol. 5, No. 1.

Nederveen Pieterse, Jan, 2015, 'Ancient Rome and Globalisation: Decentring Rome', in Pitts and Versluys (eds.).

Neira, Hugo, 1968, *Los Andes: Tierra o Muerte*, Madrid: Editorial ZXY.

Normano, J.F., 1949, *The Spirit of Russian Economics*, London: Dennis Dobson Limited.

Nugent, Stephen, 2003, 'Whither *O Campesinato*? Historical Peasantries of Brazilian Amazonia', *The Journal of Peasant Studies*, Vol. 29, No. 3–4.

Osgood, Josiah, 2018, *Rome and the Making of a World State 150 BC–20 AD*, Cambridge: Cambridge University Press.

Parsons, Stanley B., 1973, *The Populist Context: Rural versus Urban Power on a Great Plains Frontier*, Westport, CT: Greenwood Press, Inc.

Patnaik, Utsa, and Manjari Dingwaney (eds.), 1985, *Chains of Servitude: Bondage and Slavery in India*, Madras: Sangham Books.

Patnaik, Utsa, and Prabhat Patnaik, 2017, *A Theory of Imperialism*, New York: Columbia University Press.

Paz Soldán, Mateo, 1862, *Geografía del Peru*, Paris: Librería de Fermín Didot Hermanos, Hijos y Ca.

Pellew, Jill, and Miles Taylor (eds.), 2020, *Utopian Universities: A Global History of the New Campuses of the 1960s*, London: Bloomsbury Academic.

Philo, Greg, *et al.*, 1976, *Bad News*, London: Routledge & Kegan Paul.

Philo, Greg, *et al.*, 1980, *More Bad News*, London: Routledge & Kegan Paul.

Philo, Greg, *et al.*, 1982, *Really Bad News*, London: Writers and Readers Publishing Cooperative Society Ltd.

Pitts, Martin, and Miguel John Versluys (eds.), 2015, *Globalisation and the Roman World: World history, connectivity and material culture*, Cambridge: Cambridge University Press.

Pocock, David, 1971, *Social Anthropology*, London: Sheed and Ward Ltd.

Prakash, Gyan, 1994, 'Subaltern Studies as Postcolonial Criticism', *American Historical Review*, Vol. 99, No. 5.

Qadir, Shahid, and Barry Gills, 1992, 'Fracturing Socialism: a fragile future?', *Third World Quarterly*, Vol. 13, No. 1.

Raworth, Tom, 1969, *A Serial Biography*, London: Fulcrum Press.

Roscams, Steve, 2008, 'A Marxist look at the legions', *International Socialism*, No. 119.

Rostovtzeff, Michael, 1927, *A History of the Ancient World – Volume II: Rome* (Translated from the Russian by J.D. Duff), Oxford: At the Clarendon Press.

Rostow, W.W., 1960, *The Stages of Economic Growth: A Non-Communist Manifesto*, London: Cambridge University Press.

Roth, Gary, 2015, *Marxism in a Lost Century: A Biography of Paul Mattick*, Chicago, IL: Haymarket Books.

Said, Edward W., 1978, *Orientalism*, London: Routledge & Kegan Paul.

Said, Edward W., 2002, 'Representing the Colonized: Anthropology's Interlocutors', in *Reflections on Exile and Other Essays*, Cambridge, MA: Harvard University Press.

Sarkar, Ash, 2025, *Minority Rule: Adventures in the Culture War*, London: Bloomsbury.

Scheidel, Walter (ed.), 2012, *The Cambridge Companion to Roman Economy*, Cambridge: Cambridge University Press.

Scheidel, Walter, 2012, 'Approaching the Roman Economy', in Walter Scheidel (ed.).

Scorsese, Martin, and Michael Henry Wilson, 1991, *A Personal Journey with Martin Scorsese Through American Movies*, London: Faber and Faber.

Scott, James C., 2009, *The Art of Not Being Governed: An Anarchist History of Southeast Asia*, London and New Haven, CT: Yale University Press.

Seligman, C.G., and Brenda Z. Seligman, 1932, *Pagan Tribes of the Nilotic Sudan*, London: George Routledge & Sons, Ltd.

Srinivas, M.N., 1976, *The Remembered Village*, Berkeley, CA: University of California Press, Ltd.

Sennett, Richard, and Jonathan Cobb, 1977, *The Hidden Injuries of Class*, Cambridge: Cambridge University Press.

Shaw, Brent D., 2019, 'Did the Romans Have a Future?', *Journal of Roman Studies*, Volume 109.

Sherwin-White, A.N., 1966, *Racial Prejudice in Imperial Rome*, London: Cambridge University Press.

Simmons, O.G., 1959, 'Drinking patterns and interpersonal performance in a Peruvian mestizo community', *Quarterly Journal of Studies on Alcohol*, Vol. 20, No. 1.

Sivakumar, S.S., 2001, 'The Unfinished Narodnik Agenda: Chayanov, Marxism and Marginalism Revisited', *The Journal of Peasant Studies*, Vol. 29, No. 1.

Solomon, Susan Gross, 1977, *The Soviet Agrarian Debate: A Controversy in Social Science, 1923–1929*, Boulder, CO: Westview Press.

Stapledon, W. Olaf, 1930, *Last and First Men: The Story of the Near and Far Future*, London: Methuen & Co., Ltd.

Stauder, Jack, 1974, 'The "Relevance" of Anthropology to Colonialism and Imperialism', *Radical Science Journal*, No. 1 (January).

Stein, William W., 1961, *Hualcán: Life in the Highlands of Peru*, Ithaca, NY: Cornell University Press.

Stern, Steve (ed.), 1998, *Shining and Other Paths: War and Society in Peru, 1980–1995*, Durham, NC: Duke University Press.

Stoddard, Lothrop, 1922, *The Revolt Against Civilization*, London: Chapman & Hall, Ltd.

Strachan, Alan, 2023, *Adventurer: Bernard Miles and the Mermaid Theatre*, London: Wordville Press Ltd.

Sutch, Richard, 1975, 'The Treatment Received by American Slaves: A Critical Review of the Evidence presented in *Time on the Cross*,' *Explorations in Economic History*, Vol. 12, No. 4.

Sweezy, Paul M., 1946, *The Theory of Capitalist Development: Principles of Marxian Political Economy*, London: Dennis Dobson Limited.

Syme, Ronald, 1958, *Colonial Elites: Rome, Spain and the Americas*, London: Oxford University Press.

Szwed, John F., 1966, 'Gossip, drinking and social control: consensus and communication in a Newfoundland parish', *Ethnology*, Vol. 5.

Tannenbaum, Frank, 1968 [1929], *The Mexican Agrarian Revolution*. Hamden, CT: The Brookings Institution.

Tanzer, Helen H., 1939, *The Common People of Pompeii: A Study of the Graffiti*, Baltimore, MD: The Johns Hopkins Press (The Johns Hopkins University Studies in Archaeology, No. 29).

Thompson, E.P., 1963, *The Making of the English Working Class*, London: Victor Gollancz Ltd.

Torga, Miguel, 1950, *Farrusco the Blackbird and other stories from the Portuguese* (Translated with an Introduction by Denis Brass, illustrated by Gregorio Prieto). London: George Allen and Unwin, Ltd.

Toynbee, Arnold J., 1965, *Hannibal's Legacy: The Hannibalic War's Effects on Roman Life* (2 Volumes), London: Oxford University Press.

Treggiari, Susan, 1969, *Roman Freedmen during the Late Republic*, Oxford: At the Clarendon Press.

Trotsky, Leon, 1924, *Problems of Life* (Translated by Z. Vengerova, with an Introduction by N. Minsky), London: Methuen & Co. Ltd.

Trotsky, Leon, 1934, *The History of the Russian Revolution*, London: Victor Gollancz Limited.

Trotsky, Leon, 1964 [1937], 'Thermidor and Anti-Semitism', in Irving Howe (ed.), *The Basic Writings of Trotsky*, London: Secker & Warburg.

Trotsky, Leon, 1969a, *The Chinese Revolution* [1924], New York: Merit Publishers.

Trotsky, Leon, 1969b, 'The Three Conceptions of the Russian Revolution', *Writings 1938–39*, New York: Merit Publishers.

Tupayachi, Isaac, 1959, 'Un ensayo de econometría en La Convención', *Revista Universitaria del Cusco*, Vol. 48, No. 117.

Umachandran, Mathura, and Marchella Ward (eds.), 2024, *Critical Ancient World Studies: The Case for Forgetting Classics*, London: Routledge.

Valderrama, Ricardo, and Carmen Escalante, 1976, 'Pacha T'inka o la T'inka a La Madre Tierra en el Apurímac', *Allpanchis Phuturinqa*, Vol. 9.

Van den Berghe, Pierre L., and George P. Primov, 1971, *Inequality in the Peruvian Andes: Class and Ethnicity in Cuzco*, Colombia, MO: University of Missouri Press.

Venturi, Franco, 1960 [1952], *Roots of Revolution: A history of the Populist and Socialist Movements in Nineteenth Century Russia*, London: Weidenfeld & Nicolson.

Veyne, Paul, 1990, *Bread and Circuses: Historical Sociology and Political Pluralism*, London: Allen Lane, The Penguin Press.

Villanueva, Victor, 1967, *Hugo Blanco y la rebelión campesina*, Lima: Librería-Editorial Juan Mejía Baca.

Virga, Nino, 2023, *Empires Through Time: The Rise, Reign and Decline of Global Powers*, London: ChronoLegacy Publishing.

Walbank, F.W., 1946, *The Decline of the Roman Empire in the West*, London: Cobbett Press (Past and Present Series: Studies in the History of Civilization).

Walicki, Andrzej, 1969, *The Controversy over Capitalism: Studies in the Social Philosophy of the Russian Populists*, Oxford: Clarendon Press.

Walicki, Andrzej, 1975, *The Slavophile Controversy: History of a Conservative Utopia in Nineteenth Century Russian Thought* (Translated by Hilda Andrews-Rusiecka), Oxford: Clarendon Press.

Walicki, Andrzej, 1980, *A History of Russian Thought: From the Enlightenment to Marxism* (Translated by Hilda Andrews-Rusiecka), Oxford: Clarendon Press.

Wertheimer, Mildred S., 1924, *The Pan-German League 1890–1914*, New York: Columbia University (Faculty of Political Science, Studies in History, Economics and Public Law).

Whittington, Harry, 1964, *Samuel Bronston's The Fall of the Roman Empire*, London: Frederick Muller Ltd.

Wilkie, Raymond, 1971, *San Miguel: A Mexican Collective Ejido*, Stanford, CA: Stanford University Press.

Williams, Gavin, 2016, 'Slaves, Workers, and Wine: The "Dop System" in the History of the Cape Wine Industry, 1658–1894', *Journal of South African Studies*, Vol. 42, No. 5.

Wilson, Francis, Alide Kooy, and Delia Hendrie (eds.), 1977, *Farm Labour in South Africa*, Cape Town: David Philip.

Wilson, Peter J., 1973, *Crab Antics*, New Haven, CT: Yale University Press.

Wolf, Eric J., 1966, *Peasants*, New Jersey: Prentice-Hall Inc.

Wortman, Richard, 1967, *The Crisis of Russian Populism*, London: Cambridge University Press.

Wyke, Maria, 1997, *Projecting the Past: Ancient Rome, Cinema and History*, London: Routledge.

Yamaguchi, Sakiko, Raphael Lencucha, and Thomas G. Brown, 2021, 'Control, power, and responsibility: a qualitative study of local perspectives on problem drinking in the Peruvian Andean highlands', *Globalization and Health*, Vol. 17, No. 1.

Yousfi, Louisa, 2025, *In Defence of Barbarism: Non-Whites against the Empire* (translated by Andy Bliss), London: Verso.

Author Index

Subject Index

www.ingramcontent.com/pod-product-compliance
Lightning Source LLC
LaVergne TN
LVHW020938031026
849429LV00029B/336